SAIL BEFORE SUNSET

Betty and Earl Hinz aboard Horizon.

SAIL
BEFORE SUNSET

Earl R. Hinz

David McKay Company, Inc.
NEW YORK

Library of Congress Cataloging in Publication Data
Hinz, Earl R
Sail before sunset.
1. Hinz, Earl R.   2. Horizon (Ketch)   3. Voyages
and travels—1951–   I. Title.
G477.H54   910′.45′0924   79-250
ISBN 0-679-51350-7

10 9 8 7 6 5 4 3 2 1

Manufactured in the United States of America

This book is dedicated to my wife, Betty, who was the First Mate of *Horizon* on our Polynesian adventure. It was her belief that we should make this trip while we can, in her words, "sail before sunset." Her positive philosophy, which led to the adventure of a lifetime, was founded on her favorite poem, "Crossing the Bar," by Alfred Lord Tennyson:

Sunset and evening star
   And one clear call for me!
And may there be no moaning of the bar,
   When I put out to sea,

But such a tide as moving seems asleep,
   Too full for sound and foam,
When that which drew from out the boundless deep
   Turns again home.

Twilight and evening bell,
   And after that the dark!
And may there be no sadness of farewell,
   When I embark;

For tho' from out our bourne of Time and Place
   The flood may bear me far,
I hope to see my Pilot face to face
   When I have crost the bar.

Contents

APPENDICES

Introduction

Our situation amused us for we had grown up as conservative members of the midcentury establishment so battered and bruised by the restless youth of the 1950s and 1960s. Now we were to leave that establishment and join in the cruising world dominated by those young and resourceful persons who shun the crowded cities and their man-made problems. We were to be an anachronism in the growing cruising world—too old to pass ourselves off as carefree vagabonds, yet too young in spirit to retire to obscurity.

Why were we out there on the trackless waters of the immense Pacific Ocean? It was simply a desire to see for ourselves the islands and peoples of the South Seas made famous by book and movie. Travel agency ads not withstanding, we felt that there was only one way for us to see these magic isles, and that was by small boat. I had already spent too many hours of my life waiting in airports and being shepherded about by professional help to think that one could see the real character of local people by flying or for that matter by cruise ships. We were to find that the peoples of the Pacific Islands are still deeply tied to the sea, and the seafarer, however poor, is a welcome person in their midst. No sophisticated airline or ship terminals, stereotyped travel attendants, or air-conditioned hotels for us. Instead, colorful waterfronts, local persons in native garb, and a tangy salt air of precivilization purity.

As for age, we found ourselves among the senior members of the cruising community. Mostly, the boats were homes to persons in their 20s and 30s who were not yet hooked on the materialistic needs of modern urban society. A modest boat kept seaworthy, casual dress consistent with local custom, and a friendly nature was their way of life. We were to find countless friends among these sincere young people who are practical idealists and live in a healthy world of their choosing.

But we were also to find a large number of establishment types, who, like ourselves, still had the red blood cells of adventure flowing through their veins. Some had never sailed before and started with a new boat. Others were old timers at the game and had boats of salty but proven vintage. There was no pattern of experience or boats—only consistency of purpose. People happy to forget the constraints of urban living and eager to make their own future.

None of these fitted the stereotype of South Sea wanderers—bearded and carefree, with their arms around island girls. What stereotyped perception overlooks is that the cost of the modern cruising boat may require a lifetime of work, and many of us arrive at Paradise Island with grey hair. Then there are the many others who continue to work, docking their cruising type boats at local marinas unaware that they, too, have the means to split from the 9-to-5 world and create an unbelievably satisfying way of life for themselves before it is too late.

We long ago lost count of the number of friends and acquaintances who had said, "I wish I could do that." As our boat was gradually transformed from a "Tupperware" product to a cruising reality, envy of us grew. Whether they envied our boat, our plan, or our determination, we do not know. But on our return it was no longer envy—it was a solid belief that you can do it yourself.

There is an old proverb credited to the Chinese which says that every journey starts with but a single step. Sometimes that step can be pretty obscure until the journey itself becomes visible. Ours was a $1000 windfall from a retirement fund paid in 1958 on the occasion of my leaving a San Diego aircraft firm. Retirement was furthest from our thoughts, so we blew the entire sum on our first boat—a 19-foot day sailor appropriately named *Idiots Delight*. Ten years later another job change occurred, this time involving a transfer to Los Angeles and forcing us to sell our house in the small city of Riverside. By now, our son Eric was a young man in college and we no longer needed a large house, so we moved into an apartment in the big city and banked the house sale proceeds. We then set about to find ways to invest for the future as bankers tell us to do. An early retirement at age 55 appeared possible in a few more years, and we decided that our best investment in the future should involve ourselves and the enjoyment of life. Once again, the boat won out. Now, however, it was to be a cruising boat of adequate size and capability to take us anywhere in the world. Exactly when or where was yet to evolve, but, having made the decision, we devoted all our free time to buying, equipping, and provisioning a long range cruising boat to be named, appropriately, *Horizon*. So it was that our love for water and sailing were to take us on a 17,000-mile odyssey through the fabled islands of the South Pacific.

San Diego, California

1

A Changing Lifestyle

Our dream of visiting the far off islands and peoples of the Pacific was becoming a challenge. To make it real required effort, and we were finding that our resources of time, patience, and money were being severely tested. We had to procure a proper boat, prepare it for at least two years of self-sufficiency, and then put our personal and business lives in order. How long would the preliminaries take? We could only guess at our capability to put everything together for the first time while maintaining a more or less conventional life within our society. One year seemed like a reasonable time for selecting the boat that would become our cruising home, with an additional two years devoted to outfitting it.

Now our problem was to propose to ourselves a departure date so that we could back off the estimated 3 years necessary for preparation. Our grand rationale for this exercise turned out to be really pretty simple—do it before you're too old to enjoy the rigors of sailing, but not before you have assured yourselves of some form of continuing income.

Early retirement for me at age 55 appeared to be a real possibility, combining a still capable physical condition with some continuing financial return from an engineering career. Betty, who had in recent years returned to her nursing career after many years as a homemaker, was also in good physical condition and was willing to resign after we had put all the other pieces together. And so, as the 52nd year of my otherwise conservative life passed into history, we set about in earnest to make our dream come true.

Boat shows, visits to manufacturers, talks with brokers, and an occasional sea trial became a way of life for us. My business entailed some travels about the country, making it possible to investigate cruising boat designs on both coasts. While Betty was happy to leave the technical aspects of boat selection up to me, she wanted to get the feeling of large cruising boats, so she accompanied me on much of the search. Our earlier experiences with both wood and fiberglass boats had convinced us that fiberglass was the best for durability and low maintenance. We therefore focused our search on fiberglass boats, and,

With boot top awash, Horizon *departs her home port of San Pedro, California.*

finding few modern cruising designs on the used boat market, we turned to new construction. The year we had allocated to boat selection passed quickly and the number of candidate designs narrowed until we were left with one—a stock 41-foot ketch of unusual design built by Morgan Yacht Company in St. Petersburg, Florida. Conceived for charter service in the Caribbean, it was an ideal boat for our purpose— good sailing rig, comfortable cabin arrangement, and solidly constructed to withstand the abuses of chartering. It was made of fiberglass with a teak interior, aluminum spars, and diesel auxiliary power.

Once we selected the boat, little time was lost by either the Long Beach yacht broker, with whom we placed the order, or the factory, which was to build it. Our order was signed on May 13, 1972, and I visited the factory in late May for final decisions on options and minor changes. At that time our dream was standing in the warehouse in the form of 55-gallon drums of resin and bolts of glass cloth. A warm heritage is something that the modern fiberglass boat does not have. Hull number 95, about to become our boat, was moved off Morgan's production line on July 3 and readied for delivery overland by truck and trailer to the West Coast. We were subjected to a myriad of highway regulations regarding oversize loads, special permits were needed to carry this 14-foot wide load along the eight-state route to the Pacific coast. Finally, word was received from the truck convoy on Saturday, July 29, that they had arrived in Tucson, Arizona, where they would wait until Monday, since it was illegal to carry such an outsize load on California highways on a weekend.

With great anticipation we drove to the Long Beach Marina Shipyard the following Monday morning for our first glimpse of our dream coming true. We were soon greeted with the incongruous sight of a boat finishing its first passage of 2400 miles covered with dirt!

A few more weeks were to elapse while the yard rigged the boat and made it ready for launching. Commissioning took place on September 30, just five months after the boat was ordered. With a bottle of good California champagne shattered over the massive stemhead fitting, Betty christened the boat *Horizon,* and our dream took on a physical form.

Over the next two and a half years, countless hours (and dollars) were spent in customizing *Horizon* to our satisfaction. Most of this work was done with the help of a longtime friend, Norm O'Brien. A bachelor with few time commitments outside of his professional career and an occasional golf game, Norm labored with us hour by hour as *Horizon* began to take on a cruising character. Sails, refrigeration, wind vane self-steering, navigation station, ground tackle, and the like were assembled and installed. As the most important items were completed, they were scratched from the work list, only to be replaced by less vital ones, and so the list seemed to perpetuate itself. Fearing that the boat itself was to become our objective rather than the cruise, we set February 1975 as our jumping-off date. Our work priorities were then reordered to stay within the remaining weeks. A large number of cosmetic and convenience items were never completed, but all of the safety at sea installations and day-to-day living accommodations were carefully finished. Even though our departure date had been arbitrarily set, we were satisfied with our completed modifications, so we happily snipped off the remaining work list and got ready to leave.

Well over a year later while we were enjoying the tropics, *Yachting* magazine asked me for an evaluation of this stock boat converted to a world cruiser. I was happy to report that it was working out fine. (Our first-hand evaluation appears in Appendix A.)

While the boat was being customized, Betty, besides continuing her work as a nurse, was planning and buying provisions. Each week the apartment grew more and more like a warehouse. Buying small quantities of provisions over long periods was to soften the last-minute purchasing blow by some fifty percent. Working toward a six-month period of self-sufficiency, Betty estimated we needed about 1000 pounds of food—mostly canned goods with a heavy emphasis on meats, which we knew would be scarce in the islands. On a smaller boat we might have become sorely pressed for stowage space, but on our boat this was not the case nor did we regret the large initial food investment. As we traveled further west and until we reached New Zealand, we lived off those provisions supplemented only by locally procured fresh fruits and produce and occasional purchases of tinned food from skeleton stocks at island stores. Few cruising boats were better provisioned than *Horizon,* nor did many enjoy 3 good meals a day such as Betty skillfully prepared on her two-burner kerosene stove. Betty's only concession to the elements was one big storage bin full of prepared one-dish meals, such as canned spaghetti, stew, chop suey, etc. These one-dish meals were reserved for those occasions when the seas turned rough and cooking became a problem.

As provisions were accumulating in the apartment and a variety of spare parts and tools were being assembled in the garage—threatening to displace the automobile—we attacked the problem of where to stow it all aboard *Horizon.* The boat seemed to have a multitude of shelves, drawers, lockers, and bins in her 40-foot length and 14-foot beam, but we later wished that there were even more built-ins as rough seas have a way of scrambling unconstrained goods. We approached the stowage problem by first making a general arrangement plan of the entire boat, identifying each compartment and then designating each individual stowage place within that compartment. All stowage was above the cabin sole, there being no bilge in this shoal draft boat.

First space assignments went to the comfort of the crew. Adequate forecastle space including the port bunk were given to the crewman, and Betty and I as owners took the aft cabin. One glaring error in cabin layout (unavoidable on our tight schedule of boat modification) was the placing of the navigation station in the aft cabin. While it was an ideal use of space, we later found that it greatly reduced our privacy inasmuch as the crewman occasionally needed to work a navigation problem or refer to a chart.

Initially we made no bunk commitments in the main cabin since we wanted to retain it purely as a dining area and social saloon and for the occasional use of guests. Exceptions to this occurred at sea when rain or heavy seas forced us to close the aft cabin companionway. Then Betty and I often took to sleeping in the main cabin between watches. When sailing to windward in rough seas our crewman also found it preferable to sleep in the main cabin.

With the living space arranged, we set about categorizing all the remaining stowage spaces as food, medical, spare parts, and tools. A loose-leaf notebook of four sections became our storage record and key to the 70 individual hiding places aboard *Horizon*.

Vermin aboard the boat had no particular appeal to us, yet we knew that the hot, humid climate and the less sanitary environment of the tropics raised the likelihood of infestation. We started with the advantage, however, of a clean fiberglass boat having few cracks and crannies in which vermin could hide or breed. Betty took the extra precaution of washing all of the stowage bins, drawers, and shelves with a strong solution of borax, which left to air dry, repels cock-roaches. To prevent worms and bugs, she put bay leaves into all the bulk containers of dried foods such as flour and rice and into the plastic bags that were placed around each paper container of dried products. And in a further attempt to lock the door before the horse was stolen, we were very careful to bring aboard only clean paperboard containers and boxes, which we felt sure harbored no roaches or their eggs. This became more difficult as we went further south and warehouse cleanliness steadily deteriorated. We were also warned that roaches inhabit clusters of fruits, so we thoroughly dunked in clean sea water all local produce before bringing it aboard. Our final record over the entire trip was two roaches seen aboard and one captured.

We were also prepared for rats, which commonly inhabit the dirtier waterfronts and come aboard by tightrope walking your dock lines. For this eventuality we brought along large aluminum pie plates to make rat guards if needed. And as a backup we also had a couple of old-fashioned rat traps. We were fortunate in never having a rat problem, but we did give one of the traps to a boat where there was evidence of a rat aboard.

We felt we should pay particular attention to fresh-water management, since we would be going into areas with questionable water purity (Mexico, for example), be away from land for long periods (four to six weeks), and be stopping at places without water reserves (atolls). To learn more about water purification problems, I called the Los Angeles Department of Water and Power and talked with their chemist. He advised the use of common household bleach, like Clorox or Purex, in the following proportions:

(a) if water is clear, add one-half teaspoon of bleach to each five gallons of water.
(b) if water is cloudy, add one teaspoon of bleach to each five gallons of water.

We followed his advice, and at no time during the cruise did dysentery affect any of our crew.

We were to find, however, that water can also grow stale and tanks can get odiferous. We learned a unique solution to this problem from another cruising yacht enroute. When faced with stale water in a tank, simply pour in a fifth of local wine per 50 to 100 gallons of water. Staleness disappears and the crew becomes happier. However, to avoid stale water in the first place, and to keep airspace odors from generating, we learned to add baking soda to each new supply taken on board, using one-half cup of baking soda per 50 gallons of water. Bacterial water purity was not to become a problem on any part of our trip. But after refilling the tanks many times we began to notice that excessive sediment was collecting, which could have been handled with the further addition of a particle water filter.

To conserve fresh water, each sink had both fresh water and salt water hand pumps—and no wasteful pressure water system. At sea, the fresh water would be turned off in the two heads so that no one would be tempted to wash body, hair, or clothes in fresh water behind closed doors. Fresh water was always available in the galley for drinking and cooking, although at sea we used salt water for all washing, and Betty did considerable cooking with it. Our water conservation plan was to be so successful that in our longest passage of 28 days we used only 60 gallons of fresh water—an overly safe margin considering that we were carrying 175 gallons. From this experience we evolved a schedule of water consumption that assumed two gallons used per day at sea and three gallons used per day in port when the salt water supply was turned off.

Betty and I had discussed the matter of crew over many cups of coffee with no decision. As a two-person team we work well together, and between us we had all the necessary skills. But we were troubled by the need for 24-hour watches at sea, which seemed quite demanding for two people and impossible for one. We continued to outfit *Horizon* for handling by two persons but with an option to carry a crewman if desired. The decision was ultimately forced on us by the insurance company, which would not give us extended cruising coverage unless we had a three-person crew. Now we set about in earnest to seek a crewman. We advertised in *Sea* and *Pacific Skipper,* both West Coast boating magazines, as well as in the many freebie boating tabloids that get good distribution around the marinas. Simultaneously, we asked the editors of the Cabrillo Beach Yacht Club *Lighthouse* and the Redondo Beach Power Squadron *Signal Halyard* to run the same ad, which went as follows:

> CREWMAN WANTED for South Pacific
> fun cruise. Navigation experience
> desired. Write P. O. BOX ——.

Now the cat was out of the bag, and friends and acquaintances sensing adventure began asking questions about our itinerary. At first we were more than optimistic that we could find our crewman from among our circle of boating friends. But disappointment soon set in, for most of our friends were established in business and community, and, unlike us, they were unwilling to separate themselves from the security of the life that they were used to. At best, we had offers to crew to Hawaii or Tahiti or on some other leg of our cruise, which matched their vacation schedules. We knew that such a transient crew approach would not satisfy the insurance company nor did we want to have crew replacement problems along the way. Little did we know how naive was this reasoning.

With no likely candidates among our acquaintances, we turned to screening the letters of inquiry now beginning to come in. Responses to our ad came from retired merchant marine officers as well as new high school graduates. Most sounded sincere, but many lacked what we thought was adequate experience. To shorten our ad we had asked only for navigation experience, knowing that any person with that experience would also have general seamanship experience. We found that this, indeed, was the case, and we received several qualified inquiries, which I answered by telephone. Again, the biggest issue became the length of the cruise—none were interested in a two-year round trip, so we scaled it back to a one-year outbound passage only. Now we started to get some real interest from potential crewmen, since most had in mind an around-the-world trip for which we would furnish transportation for the first and most interesting part of their journey.

But still another problem seemed to bother many candidates. There were buddies who wanted to travel together, and, while *Horizon* had accommodations for four people, we had no intention of taking along an unneeded hand. One of these inquiries had come from a Swede who together with an Australian buddy wanted to crew on a boat going to the South Pacific. We really became interested when we received a second letter from the Swede informing us that his friend had flown home on an emergency and would we be interested in him alone? His credentials were ideal—28 years old, a yacht masters license with supplementary navigation training, with three years aboard a 116-foot ketch on an around-the-world cruise. Several telephone calls later we reached an agreement that he would join us for as far west as we went provided that he was financially able to take care of himself after leaving *Horizon* and continue to Australia or back to the U.S.. At this time we had no idea how far west we would go, so the arrangement was fair and Sven of Stockholm, Sweden, became our first crewman. At this time we were congratulating ourselves on our choice, little realizing that our inexperience in cruising boat crew problems was to make us experts in personnel administration and labor relations before we were through.

Two weeks before our departure date Sven arrived at Los Angeles International Airport with his wife, who wanted to see *Horizon* and meet Betty and me. In the next two weeks Sven applied himself diligently using his seaman's talents to getting *Horizon* ready for the sea—installing ratlines, reinforcing sails, tuning and checking rigging. Marina onlookers claimed he spent more time in the bosun's chair than on the deck. We can honestly say that during Sven's tenure on *Horizon* she never looked so good nor was any boat of the cruising fleet any more shipshape.

Sven carried all the dignity of a professional seaman and had much of the Old World deference to rank. This was to bug me on more than one occasion. I have always been a do-it-yourselfer and enjoyed rowing the dinghy ashore or to visit other boats. Sven, however, would have none of that, and he told us more than once that it was the crewman's duty to take the captain and his lady on their visits. Although fearful of growing flabby through lack of exercise, I finally acceded to his philosophy.

For months before our departure we had been hearing rumors of attacks by local people on cruising boats anchored in Mexican or Latin American waters. These reports even alleged piracy on the high seas. Knowing the vulnerability of a cruising boat in an isolated anchorage, we believed the reports and concluded that some means of self-protection was needed. But what? We needed some expert help at this point, so Betty and I took our problem to the nearby Torrance City Police Department. Our mission so baffled the receptionist that it took her a full half hour to find a person to talk with us. We were then escorted into the chief's office to talk with his uniformed aide. At first he, too, did not understand what the Torrance Police could do for a cruising boat in foreign waters. But soon our arm-waving descriptions of hypothetical coastal cruising situations began to get his attention. Then his thinking changed from sophisticated law enforcement to what he would do in our situation. Surprisingly, this man carrying a gun even then, advised against the use of firearms in an isolated confrontation. Our faith in television westerns was crushed! Not to defend yourself with a Colt .44 seemed like heresy, but he argued that any attacker who was so determined that he could be thwarted in no other way probably had his own guns and we on *Horizon* made a better target than he in a skiff. Further, the attacker would probably not be alone and your chances of ultimate victory were poor at best—especially if local justice gets hold of you for shooting up its citizens. His advice was, simply, don't use a gun in a futile attempt at defense, try to thwart the boarding by some other means.

At this point the conversation went wild with ideas but soon boiled down to a few practical solutions that could be implemented without making *Horizon* an armed ship. Friendliness and reasoning at a distance were first advised with a casual show of force on the part of the entire crew. Maybe even a simulated gun such as a CO_2 target pistol in the waistband of a swimming suit would help deter them. At night, especially, a flare pistol could be used to advantage since when fired at short range its dazzling light would probably alarm most unsophisticated people.

The next hypothetical situation addressed an actual aggressive boarding. He suggested two techniques easily performed by untrained persons. One was simply a small baseball bat, which can give someone on the boat deck a decided advantage over the boarder trying to climb over the lifelines. We found a Little League bat of sound ash to which we attached a stout nylon wrist loop so it could not be easily pulled away from you. The second boarding defense measure followed Betty's inquiry about the use of Mace gas. While it is outlawed in California, Mace could still be obtained in some other states and is a very effective short-range deterrent. However, our policeman advised us of a simpler and equally effective deterrent—a common aerosol can of oven cleaner! It is a common household item not normally thought of as a weapon, but its spray directed at the face of a would-be attacker would temporarily stop him. The baseball bat and a shove overboard would, we hoped, wrap up the incident.

After two hours of discussing boat defense techniques with a trained policeman, we felt better about our chances of enjoying isolated anchorages. As we parted, he said that a good policy is to be friendly and firm from a distance. Or, better yet, completely avoid questionable areas and not expose ourselves to unnecessary hazards.

While Betty and I continued to get the boat ready we also whittled away at our list of extracurricular chores. Being part of the establishment for so long had implanted in us a faculty for orderliness that underlay all of our planning. The thought of lost mail, bills going unpaid, checks not being deposited, or loss of contact with friends led us in search of some responsible individual who could be our alter ego for a couple of years. At first, we thought about enlisting the services of a relative or friend to act on our behalf, but on second thought it didn't seem right to burden a volunteer with dull administrative details while we were having all the fun. About this time, a couple came into Betty's clinic for overseas shots before sailing into the Pacific. Betty learned from them that their attorney, Ralph George, of Torrance had established a simple legal procedure that enabled a bookkeeper to handle all of their accounts while they were gone. We hastened to the same attorney and, with his assistance, arranged for MS Bookkeeping Service, run by Shirley Harding, to handle our few continuing but important financial matters and to collect our mail for us. Our agreement with Shirley read:

In my capacity as bookkeeper with Power of Attorney during the absence of
EARL R. HINZ and BETTY F. HINZ
it is my responsibility to perform the following activities per their detailed instructions.
1. Endorse and deposit all income to checking account.

2. Disburse checks from that account to pay authorized expenses as designated by Mr. Hinz.

3. Maintain records of account, proof of receipts and disbursements.

4. Prepare and submit Federal and State Income Tax statements as required for the year ending 12/31/75. (To be amended if required on return of Mr. and Mrs. Hinz.)

5. Collect and assemble personal mail, to be collected from time to time by Eric Hinz or Norm O'Brien.

6. Perform any other bookkeeping functions that may be required and not designated at this time.

Fees for my services are to be at the rate of $10.00 per hour and apply only to actual hours spent. It is estimated that these duties can be satisfactorily performed in less, but not more than five hours per month.

For convenience we also established our post office box in the same branch as the bookkeeper's so she could easily collect our mail for forwarding.

But we were to find that a post office box is not always an acceptable address. We weren't surprised that the state motor vehicle bureau required a street residential address, but we were flabbergasted when the Coast Guard insisted on a street address for a documented yacht even though the vessel and owners were at sea! This crisis was surmounted in turn by using our bookkeeper's business address, which was more valid than any other we could think of. I might add that our business-in-absentia system worked well, and we lost not a single piece of mail nor did any creditor come looking for us.

Because cruising is based on opportunity as much as desire, we were not going to be ruled by an itinerary. However, we did have to get navigation charts, sailing directions, and light lists for probable areas of visit, and this led us to make a preliminary itinerary at least. It was to start with Mexico and take us through the South Pacific to the Fiji Islands and New Zealand. Neither Betty nor I spoke any Spanish, and we reasoned that with the continuing friction between yachtsmen and locals in Mexico, we would be better off if we could learn at least a little of their language. So, off to night school we went for a 30-hour course in survival Spanish. It paid off on many occasions in Mexico making us a little more *simpatico* than if we had shown no interest in their language. While it would also have been of some use to know French for our 3-month stay in French Polynesia, the island people would rather speak Tahitian, and that would have been the language to learn.

Time was passing faster now and it was no longer marina speculation on whether or not we would make a long cruise. *Horizon* was sitting lower in the water every day as supplies and provisions were put aboard. But we still had our primary ties to society—our jobs. We were not eager to cut off our income too early, yet our departure date of February 15 was approaching at an alarming speed. Again, with our usual decisiveness not necessarily founded on a rational base, we picked January 15, 1975 for job termination. Betty resigned from the medical clinic, and I retired from the aerospace industry. Our lives immediately changed from a well-regulated 5-day work week with holidays to a hectic 7-day per week, 15-hour per day effort to gracefully leave our urban life and take up a new life on the sea. It was not easy. In fact, it was traumatic at times. For over 30 years we had worked at being a successful part of a modern society, and now we were deliberately cutting the umbilical cord of security. But, as a close friend observed, if you don't do it when you can, you'll regret it the rest of your lives. We wanted to do it, so we pressed forward with our plan on an ever-shortening time scale. Finally, we put our furniture into storage, sold the cars, and moved onto *Horizon* with Sven. We departed our home port of San Pedro on February 18 for San Diego, where we would finish our outfitting and provisioning and obtain the necessary Mexican entry papers and fishing permits.

The adventure of a lifetime, dreamed of by many but realized by few, was about to begin for us. It was only our unbounded enthusiasm that overcame occasional melancholy thoughts of:

—departing from a social niche developed and nurtured by us over many years
—leaving our son to finish college and make his own entry into the world
—quitting our careers, which we had both enjoyed
—putting away all the prized possessions we had accumulated over years of close family living
—heading into a new world of unpredictable challenges, not knowing where our wanderlust would take us

2

South Along the Mexican Coast

We hadn't been many hours at sea before we discovered that we had loaded the boat so far down that the galley sinks would no longer drain by gravity. In fact, water was standing two inches deep in the bottom of the sinks, making them quite useless and becoming our first enroute mechanical problem. It should not have surprised us that the boat was sitting so low for we had put on board at least 1000 pounds of food, 175 gallons of fuel, 170 gallons of water, spare parts and repair materials for everything, plus the crew and their gear.

The sink problem was easily solved by installing a diaphragm hand pump, which has large flapper valves that readily pass bits of garbage and debris that accumulate in the sinks. Considering that we didn't have many options on fixing the sink, the Whale brand diaphragm pump worked admirably well for the entire cruise.

Light winds prevailed over this short passage, and it took us 34 hours to sail the 85 miles. Arriving late in the evening, we checked in at the San Diego Yacht Club guest dock and then moved to our assigned slip for the night. Our slip arrangement had been made previously by Bob Sharp, a long-time sailing friend of ours, who also loaned us a car, which made our final provisioning much easier.

One important reason for stopping at San Diego was to get our clearance papers to enter Mexico. While this could have been done in Los Angeles, the Mexican Consulate in San Diego clears more yachts into Mexican waters so their procedure is better established. Besides, the consulate in San Diego is more easily accessible. Visas are not required for boat travel in Mexico, and our passports did not get a single Mexican imprint. Instead, one gets a Tourist Card, which serves the same purpose. I had decided earlier that we would attempt to pursue our own official paperwork in foreign countries rather than use ship's agents. Looking back, only Mexico posed any problem of port formalities, and even then the experience of working them out with our limited Spanish was worth the trouble. We found the Mexican officials to be friendly and cooperative but obsessed with rubber-stamping every square inch of paper until the wording was illegible.

Because of heavy pleasure boat traffic into Mexican waters, a set of standard entry forms has been prepared in Spanish containing the request for consular clearance as well as crew lists for port entry (available from "Crew List," Babe Baldwin, P.O. Box 6354, San Diego, CA 92106). We obtained a set of the forms, filled out the consular clearance request form, and drove downtown to the consul's offices. After only a couple hours of waiting, we were relieved of $8.00 for the consular permit and a total of $48.00 for fishing licenses for three months for the three of us. In return, we were given a sheaf of papers to take along with us—all written in Spanish, of course. If copies of documents seem important in America, they are a traveler's lifeblood in Mexico. Consequently, I had many copies made of our new well-stamped authority to travel in Mexico. This turned out to be a wise step since each port, customs, and immigration official felt he had to have a copy of every document.

Word got around the San Diego Yacht Club of our impending departure, and friends gathered for an impromptu farewell dock party. To our delight, our son Eric came down from college to join in the farewell. At 11:30 Saturday, March 1, amidst a big cheer, we cast off the dock lines and motored out into the main channel to set sail. We were not to depart alone, for Milt Statford's Cal 48, *Vision,* and Bob Sharp's Cal Cruising 46, *Wind Rose,* fell in with us for a round of picture taking. The wind cooperated and we departed San Diego at five knots on a comfortable beam reach. At 1500 our escorting boats turned back, and we waved a special farewell to Eric aboard *Vision.*

Now we were alone—sailing south into the foreign waters that would be our world for many months. It was a lonely feeling as our friends dropped behind, but, anticipating adventure, we set our watches and sailed on south past Mexico's Coronado Islands.

Most cruising boats going south from San Diego make Ensenada their first port-of-call and affect an entry clearance there. But we had been to Ensenada so many times on the Annual Newport Beach–Ensenada yacht race that we elected to bypass it and make our official entry further south.

The coast of Baja California is basically inhospitable—rocky, with many headlands having reefs and shoals in abundance. While the ocean current well away from the shoreline follows a southerly movement, inshore the headlands cause large eddies, and the current can flow in any direction, causing many boat and ship disasters. Many anchorages are comfortable in the prevailing northwest winds but become untenable if the wind hauls into the west or south. All in all, longer offshore passages with less shoreline exploration are a safer procedure.

Our first anchorage in Mexico was in the lee of Isla San Martin, 145

Isla San Martin, our first foreign landfall, 145 miles south of San Diego.

miles south of San Diego. Isla San Martin is a barren, windswept, extinct volcanic cone rising to a height of 497 feet with a navigation light at its summit. A transient fishing camp, abandoned at that time of year, was the only other sign of civilization on the island. We had no particular urge to climb the summit so we contented ourselves with a closer look at the island shoreline and otherwise busied ourselves with making life more comfortable aboard *Horizon*. One other cruising boat joined us at the open anchorage as well as several fishing boats, which would put in late at night and leave early in the morning.

We stayed two nights at Isla San Martin and then took a short 10-mile sail to Bahia San Quintin, where we anchored off the beach well protected from the northerly winds. We had thoughts of visiting ashore the next day, but when we awoke in the morning the wind had swung into the SSE and we were now holding off a lee shore. This was no place for us to leave the boat, so we again weighed anchor and started the 200-mile passage to Bahia Tortuga, a safe closed harbor. Winds along the coast became frustratingly light and our sailing speed varied from 0–3 knots with sails down for hours at a time to reduce slatting wear and tear on them.

However dull the sailing was at this point, it was brightened by a surprise birthday party for Sven. He was welcomed into his 29th year with a chocolate cake, which Betty had secreted aboard (frozen) at San Diego. His unbridled passion for chocolate was further satisfied with a gift of a king-size chocolate candy bar. His chocolate mania was to seriously strain our supply of powdered drinking chocolate aboard.

The weather continued cool with some fog and heavy dew at night. We had put aside our yachting clothes when we left San Diego in favor of thermal underwear, wool sweaters, blue dungarees (real bell bottoms, the only kind for boat work), boots, knit caps, and waterproof gloves. With this protection we were quite comfortable on the long night watches.

Bahia Tortuga lies 35 miles southeast of Isla Cedros and its smaller rocky neighbors, Islas San Benitos. These islands, setting off a coastal headland, Punta Eugenia, cause a natural restriction to the flow of coastal traffic, and, as we drifted by them during the night of March 8th, we counted the lights of seven other vessels at one time in our vicinity. Dawn of Sunday, March 9, broke clear with a dropping barometer and an increasing northeasterly wind. Soon we were making 5½ knots headed east for Bahia Tortuga—we thought. But we had not reckoned with a strong current, and by the time we closed on the unrecognizable shoreline, we had been swept far south of Bahia

Cabo San Lucas on the southern tip of Baja California.

Tortuga. Faced with tacking into a northeasterly wind against a southeast flowing current was too much for us to accept, so we elected to forget that harbor and just continue south on the good reaching winds. In two more days of sailing we covered the remaining 245 miles to Magdalena Bay and entered this magnificent 80-square-mile undeveloped bay and anchored in the lee of Punta Arena.

Now for the first time we felt that we were in foreign waters, when local fishermen from Puerto Magdalena, five miles further inside the bay, stopped by to trade us some lobster for whiskey. Our trading stock, however, was made up of wine, and for two fifths of port we were able to get four live lobsters. We probably could have gotten the whole fishing skiff for two bottles of bourbon.

Punta Arena gave us our first close look at a Mexican fishing camp, abandoned for the season. This was a shark fishing camp as evidenced by the many mounds of sun-dried shark skeletons. The most sophisticated buildings were small shacks of pasteboard and corrugated iron, while the least sophisticated were merely brush-covered lean-tos. There is no drinking water here and piles of fruit juice cans tell the story. Surprisingly, few *cerveza* (beer) cans were found. But it was not always this desolate at Punta Arena, for on the north side of the point are to be found ruins of machinery and their foundations. In earlier days attempts were made to process whales and can fish, but the lack of water and plain isolation spelled the industry's early doom. Now only the nomadic fishermen from La Paz work the fertile waters of this area. But the whales are still there. Magdalena Bay is one of several bays along Baja California's west coast where the California gray whale spends the winter mating season, and we were fortunate to see two of the leviathans in the shallow waters of Bahia Magdalena.

After a few days exploring Punta Arena, we motored 15 miles along a Z-shaped channel to Puerto San Carlos, an official Port of Entry. The anchorage in Puerto San Carlos is not good since it is in a strong tidal stream and about a half mile from shore across a tidal flat. This was to be the start of my disillusionment with the inflatable dinghy as a shoreboat, we had to row against both wind and wave going ashore.

After getting our papers cleared at the port captain's office, we walked the half mile of dusty road to the small village. Here we bought our first fresh foods in weeks, but only those that would be cooked or peeled before eating. We had little desire to encounter Montezuma's revenge. While the town was dry and dusty, it was neatly tended and had a first-rate children's playground and town square. The local citizens we found to be a friendly lot, responding cheerily to our "buenos dias," rendered with a strong *Americano* accent.

Departing Magdalena Bay, we marked two significant events in quick succession. At 1715 local time on March 17 at 24° 20′ N. latitude and 111° 55′ W. longitude, *Horizon*'s water mileage at last exceeded her road mileage in the overland delivery from Florida to Long Beach. And on the following day we crossed the Tropic of Cancer at high noon and immediately started to feel warmer. This 145-mile passage to Cabo San Lucas used up two days of sailing time in very light airs, and, finally, we gave up and motored the last 20 miles in an early morning calm.

Cabo San Lucas is a small, quiet resort town sustained in part by a fish cannery. There is no shipping, as such. All products arrive or depart by truck, mostly on the large ferry boats that connect with the mainland port of Puerto Vallarta. The topography of Cabo San Lucas must be classed as transient since every few years a violent summer tropical storm will flood the town rearranging both land and buildings. In the past year a river overflowed, wiping out the port captain's office and dumping sand and assorted debris into the newly created inner harbor. We had initially anchored in this inner harbor for convenient access to the town. But we found it too dirty and busy for comfort and so moved to the outside bay. There we could swim off the boat and enjoy beautiful beaches.

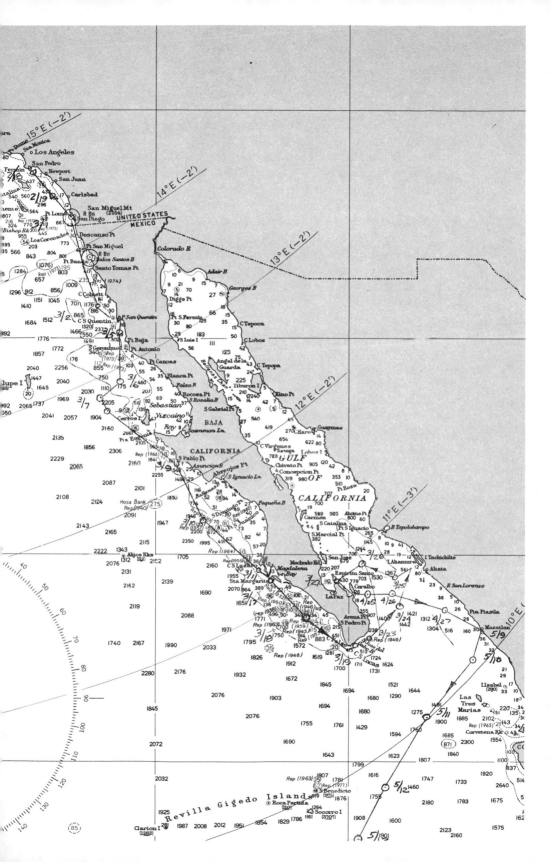

There had been little need for us to do much shopping yet, but we noted that canned goods prices are considerably higher and fresh food prices considerably lower than in California. We were able to purchase excellent potatoes and oranges in Puerto San Carlos and Cabo San Lucas at reasonable prices—also tasty tree-ripened bananas. Tops in this country, though, is the local bread called in Spanish *pan* ("pahn"). It is baked daily without preservatives, and we literally waited by the brick oven at the *panderia* for the first of the day's output and were never disappointed. The price was right, too.

Cabo San Lucas is a crossroad for yachts traveling down the mainland Mexican coast, up the coast of Baja California from whence we had come, or north into the Sea of Cortez, which was our next leg. Sailing the 140 miles to La Paz turned into a real challenge for us. By all standards (except in the Sea of Cortez) it should have been no more than a three-day sail. But it turned into a four-and-a-half day encounter. The first two days were sailed against a north wind on a port tack, which took us close enough to the mainland of Mexico to see the lights of the coastal railroad town of Altata. Then followed two days of light winds as we starboard tacked back to the Baja coast and on the fifth day a southwest wind right on our nose forced a beat into Canal de San Lorenzo, the entrance to Bahia de La Paz. In all, we had traveled 280 miles, or twice the rhumb-line distance between Cabo San Lucas and La Paz—a real test of a purist's patience.

Our arrival in La Paz coincided with their big Easter religious holiday, so we had to delay transacting our official business with the port captain and immigration until the following Monday.

Now after a month of cruising down the Baja coast and into the Sea of Cortez we formed some new thoughts on our neighbors to the south. Traveling by small boat brought us into contact with people in coastal villages who are still unspoiled by tourists. While our knowledge of their language could only be described as "survival Spanish," we have had little difficulty in getting our official papers handled or in obtaining supplies. Nor did we notice it to be a land of *manana*. The Mexicans do observe different working hours to adapt to their more tropical environment and some adjustments had to be made on our part. However, when they are open for business we have found them to be attentive and efficient.

La Paz kept us in her grasp for four weeks of beautiful sunsets. Situated on the east side of a large bay, the sun sets over the Sierra de la Giganta to the west, which is usually topped with garlands of clouds changed daily to the delight of the viewer. A beautiful setting for our evening social hours.

Enterprising Mexican youngsters provide trash pickup for yachts at La Paz.

Ciudad La Paz, "City of Peace," became a permanent settlement only in 1811. And its future was assured in 1830, when it was designated the capital of all Baja California. Its history, however, goes back to the 16th century when Spanish explorers discovered the site in 1534. Succeeding years saw pirates, vengeful Indians, missionaries, and inhumane soldiers occupying center stage in the beautiful bay at the edge of the Tropic of Cancer. A mixture of early Indian, Spanish, and Mexican life continued for 277 years before the seed of today's city took root. Black pearls were the mainstay of the economy for 400 years until in 1940 a mysterious epidemic wiped out the flourishing industry. But by then sportfishing had caught on, and La Paz continued to thrive; now it boasts a population of over 50,000.

La Paz has but one enemy—the wayward tropical storm. As happened in 1968 and again in 1976, these storms can wreak havoc with wind and water when they unpredictably follow a northerly course rather than the normal westerly movement from their breeding grounds off Acapulco. The sailor plying the Mexican west coast waters should beware of the eastern north Pacific hurricane season extending from June through October.

La Paz is still a frontier town with all the delights of old Mexico—

lovely architecture, friendliness, informality, street venders, and dirt roads. But it is rapidly coming of age. Baja California Sur is now officially a state of Mexico and the President of Mexico installed the first elected governor at La Paz in April 1975. We had a first row exterior seat to the proceedings as the reception was held on one of the new ferry boats tied up to the Federal Pier where we and others normally landed our dinghies.

Besides now having an elected governor, the city of La Paz can boast its first modern laundromat equipped with Maytag washing machines. Predicted by many locals to be a losing venture in a land where women are traditionally subservient to the wash tub, it has surprised everyone with its popularity. In fact, it was so popular that we resorted to washing during the siesta hours of 1200 to 1400 in order to avoid waiting.

Adding to our great enjoyment of La Paz was the warm hospitality of Mac and Mary Shroyer. The Shroyers operate a fiberglass boat-building shop and run a fleet of Grand Banks sport fishing boats under the name Embarcaciones Baja California. They themselves have sailed to La Paz from California, and we found them interesting and sympathetic to the needs of the cruising yachtsman. One of the small but important challenges presented to the crew of a cruising boat is where to get a fresh-water shower ashore to refresh themselves after a salty passage. Mac kindly solved that problem for us by offering the use of his shop's shower facilities.

Several enterprising youngsters have made the La Paz yacht harbor a source of business, which is of benefit to the anchored cruising boats. One group tends the dinghy dock at the Federal Pier helping boaters on and off this high, narrow stone walkway. An occasional small tip also gets security for your dinghy while you are ashore. A second group uses fishing skiffs—sometimes with outboards and sometimes awkwardly propelled by a single oar—to provide trash pickups from the boats. Never pushy, the kids are fun to deal with, even using only survival Spanish. But we noted that when their business got too profitable, they seemed to disappear, presumably to spend their profits.

The highlight of our La Paz visit was Eric's arrival for his college graduation vacation. He was followed a few days later by his girl friend Lynda, on a week's vacation from her job. We motored to the islands of Espiritu Santo and Partidas, twenty miles north of La Paz, and we went cove-hopping for the week.

Although the islands are dry and barren, they are great for climbing and the numerous sandy beaches and inlets made beachcombing a

A lunch stop at Isla del Espiritu Santo.

delight. Fish abound in the area, and, while we didn't do any fishing ourselves, we did enjoy Sierra mackerel given to us by another cruising boat, and we traded .22 caliber rifle shells with local fishermen for some delicious Cabrilla. The week ended all too soon, and returning to La Paz, Eric put Lynda back on the airplane to Los Angeles and the four of us made ready for the trip to Mazatlan.

Our 240-mile leg from La Paz to Mazatlan took three days of wind frustration on light easterlies (NE to SE) followed by a most delightful fourth day of downwind sailing with the self-steering vane doing all the work. We held 5–6 knots all that fourth day and into the evening, reluctantly giving it up at about 2200, when we arrived at the Mazatlan harbor entrance under a full moon. The crossing had its interesting moments of ferry boats, tankers, and fishing trawlers during the night and porpoise, pilot whales, and jumping manta rays during the day.

Experienced sailors of Mexican waters advise against putting too much dependence on the local navigation aids and we did find them to be at great variance with their descriptions published in *Light Lists* and on charts. Many lights were not operating and others had characteristics widely different from the published information. None of the lights were visible from the stated distances. What we thought might be

Mexico's most important navigation light—the Cabo Falso light at the tip of the Baja peninsula—was not working the night we passed it.

Normally we wouldn't consider making a night entry into a strange port, particularly in Mexico, with its doubtful navigation aids. However, in the case of Mazatlan we made a valid exception, being clearly guided to the harbor entrance by the powerful light, 515 feet high atop Isla Creston at the harbor entrance. We furled our sails in the lee of Isla Creston and in the company of local commercial fishing boats, made a comfortable night entrance into the harbor.

Sailors planning to visit these waters, should carry plenty of fuel or have lots of patience! We had been told of poor sailing winds along the Baja coast and in the Sea of Cortez and we are now believers. From San Diego to Mazatlan we had traveled 1400 miles and sailed almost 1300 of them. In doing so, many hours were spent becalmed with sails down, which, while preserving your sails, can be very trying to your patience. While we could have resorted to the engine—we have a 1000-mile cruising range under power—sailing is our game, and besides, sailboats make poor motorboats. Overall we had averaged 65 miles per 24-hour day, which gives an idea of the poor sailing winds.

Although we had not done much motoring (only 23 hours between San Diego and Mazatlan), we did run the engine each day to recharge the batteries and cool down the refrigerator. Engine running time must satisfy both the needs of the ice chest and batteries, but we found that the ice chest cooled down faster than the batteries could be charged with their automatic voltage regulator in control. Not wanting to run the engine for unnecessarily long periods at low charging rates, we added a manual charge control in parallel with the automatic regulator. This gave us the option of manually controlled higher charging rates to 40 amperes for short engine-running periods or the normal use of the automatic regulator for extended periods of motoring. Care must be taken when using the manual mode to prevent overcharging and boiling away the battery fluid.

Without a doubt, mail was our single biggest problem in cruising Mexican waters. Both letters and packages went astray, and airmail takes 7 to 10 days coming or going. In the past, port captains have held mail for yachts, but now, at least one, in La Paz, is declining to do so. *Poste Restante* may in the long run be the solution. But one must be specific when calling for mail, since at least the Mazatlan post office differentiates between "general delivery," which is for local patrons and *Poste Restante* for the transient patrons. The posted lists of persons having mail usually pertains to general delivery customers, the rest still have to ask for theirs at a window.

It is inevitable that at some point in a long cruise, there will be a maintenance problem, which will require sending back to the States for parts. If it happens in Mexico, the bureaucratic customs procedures are likely to be infuriating.

The yacht *Moorea* had its diesel engine injector pump drive shaft break while crossing to Cabo San Lucas, and they returned under sail to Mazatlan, where they telephoned Newport Beach for a replacement part. It was shipped promptly via a U.S. airline, only to end up sitting for days in the custom house. This in spite of having a local agent handle the paperwork.

In another instance, the yacht *Saga* suffered transmission damage while at La Paz. They removed the unit from the boat, packed it in a box, and took it to Los Angeles by air as personal baggage. Once repaired, it was brought back through Mexican customs as personal baggage with no problem. So with air travel as cheap as it is, it may be wise simply to fly from Mexico to California to get parts or repair work done. Certainly it will be quicker and less frustrating.

Mazatlan is an enticing port of call for both cruise ships and yachts. During our 12-day stay in this beautiful harbor, no less than 7 cruise ships docked for a day's visit. Many cruising boats call here since it is located due east of Cabo San Lucas and is a convenient stop no matter which way a yacht is headed along the Mexican coast. Its popularity among yachtsmen is further heightened every two years when fifty or so racing boats make it their goal in a race from Los Angeles.

The city of 120,000 persons developed as a fishing port around its natural harbor, but it later expanded as shipping of agricultural products and minerals from the interior of Sinaloa became important. More recently, it has been discovered by vacationers who arrive by car, jet plane, ship, and yacht to enjoy the tropical climate, extensive uncrowded beaches, and exciting sportfishing.

Mazatlan is not an old city, having been founded only in 1822, mostly as a result of enterprising Germans who settled there to sell agricultural equipment to the neighboring inland regions. Prior to their arrival, the natural harbor had only been used occasionally for careening of ships and to pick up fresh provisions. After becoming a permanent settlement, Mazatlan had a rather tempestuous youth as a battleground, which saw a rebellion against General Santa Ana, trouble with the Americans and French, and civil strife amongst its own people. It wasn't until 1875, when the imposing cathedral on the plaza, the Basilica of the Immaculate Conception, was started, that a real peace was realized.

The flavor of Mazatlan's heritage still exists in the blocks of old

The rugged shoreline of Mazatlan.

houses whose tall window gratings face the narrow streets but whose interiors open onto spacious secluded patios. These buildings of the old colonial period are in marked contrast to the modern homes, stores, and hotels, which are stretching ever northward along the coast.

For local color, it is hard to beat the one-block-square people's market, composed of about 200 privately operated stalls offering local crafts, clothes, fruit and vegetables, meats, breads, etc. We regularly saw one merchant sitting on his haunches displaying garlic buds for sale on an inverted box. It seemed primitive, but it was his business. This marketplace, together with the adjacent twin gold-spired cathedral and the main plaza, is the center of old Mazatlan and a place of discovery all in itself.

While tourism takes to the North Beach, light industry moves further inland along the upper harbor reaches. With the interesting parts of the city spread so far apart, it was impossible to see them solely by walking so we used the local bus system to advantage. While not a very sophisticated system, it provides a needed service at the low cost of one peso (about 8¢ then), and it added much enjoyment to our stay.

Following a few days of sightseeing in Mazatlan, Eric flew back to Los Angeles, and Betty, Sven and Earl turned to making the final preparations for the 3000-mile crossing to the Marquesas Islands. Betty did the final shopping and stowing of provisions—mostly fresh fruits, vegetables, breads, eggs, and other perishables. Fortunately, we had done most of our reprovisioning in La Paz at a modern supermarket, which rivals the best in California and turns out to have a better selection and lower prices than anything here in Mazatlan. The supermarket also accepted Master Charge cards, which helped the ready cash problem. We found fruits, vegetables, and meats relatively cheap in Mexico, but canned goods and shellfish are often double the U.S. price. Soft drinks and beer were selling for 32¢ per can with no case discounts, which we look for when reprovisioning. Liquor was generally cheaper, but local wines were higher and not as good as the California wines. Mexico has a virtual embargo on wine imports in order to protect their fledgling industry, which needs to gain more experience at this point.

After taking aboard the additional supplies for the long passage that would eventually take us to Tahiti, our next provisioning port, we found *Horizon* to be quite crowded down below. So we set about to make it more accessible as well as secure in case we should encounter heavy weather. In doing this, we converted the remaining pilot berth in the main cabin to stowage for boxes of eggs, oranges, and paper goods—things which are fragile or bulky and can't be jammed into lockers. The resulting stowage was inherently secure, being constrained by the cargo net leeboard we had installed for sleeping purposes. Now with only three people aboard, the extra berths were no longer needed.

There was also a variety of other produce to care for, such as carrots, onions, limes, potatoes, and cabbage. Some of these were stowed in nylon mesh bags hung where space permitted. The bulk, however, were slung in individual pockets tied in a continuous length of nylon netting left over from making our overhead life jacket containers. The pockets were strung along a handrail over the now-converted pilot berth and provided well-ventilated storage out of the way of normal living space.

In searching for alcohol to preheat the Primus kerosene stove burners, we had been referred to a liquor store that carried 180-proof drinking alcohol. There was no question but that it would provide a preheat! But we wanted something a little less exotic and eventually found industrial alcohol in a hardware store at half the price ($1.25 per liter); it worked well, although it did not have the most pleasant burning odor.

With our large fuel tankage and little engine running we had no urgent need to add fuel, but we topped it off anyway in La Paz and

Mazatlan. In La Paz it cost 20¢ per gallon, while in Mazatlan it cost 35¢ per gallon at Heimpel's sport fishing dock. In one case it was a 25% markup on wholesale, while in the other it was a 100% markup.

While reprovisioning was taking place, Sven was reinforcing the genoa with leather wherever we felt excessive wear might take place during the long passage. The leather he used was cut from a full steerhide tanned for jacketmaking, which we had purchased in La Paz for $10.00 to be used just for this purpose. This investment saved much wear on the sails besides the work of repairing them at sea.

Horizon was again setting low in the water, loaded with the best of Mexican produce, *pan,* and *cerveza.* The time had come to leave the shore of the North American continent and head into the South Seas. Friday, May 9, was picked for a departure that almost didn't occur.

Port clearance procedures seemed to vary greatly in our Mexico travels, even though the ports are nationalized under the Secretaria de la Marina Nacional. Puerto San Carlos, where few boats make their Mexican entry, had no requirement for a temporary boat import permit, and we were naively satisfied that they knew what they were doing. It came as a rude shock to us when I requested my clearance papers at the port captain's office to leave Mazatlan and was told that he could not issue them because I had no paper entitled *Permiso de Importacion Temporal.* Now what to do? My survival Spanish was rapidly failing me. Port Captain Luis Seemann took my problem from his secretary since the two of us were making no headway. He advised me to go to a ship's agent for help since I was now deep in the intricacies of Mexican maritime law.

On his advice, I hastened back to the yacht harbor to Bill Heimpel's sport-fishing offices, since they also act as agents for visiting boats. With a stroke of luck I found one of their operators not busy with the sport fishing crowd, and he took my problem over the telephone to the marine customs officer. It took a lot of Spanish before even he understood what I needed—apparently few are ever trapped without the permit. Then he sat down at his typewriter and composed a letter from me to the chief of marine customs requesting a Certificado de Solvencia, attesting that I owed no bills in Mexico and requesting permission to set sail.

A half hour later and $5.00 poorer, I made my way to customs, which was located away from the waterfront in a picturesque old fortresslike building with ceilings at least 20 feet high. There I found two unoccupied English speaking allies on their staff. One took my letter and flitted back and forth between rooms giving every office a chance to measure my predicament and pass judgment. The second kept me occupied with small talk to help pass the time and keep me contained. Finally, the leg man returned with all the approvals, and my chatty friend then typed up the certificate and secured many stamps and signatures to give it an official appearance.

It was now mid-afternoon and very hot, but I made all possible haste back to the port captain, who now not only gave me an engraved clearance certificate, but also handed me a parcel. It was our long-lost package from Eric, sent airmail six weeks earlier in care of Mac Shroyer at La Paz. Where it had been was a mystery, but Mary Shroyer had just received it and had the captain of the La Paz–Mazatlan ferry hand carry it to the port captain at Mazatlan. It arrived with perfect timing, for within one hour we had weighed anchor and departed Mazatlan for the Marquesas Islands.

Horizon's Pacific cruise was off to a good start and already memories were accumulating such as:

—the stark beauty of the Baja California coastline
—a feeling of loneliness and isolation at the Mexican fishing camps
—the simple friendliness of the Mexican on the street and his delight in helping us speak Spanish
—the colorful marketplaces
—eager anticipation of mail from home, which never left us the full cruise
—the satisfaction of living a life on our own
—a feeling of peace with the world as we watch yet another gorgeous sunset from the deck of our boat

3

The First Long Passage

South-southwest by the compass was our initial heading as we departed Mazatlan for Nuku Hiva. We would be sailing somewhat south of the great circle course to avoid the Islas de Revilla Gigedo, which lie about 300 miles off the Mexican mainland. These four small volcanic islands are barren except for sagebrush and cactus and a few spots of grass. Considering all of the detached rocks in their vicinity, they seemed quite inhospitable and not worth a close look compared to the lush islands that we knew lay ahead of us. So we shaped our course to avoid them safely.

Progress was slow for the first five days as we sailed in coastal winds of 0–8 kts., mostly from the west and northwest. The skies were overcast, making celestial navigation difficult, but since we were on a safe route careful dead reckoning would serve our purpose in the absence of clear skies. The daily distance made good (noon–to–noon) averaged only 83 miles per day including currents, and some of the time we drifted with the sails down to reduce the slatting wear on them.

These first slow days of the long passage were not wasted, since we used them to develop a routine of life at sea, which, with only minor changes, we were to use for the rest of the cruise. While we did not want to get too regimented on a fun cruise, we all also felt that it was worthwhile to have a daily schedule of simple proportions at least.

We had earlier decided that we would stand 24-hour watches when sailing as a precaution against collision, and this had been the principal reason for taking along a third crew member. Beyond that we could find only two events of real consequence that would set our routine—these were eating habits and times for celestial observations. Even these are not rigorous, since weather can randomly affect both. Our simple watch criterion said that the skipper and crewman would alternate 3-hour cockpit watches. Betty, however, insisted on one regular watch, but not one that would interfere with galley duties. She settled on the 2100 to 2400 slot to allow her to "wind down" after the supper hour and have a quiet smoke by herself. Little did she (or we, for that matter) realize that more unusual occurrences were to happen on that watch than any other over the succeeding months.

Our watch schedule, which stood the test of 17,000 miles of sailing and had the stamp of approval from three very different crewmen was as follows:

This system rotated each day and skipper and crewman thereby alternated, taking the morning sights and reducing them after breakfast to establish our daily position. The six-hour-long daylight watches (0600–noon and noon–1800) were not tiring, and the equivalent time off gave the crewman or skipper an extended period to really relax and do things of personal interest.

The safety of the solo night watches at sea was to give us some concern. If for any reason the person on watch were to fall overboard, chances are that the sleeping crew would not hear him, and the self-steering system would simply keep the boat sailing on into the night. Even if we heard the person go over, the chances of finding and retrieving him are not in his favor. So to the night schedule we added two rules: always wear deck shoes and use your safety harness at all times.

As our routine of life at sea evolved we began to appreciate little gadgets that we had put aboard, such as the flat metal-mesh heat distributor used for slow cooking. Betty put it to work for toasting bread on the kerosene stove, and it was far superior to any of the other so-called toasters that we had tried over many years of boating. And the ever present problem of keeping dishes, pans, and other galley wear from sliding on the hard-surfaced countertops was cured by covering the surfaces with rubber webbing bought months earlier at a restaurant supply house and now put to work. With dish and pan clatter arrested in the galley, we turned to quietening the rigged blocks, which were forever banging on the decks. Remembering our nylon carpet

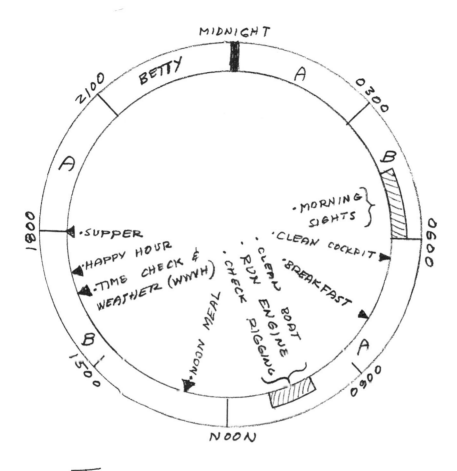

THE
DAY's
ROUTINE AT SEA

squares that we originally used at dockside to protect the decks from dirt and hard shoes, we cut them to fit under all free blocks as thump pads, and that made life below in our "fiberglass drum" much more pleasant.

There are as many different techniques of navigating small boats as there are navigators to develop them. They range from the self-confident person who taught himself enroute, to the experienced hand who has done it all before. I fell into the latter category, and having made navigation a hobby over the years, I set up a procedure to be followed, which was simple but precise enough to give us a good understanding of the local ocean currents and confidence in our position. Precise dead reckoning is the basis for it, using hourly navigation and weather recording. This was done by the person on watch using "The Offshore Log," a navigation workbook, which I had developed earlier for use in navigating small boats. With this information I could easily determine and plot our DR positions for 0600, 1200, 1800, and 2400 local times. That DR position closest in time to celestial sight taking (usually the 0600 DR) was then adjusted to correct for currents based either on the Pilot Charts or from the prior day's run or both. Using considerable judgment, which improved with time, we were able to establish a reliable estimated position for use in the celestial data reduction. No big thing at all—just a routine, repetitive process that got easier and more precise each day.

But the real satisfaction of blue water sailing comes with the daily celestial position fix, which if done right, tells you precisely what your progress has been for the past 24 hours. There are always uncertainties in the upcoming day's weather, so the person on the dawn watch (Sven or myself) would take a round of sights at morning twilight. Should clouds obscure the morning sky, we then resorted to sun lines during the day. Evening fixes were rare, being used mostly for night approaches to land, since working up sights at night just never seemed like fun. But on the other hand, star gazing to pick out suitable navigation bodies in the peaceful early hours of the morning was always most interesting. Particularly when bright, unidentified stars would show up slowly moving across the dark sky, and suddenly you realized that you were tracking a satellite! In only a few mornings of star gazing you develop your own list of favorite navigation stars and planets, which turn out to be useful for many succeeding days.

After a few weeks of practice we became very proficient at simple two-body fixes, which, when carefully done, we felt to be as accurate as three-body fixes or runs of sights. On the whole, sight taking on a small boat is difficult, so we concentrated on getting just two good sights at any time, and this became our standard procedure.

In sight reduction we had a difference of opinion, since Sven had been trained using HO 249–Air Navigation Tables, which is probably the most commonly used system on small boats. I, however, had tried it in earlier years along with HO 211, 214, and 229–Marine Navigation Tables, but I had found its precalculated convenience limited my selection of bodies to "shoot." Consequently, I put a 3-volume set of HO 229 tables aboard covering the latitudes 0–45°. With these I solved all of my sights with equal ease just as fast as Sven by using my newly developed "Sight Solver," which did away with forms and procedural errors.

The end result of dedicated navigation work is a small pencil mark on a chart that represents your position in the vast ocean area. For the first few days out, the noon position dots move ever so slowly. But after many days your track seems to come alive, and your destination becomes an irresistably attractive force. On passages lasting several weeks, morale is an important consideration, and even a pencil mark moving inevitably towards a destination is worth a toast at Happy Hour.

From the sixth day on, those daily position marks started getting further apart and we then knew we were finding the tradewinds at last. Although the winds started more north than east, they were steady and we enjoyed pleasant sailing at an average of 108 miles per day on winds to 10 kts. On our tenth day out the winds swung into the east and we had the first rain, which then continued more or less—mostly more— for seven consecutive days.

On the twelfth day we fell into the Doldrums—literally and figuratively. With almost continuous rain and progress reduced to 68 miles per day for four consecutive days, our spirits sagged. Winds boxed the compass and were mostly 0 to 6 kts. Even the best squalls couldn't generate winds of over 15 kts. and drifting occurred all too often. Our longest period of drifting was the night of May 20 from 1700 to 0200 the next morning, during which the rain deluged us. We captured about 5 gallons off the cockpit awning, which was used for coffee and rinsing some of the salt out of our clothes. Our rain catcher had not yet been completed or we would have caught more of the sweet, soft rain water.

The Doldrums are more formally known as the "intertropical convergence zone" or the "belt of equatorial calms." But by any name they still are an undesirable sailing area. This region of light and variable winds laced with squalls and thunderstorms is the product of the convergence of the northeast and southeast tradewinds. It tends to be wider in the Eastern Pacific than in the Western Pacific and, while it also always lies north of the equator in the east, it sometimes droops below the equator in the Western Pacific. The worst weather of the

Doldrums occurs where the winds of the Northern and Southern Hemisphere meet at their widest angle, which is in the Eastern Pacific. Consistent they are not, so the sailor takes his chances. In my crossing of them in the Los Angeles to Tahiti race in 1970, they were hardly noticeable.

On the other hand, they can be quite miserable, as we see from a description given by Commodore Arthur Sinclair, aboard the frigate *Congress* on a South American cruise in 1817–1818:

> This is certainly one of the most unpleasant regions in our globe. A dense, close atmosphere, except for a few hours after a thunderstorm, during which time torrents of rain fell, when the air became a little refreshed; but a hot glowing sun soon reheats it again, and but for your awnings, and a little air put on circulation by the continual flapping of the ship's sails, it would be most insufferable. No person who has not crossed this region can form an adequate idea of its unpleasant effects. You feel a degree of lassitude unconquerable, which not even the sea bathing, which everywhere else proves so salutary and renovating, can dispel. Except when in actual danger of shipwreck I never spent twelve more disagreeable days in the professional part of my life than in these calm latitudes.

We entered the Doldrums at 11° N. latitude, which is about 2° north of their normal position for that time of the year. They were also only about 4° wide at this longitude instead of the average 5°. Surprisingly, we were able to get two celestial fixes off the sun while in the cloudy Doldrums. As Betty remarked, the Doldrums would have been much worse if they had been the glassy calm variety. The moral is "be pleased with what you have."

We came out of the Doldrums into the southeast trades very abruptly. At 0200 the morning of May 24 (day 15) there was no wind, but it had quit raining. At 0300 we had about 3 knots of wind from the south. At 0600 it had risen to 10 knots from the south-southeast and we were sailing again. From then until we raised Nuku Hiva on the twenty-seventh day, the Trades never faltered and we had glorious sailing averaging 126 miles per day on southeast and east winds. On one day we logged 175 miles but such progress was offset by other days such as the one when we netted only 71 miles. These variances in daily distance traveled came mainly from ocean currents. We rode a very favorable 2.4 knot current on the day with 175 miles progress. The 71-mile day occurred in the ocean region between the east-flowing equatorial counter current and the prevailing westerly currents driven by the

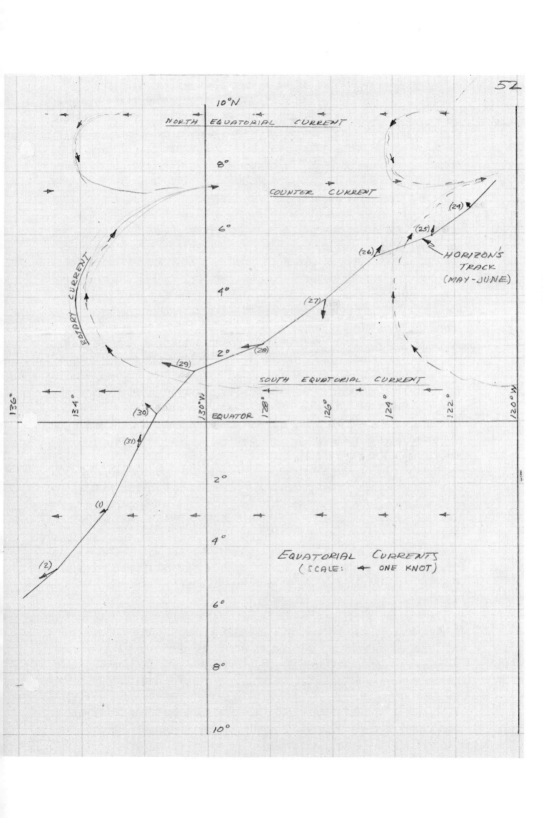

52

southeast tradewinds. On this day we had encountered a northeast current flowing at 1 knot setting almost dead against our course.

The surface currents of the ocean are caused predominantly by winds blowing over the surface of the water. Consequently, surface current patterns are somewhat similar to the wind patterns, particularly over the open ocean. Anomalies do occur, however, and one of them is the equatorial counter current. The converging west-flowing ocean currents from the two hemispheres actually remain separated by a narrow eastward flowing current near the equator. This counter current occupies a narrow band of about 1 to 2° width north and south, and, as one would expect, unusual water motion occurs as these opposing principal flows separate. I call it a rotary current, which acts like a bearing rolling between two flat plates. We were able to track these currents for many days during which we experienced excellent navigation conditions. Our observations of the currents in this region are shown in the chart below along with the average current data extracted from the monthly Pilot Chart. The small arrows along our course represent the local currents, and they seem to pull and push the course line out of position, which, indeed, is what is happening.

Small-boat sailors have often reported erratic sailing in this region of normally steady easterly trade winds. The explanation for it lies wholly in the counter and rotary currents of the area, which have a significant influence on the slow-moving sailboat. Today's sailor should hardly be surprised by the presence of this unusual current pattern since it is indicated on the Pilot Charts.

Highlight of the long passage south was the equator crossing that took place on May 30 at a longitude of 131° 50′ W. Betty as the only Pollywog aboard was duly initiated into the Court of Neptunis Rex by old Shellbacks Earl and Sven. As part of her tribute to Neptunis Rex, Betty posted a letter at the equatorial mail buoy, and, wind and tide willing, we'll discover in a couple of years who received it. There was a tear in my eye at the event, however, since that bottle had contained the last of our Mexican tequila. We have learned to enjoy many foreign ways of life!

Days in the southeast trades were comfortably warm, making the fantail showers with buckets of salt water a real pleasure. We had only two days of rain during the last twelve days of the crossing, and we were able to get good celestial navigation fixes every morning. We took only one evening fix and that was in preparation for a night approach to the Marquesas Islands.

Making a landfall never ceased to give me a thrill, and this time it was superlative—both geographically and navigationally, as the uninhabited island of Ua Huka in the Marquesas group came into view shortly after noon on June 4. Sailing onward we passed into the lee of Ua Huka at 2330, and the breeze carried a fragrance of flowers beyond belief! At 0300 on the morning of June 5 we arrived off the southeast corner of Nuku Hiva where we heaved-to until daybreak, after which we sailed into beautiful Taiohae Bay.

Twenty-seven days of sailing in all kinds of wind and wave, except storms, had taken us from Mazatlan to Nuku Hiva. The crossing had variety but no unusual drama. A distance of 2845 miles was covered, which included a dogleg to avoid the Islas de Revilla Gigedo off of mainland Mexico. Our 105-mile-per-day overall average satisfied us for a cruising passage, which crossed the Doldrums with its light confused winds and uncooperative currents. We had trolled for fish the entire distance with disappointing results catching only one (but delicious) Skipjack. The seas, in fact, were quite barren except for small flying fish and the large soaring birds that feed on them. Surface traffic consisted of five ships whose lights we saw during the night and a tanker and Japanese fishing trawler, which we saw during the day.

We had entered the great area of the Pacific known as the Polynesian Triangle. It is anchored on the north by the Hawaiian Islands, at the east by lonely Easter Island, and in the Southwest by New Zealand. In an anthropological sense, all these people are similar in racial characteristics, that is, they are all Polynesians as distinguished from Melanesians or Micronesians, with different physical features.

The Polynesian Triangle encompasses 10 million square miles of the most beautiful cruising waters on the surface of the earth. Within this area are over 360 islands with a land area of 10,000 square miles, excluding New Zealand. That gives almost 1000 square miles of water for every square mile of land and you can now begin to understand the origin of the seafaring nature of the Polynesians. Over this vast area of the Polynesian Triangle there are only 1.2 million persons (again excluding New Zealand) and over half of these people live in Hawaii.

The 360 islands are not evenly distributed over this vast area. In some cases they are chains of islands rising to the surface from submerged chains of mountains. The southern Cook Islands and Austral Islands are part of the same chain, but others like the Marquesas are simply tops of closely spaced seamounts. Over the years the neighboring islands have become politically associated, and today there are eleven identifiable groups of Polynesian Islands. Except for New Zealand, all groups lie within the tropics, that is, between the Tropic of Cancer in the Northern Hemisphere and the Tropic of Capricorn in the Southern Hemisphere.

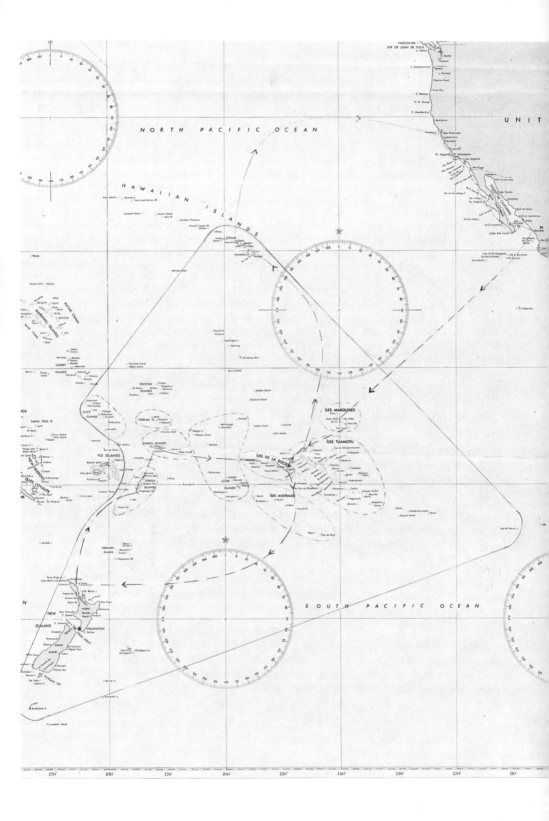

Island Groups of the Polynesian Triangle

Island Group	Number of islands	Land area sq. mi.	Population (1967/1971)	Government
Hawaii	8	6425	770,000	State of the U.S.A.
Marquesas	12	492	5200	
Tuamotu	76	343	6700	French Polynesia—a French
Society	14	646	81,000	Overseas Territory
Austral	7	63	4400	
Cook	15	93	21,600	Independent
Samoa	15	1211	172,400	Western Samoa—independent Eastern Samoa—U.S. territory
Tonga	200	269	87,400	Kingdom
Tokelau	3	4	1700	New Zealand territory
Tuvalu	9	11	5800	Independent
New Zealand	2	103,100	2,864,000	Commonwealth of British Empire

Now we were at our first islands of paradise and we took time to reflect on the events of the past days. Our collective thoughts recalled:

—The way one day at sea melts into another without boredom
—How unusual the equatorial countercurrent and how significant its effect on sailing progress
—The fun of initiating a "Pollywog" into the Court of Neptunis Rex
—The feeling of isolation one has on a long passage
—The simple pleasure of showering in a rainfall
—The beauty of sunrise and sunset in the tropics
—Nights of quiet solitude "ghosting" along under starlit skies

4

Marquesan Magic

No group of islands captures the spirit and romance of the South Seas more completely than those of French Polynesia. Known to Spanish and Dutch explorers as early as the sixteenth century, it was not until the eighteenth century that the islands came into scientific prominence with the explorations of Captain Cook. Even then, these islands half a world away from Europe were of little consequence until the ill-fated breadfruit expedition of Captain Bligh on the HMS *Bounty* in 1788. From then on the islands were to become unwilling hosts to a multitude of explorers, whaling ships, and missionaries. French and British rivalry backed up by naval forces soon convinced the Tahitians that they would have to pledge loyalty to one or the other of the European powers for their own protection. In 1843 France took formal possession of Tahiti and Moorea and, during the remainder of the nineteenth century, annexed all the islands of the Society, Marquesas, Tuamotu, and Austral groups in to what we know today as French Polynesia.

French Polynesia lies near the center of the Polynesian Triangle and is thought to have been settled in about the fifth century by Polynesian mariners arriving from the Gilbert Islands in Micronesia. Lost to history are the real details of settlement of the four island groups, comprising 109 islands of 1544 square miles, spread out over an ocean area of 1,540,000 square miles. While the original center of religious and political power was on the island of Raiatea, Tahiti, because of its large size and great fertility became the most populous of the Society Islands and eventually gained political dominance over its neighbors. Today Tahiti is the seat of government for French Polynesia, which has resulted in all the peoples of this area being called Tahitians.

The islands of French Polynesia contain a cross section of the geologic history of Pacific land masses. The Marquesas are the high islands, young in age, too new to have developed any appreciable fringing coral growth. At the other extreme, the islands of the Tuamotu Archipelago are the true atolls—lagoons ringed by coral reefs, which long ago swallowed up the remaining land masses. These are the low islands. Between these two geologic extremes are the volcanic reef-fringed islands called the Society Islands, which have become the principal islands of French Polynesia. They have the fertile coastal plains of volcanic ash for growing food plus a protective barrier reef that shelters the inhabited shoreline, provides a haven for fish as well as local outrigger transportation, and now makes possible safe harbors for modern ships. Tahiti in the Society Islands is a near perfect combination of mountain, coastal plain, shoreline and reef. It is not at all surprising, then, that Polynesian civilization concentrated there. This natural environment plus an intelligent people have created a Pacific paradise to be envied by all. French rule is accepted for its benevolent nature, and the local economy is booming along with French financial aid.

The five principal inhabited islands of the Marquesas group (Nuku Hiva, Ua Pu, Hiva Oa, Tahuata, and Fatu Hiva) support a population of just over 5,000 persons. But at one time late in the eighteenth century, the population was estimated by European visitors to number 60,000 persons. At that time the island of Ua Huka was also inhabited, but today it has only transient visitors at its small airport, which serves all the Marquesan islands.

Like most Pacific island groups, the Marquesas chain runs from Southeast to Northwest paralleling the Southeast trade winds. With two ports of entry, Atuona on Hiva Oa and Taiohae on Nuku Hiva, one is eventually faced with sailing to windward to see all the islands. We chose to enter at Taiohae and take our lumps going to weather later.

We got our first negative impression of French administration from the French gendarme who said we could not apply for a 3-month visa at Taiohae, but had to go to Papeete for it or leave French Polynesia after only a 30-day stay. Not having brought all the necessary papers to the gendarmerie for obtaining entry, we had to go back to the boat for

The island of Ua Pu in the Marquesas is little visited because of its poor anchorages.

them and on our return, the Frenchman had left and his Tahitian deputy was in charge. Repeating our visa request to him (he spoke English), he said it could be done and took our papers including some customs forms we filled out on the spot. A few days later he had secured approval by radio to give us a 3-month visa, although we would still have to stop at Papeete before the 3 months were up to complete the paperwork. We were to find throughout French Polynesia that the French administrators were generally stiff and uncooperative compared to the Tahitians who in subordinate roles seemed to enjoy helping the cruising people enjoy their lands.

We stayed at Nuku Hiva for two weeks, partly to rest ourselves after the crossing and to make minor boat repairs, but mostly to learn the Marquesan way of life. All this took place at Taiohae and Tai Oa Bays. Many yachts make their official entry at Taiohae, and there were 13 present on one day. Over the two weeks, possibly 20 had entered—one single-hander from France and one from the U.S., a West German boat, two from Papeete, another from France, and one each from Connecticut, New York, and Miami. And the rest? You guessed it— California. The boat from Miami was *Rigadoon,* a 38-foot Ingrid design, which had already circumnavigated the world once and was on its second trip around. We felt somewhat awed at this point to be in the presence of such cruising experience.

The most unique boat was *Scud* from Noank, Connecticut, an authentic replica of *Spray,* in which Joshua Slocum sailed around the world at the turn of the century. *Scud* was home built and sailed by a family of five (with children 10–13 years). Authentic right down to the wood stove, kerosene lanterns (not lamps), and, of course, engineless. *Scud* had already circumnavigated the Atlantic and was on its way to San Francisco. It was from *Scud* that we first learned the meaning of "Yachtie helping Yachtie." In a port of call such as Nuka Hiva, there are virtually no hardware supplies nor sailing charts available. We needed charts of New Zealand since it now appeared possible for us to reach there before the year was over. *Scud* needed some Primus pump washers, which we had, so since they decided not to go to New Zealand, we traded items to our mutual satisfaction. We were to do this many times more as unexpected needs arose. As long as there was another yacht in the harbor, we never felt alone.

The French have established socialized medicine in the Marquesas, so all treatment, medical and dental, is provided free by a small but modern and well equipped hospital and dental office. Visitors are eligible for treatment also, since there is no other source of medical help. More than one yachtsman has taken advantage of it because of a very viable staph germ, which plagues the area and causes severe infections of open sores, however small, literally overnight. We fortunately escaped those problems. But we did not escape a dental problem, for Betty had cracked the top off of a molar and, besides having a jagged edge, she knew it would deteriorate if not covered in some fashion. So, she took it to the resident government French dentist who, incidentally, conducted his practice in shorts. His remedy was simply to pull it. Betty, not wanting to lose a repairable tooth, declined his offer. In Papeete she was to get the same response from two private practice dentists, so she waited until New Zealand where a dentist properly built over the fracture.

And there's no escaping the nau-nau fly which inhabits beaches, valleys with streams, and other moist areas. It looks like a small gnat or tse-tse fly and quietly draws the victim's blood after injecting an anticoagulant fluid that later causes local swelling and great itching for up to two weeks. Vigorous scratching is often followed by a staph infection, and this gives the hospital considerable business. Nuku Hiva supposedly is the worst nau-nau fly island, but others have them also.

The nau-nau flies were at their worst along the beach by the wash

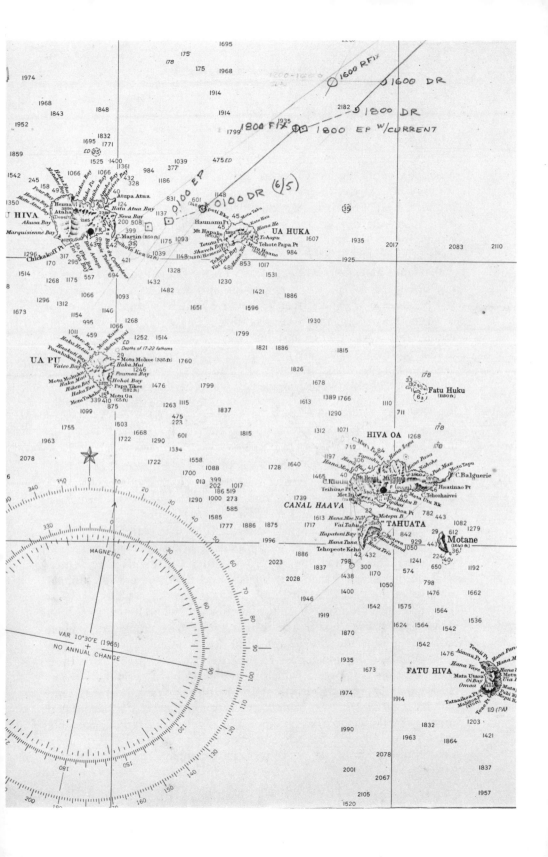

house. Since the wash house had fresh water from the mountains, we couldn't resist daily showers in spite of the nau-nau fly. Our biggest worry was taking back aboard the huge cockroaches that inhabited the wharf area.

There are three small general stores *(magasins)* in Taiohae, Maurice's being the most famous. Prices were so high, however, that we only bought day-to-day needs consisting mostly of fresh fruit and produce, beef, French bread, and bulk Algerian wine (only $1.45 US a liter!). On one day we made a major food-gathering foray into the mountains on the trail to Taipivai (read Melville's *Typee* for a great early account of this valley and its people). By noon we were stuffed with papaya and *pomplemousse,* a sweet large grapefruit. A Marquesan boy about 16 years of age helped us gather the ripe bananas and pomplemousse in a valley near his home. While he scampered barefoot through the undergrowth like a rabbit, I followed clumsily along in hiking boots I was glad to have on!

Vegetables are normally not sold in the *magasins* because people raise their own—what little they eat. But on the outskirts of Taiohae can now be found a vegetable garden wherein most of the vegetables and fruits pleasing to the European palate can be found—radishes, carrots, cabbages, leaf and head lettuce, tomatoes, papayas and pomplemousse. While a bit expensive, they were welcome after four weeks at sea.

One event of great significance took place at Taiohae on June 7—the organization of the first yacht club on Nuku Hiva. The local baker, a Chinese Tahitian named Ropa, had taken such a liking to yachtsmen (who relish his French bread and pastries) that a number of us created "Ropa's Yacht Club" in his bakery. It is complete with carved nameboard, a green burgee with ropelike letters (actually sewed-on shoelaces), and courtesy burgees from visiting yacht clubs. I presented the Cabrillo Beach Yacht Club burgee and CBYC is now an affiliate member of the Pacific Yacht Clubs Unorganized.

No account of Marquesan culture is complete without mention of the woodcarvers. Their's is a true artistic craft; they employ only hand tools except for the chain saws used for roughing out the carving blocks. Two woods indigenous to the area are used, one is rosewood and the other is toewood, which is similar to black walnut. It grows predominantly around Baie Marquisienne on the west side of the island and is relatively scarce. The harvesting of toewood is celebrated annually by the wood carvers. Once a year the wood carvers assemble by outrigger canoe at the bay and collectively harvest a self-rationed amount of the rare wood, which is all they can have for the succeeding year's carvings. After the harvest is done, they celebrate with a huge feast and then return home.

While they will carve most anything you can describe, ceremonial swords and spears, tikis, and bowls are the most common. Special items we saw in progress were a three-foot square rosewood chess table with tiki chessmen at Daniel's and a goat's foot walking stick at Uki's. We had a two-foot high wood carving made by Uki to attach to *Horizon's* mainmast over the dinette.

The Marquesan's daily schedule is set by the sun, so come nightfall the village streets are dark and empty, with but one exception—dance practice at Taiohae for the fete on July 14, Bastille Day. Every night the drums beat, the hips gyrate, and the pulses of visiting yachtsmen quicken. Aided by Aladdin lamps, the dance master directs his team through a two- to three-hour session. The final competition will be held on Raiatca in the Society Islands, and the winners go to Papeete to compete with the Tahiti groups.

Besides Taiohae, we visited Tai Oa bay about five miles away where we unexpectedly became guests of the woodcarver Daniel. When we left Taiohae on Saturday, Daniel's wife, Antoinette, had just finished her weekly shopping and was in need of a ride back to Tai Oa bay. How lucky for us! Our little favor in taking Antoinette home produced a weekend of real island hospitality. Daniel invited us to a wild goat barbecue on Saturday night after his workday was finished. His daughter Sophy and nephew Alexi also were there. (They have another daughter in school at Hiva Oa and a son who works at the Tahara'a Hotel in Tahiti.)

Wild goat is a common meat for them, and I was fascinated with the swift, clean preparation of it and the fully programmed fire, basting, and spit movement. In eating it they showed a deference to our city manners by offering us knives and forks while they ate in the traditional finger manner. The barbeque included rice, salad, and French bread, topped off with bowls of steaming French Nescafe. (Perked coffee, we find, is a rarity.)

Daniel speaks some English and Antoinette understands some, so we had little communication problem. Their home is in a beautiful valley of which they are very proud. It contains innumerable fruit trees and many coconut palms, which provide the copra crop. While only about ten people now live in the valley, there is evidence of over 1,000 once having lived there. Stone building foundations, village clearings, a wide stone road to Taiohae—all now overgrown—indicated a well organized earlier community.

Sunday is a day of rest for the Marquesans and we were invited by

Daniel to hike up the valley to see their waterfall. Along the way we picked our lunch off fruit trees—many totally strange to us. The falls is about 1,000 feet high in two steps and is said to be a huge cascade in the rainy season, which was just then starting. Late in the afternoon we returned to the floor of the valley and Antoinette deep fried, over an open fire, delicious tapioca root chips. On leaving that evening we were loaded down with mangoes, a papaya the size of a volleyball, and a huge tapioca root. Sophy also gave Betty a beautiful handmade double string of beads made from seeds. To us these gifts far overshadowed the melon seeds, garlic salt, and a few other household items that we were able to give them during our stay. Daniel seemed most pleased, however, with a Polaroid picture of *Horizon* in his bay.

Monday was a work day for Daniel, so we stopped by only long enough to say goodbye, and it was a mutually reluctant parting. The unrestrained generosity of these fine people showed again for they presented us with four hard-to-get fresh eggs as a parting gift. We will remember them forever.

Leaving Nuku Hiva we traveled south 25 miles to the island of Ua Pu. The island was presently suffering from a drought, but since this was the beginning of the rainy season it may soon have changed. The island has many small bays or bights, no real harbors, and very rocky shores. We decided to try a couple of bays even though none had any unusual character. Our first stop was at Haka Hau on the northeast coast—an open, rolly anchorage not recommended even by the villagers. We shared the dubious anchorage with a French boat we had met earlier at Taiohae. They were traveling around the world, stopping for extended periods at French possessions so that their two teenagers could go to school.

Our first day at Haka Hau we watched with great interest the loading of the copra ship, *Tamarii Tuamotu 2*. The ship's shore boat, a heavy 25-foot double-ender propelled by an outboard motor, would ride inshore on the surf, and, between breaking waves, the crew would turn it end-for-end and hold it on the beach for loading. After loading, two oarsmen, each manning a 15-foot oar, would propel it through the surf into water deep enough to allow use of the outboard. The copra bags, weighing 44 kilograms each (about 100 lbs.), are hand or horse carried to the surf and later loaded aboard the ship in cargo slings.

Copra took a new economic lease on life when the oil crisis hit the world, and prices have now risen to 30 francs per kilo (20¢ per lb. at that time) at the shoreline. The natives are in their economic glory and real coconut oil products are available again—at a price. This inflation plus the devalued U.S. dollar (from 98 down to 70 francs) has doubled the cost of merchandise since our visit to Tahiti in 1970.

Copra being ferried from Haka Hau to a trading schooner.

In addition to buying copra and other locally grown produce, these ships carry passengers throughout French Polynesia, deliver all sorts of supplies on a preorder basis, and are a floating store from which the villagers can buy supplies off the shelf. Formerly known as copra schooners in the days of sail, these interisland freighters are the lifeline of the islands.

Haka Hau is the principal community of Ua Pu and the French island administrative headquarters is there. It is probably the cleanest and best manicured village we saw in the Marquesas. Unfortunately, it was also the most completely fenced, so we were unable to add any local fruits to our stock. More flowers of all kinds grow here than on any other island in the group, but still they weren't unusually abundant. We felt the community was very uninterested in American yachtsmen, and the only personal contact we were able to make was with two small boys who visited us in their outrigger canoe minus its outrigger. That was a balancing act to behold.

All the village boats—outriggers and outboards—were launched through the surf like the copra shoreboat. We, however, took our trusty inflatable dinghy inside a small man-made groin where you risked getting bashed on the rocks instead of drowned in the surf.

We stayed two rolly nights in Haka Hau and then went in search of

Anchored bow and stern, Horizon *enjoys a stay at Haka Maii.*

Haka Maii on the southwest coast of the island. This small village is supposed to be the home of several wood ukelele carvers. There were about 200 people living here, and they have a church, two stores, a school, and an infirmary. The village chief is the appointed gendarme, so it probably is a quiet place. Many children here, as in other islands, attend a boarding school at Atuona on the island of Hiva Oa. I don't know how they are selected from the total school population, but they are obviously the brighter ones.

The anchorage at Haka Maii was small but well sheltered from the tradewinds and waves. It is about 200 yards wide, and by anchoring bow and stern, we avoided swinging into the rocks of the south cliff or the rocky reef on the north side. There was room for only one boat at a time in this bay. It was Sunday when we arrived at Haka Maii, and we expected little action from the local villagers. But by mid-afternoon nine girls and seven boys came swimming or in outriggers to *Horizon* and to our delight swarmed aboard. Beautiful children all under 15, well behaved and talking a Marquesan blue streak. After satisfying their initial curiosity they left as quickly and laughingly as they had arrived.

On Monday, our first visitor was a woodcarver who, with his son, brought bananas and mangoes to soften us up and then topped it off with a beautiful handcarved rosewood tiki. After a pleasant talk (he spoke some English and the rest was the usual charades), we determined that the two things he needed most were sandpaper and a pair of swim trunks. We gave him these from our trading stock and a more pleased individual you never saw. We talked for a while longer but were interrupted by more visitors, so he and his son left by outrigger. Incidentally, these people were careful that their outriggers did not carelessly hit our hull. Very thoughtful compared to the weekend sailors at Catalina.

The rest of the morning and into the afternoon, children with offerings of fruit and fish visited us. We soon decided that it wasn't our fair skins and gray hair that attracted them, but our gifts of Polaroid pictures. My comb was well used by all the boys who had to look their best for the picture. Polaroid pictures have a great attraction for these people but there is no end to the demand once you start and you hate to say no. The farther we got from the U.S., the more expensive film became and we took fewer and fewer pictures. But we always took some in new situations to "break the ice."

In the afternoon we attempted to go ashore to see the town and the ukelele carvers, but on close inspection the surf and the rocky beach didn't appeal to us and we returned to the boat. Betty spent the afternoon cooking some of the breadfruit while Sven and I went into the water to clean barnacles (mostly long neck variety) and other growths from the hull. Even though frustrated in our attempt to go ashore, we thoroughly enjoyed this bay and the exuberance of the natives.

Our next island stop was Hiva Oa which is the principal French administrative center for the Marquesas Islands. We were told that the town of Atuona (which we were destined not to see) is more developed than Taiohae with a greater French influence. For example, it has seven restaurants compared to Taiohae's one. It also has the Marquesas Islands' boarding school for high school students, and it is the last resting place of the French painter, Paul Gauguin. This island was also the last known scene of cannibalism, and the fierce feuds and primitive customs of the early Marquesas.

To reach Hiva Oa from Ua Pu, we had to sail 60 miles dead to windward and against the current. It took us a frustrating 32 hours in light head winds to make the passage, including four hours when we were becalmed with sails down about 10 miles from Hiva Oa. The calm was a fringe effect of a storm over the island, which brought them their

Ozanne Rohi receives burgee from skipper in front of the Hana Menu Yacht Club.

heaviest rainfall in nine months. We reached the island after dark and anchored in Hana Menu ("menoo") bay on the north shore.

During the night we were to awaken and thoughtfully review the Torrance police officer's advice on self-protection. It was pitch black and we were surrounded by skiffs with lanterns and people making ready spears and many shadowy looking weapons. We quietly waited as they moved closer and then the laugh was on us. These islanders were night fishing for shark—a common technique here. But from then on we were careful about going in the water!

In the morning, we were able to appreciate fully the grandeur of the Hana Menu. The east and west walls ranged 400 to 1000 feet high and could have been a cut of the Grand Canyon except that they were much greener. The north was open to the ocean and the south was closed by a fertile valley 500 yards wide, about 2000 yards deep, fully covered by coconut palms. While only one family occupies the valley today, it once contained over 2000 people, but little evidence remains. First, tuberculosis dealt a severe blow to the natives and in the 1800s a Tsunami ("tidal wave") wiped everything else out. One man who was high on a hillside reportedly survived.

The most exciting natural feature of Hana Menu is the fresh

waterfalls and bathing pool at the west cliff. Fed by many springs in the sheer cliff, the falls tumble through exotic tropical growth into a knee deep pool about 20 feet in diameter. The pool, which serves as a bathtub and washtub, is continuously flushed clean on about a 3-minute cycle. Imagine the delight of taking your salt-laden body into this sparkling water surrounded by hibiscus, taro, philodendron, jasmine, and other exotic tropical plants. From the falls above the pool we filled water jugs for *Horizon*'s 50-gallon auxiliary water tanks.

The host of the valley (you couldn't find a better one anywhere) is a Tahitian named Ozanne Rohi. He and his very pretty wife, Marie, speak some English, have five children, and run a very profitable copra plantation. The facilities are made up of separate thatched roof buildings, each being only one room. We were initially entertained in the dining building where Marie served us cold limeade—the limes from their trees and the cold from a kerosene Servel refrigerator. Ozanne presented us with six of the most beautiful cowrie shells we have ever seen. They are normally sold in Tahiti as souvenirs.

We also learned more about the pesky nau-nau fly. There are black nau-naus and white nau-naus. The blacks bite with a delayed action itch up to 24 hours, but the aftereffects last up to two weeks. The white's bite is followed by an immediate itch passing in 24 hours. Nuku Hiva has mostly blacks, while Hiva Oa has only whites. Moorea (near Tahiti) used to have nau-nau's, but a total spraying of the infected areas eliminated them. We wished that could be done in Nuku Hiva.

When Ozanne came to this valley in 1964, he started a guest log and picture album of visiting yachts. It is now a real who's who of cruising boats to which we proudly added *Horizon*. Last year the Hana Menu Yacht Club was formed, and it is housed in its own thatched roof building complete with battery-powered stereo, trading library, and yacht club burgees. During our second day ashore, I presented the burgee of the Aerospace Cruising and Sailing Club to H.M.Y.C., following which, Marie served refreshments consisting of a mix of fresh mangoes and pomplemousse (grapefruit).

That evening we were invited to join in a volleyball game followed by a sumptuous native feast. Besides Ozanne's family and a couple of visiting nephews, the 18 feasters were composed of the crews of the two French boats, a French professor collecting botanical specimens, and the *Horizon* crew. The feast consisted of goat, bananas, squash, and breadfruit, which had been cooking all afternoon in the traditional closed pit used by the Polynesians. Ozanne carved the goat with a wicked looking hunting knife and the 18 of us ate with our fingers. There was little cleanup to do after finger-licking, since the dogs took

Trading schooner Vaiatea *at Hana Vava, Fatu Hiva, was built in Bellingham,
Washington.*

care of the bones and the pigs took care of the vegetable skins. For the
more athletic there was table tennis in the "table tennis room" lighted
by a Coleman lamp. The rest of us talked (mostly in French) and
listened to a guitar. Ozanne does not have electricity, but he hopes to
put a 12-volt wind generator on the hilltop for lighting purposes.

After Hana Menu we decided that any other stop on Hiva Oa would
be an anticlimax, so we made plans to go to Fatu Hiva, our last island
stop in the Marquesas. It had now been seven weeks since Mazatlan,
and our supplies, while getting a little unbalanced (all cold cereal was
gone, but we still had fresh eggs), would carry us comfortably to
Papeete in July. The fresh fruits and vegetables and French bread have
helped extend our supplies, and fresh water has been abundant
although we have used very little. At sea we used mostly salt water.
With adequate supplies on board, we could skip Atuona, the last major
supply point in the Marquesas.

Fatu Hiva lies 60 miles SSE of Hiva Oa and the passage was made
overnight against steady tradewinds of 10–15 knots and relatively calm
seas. We arrived at Hana Vave on Sunday, June 29, at 0730. Being the
only boat in the bay, we anchored centrally off the beach, but it was

still in 9 fathoms. We had been advised to anchor securely because of strong wind gusts that come out of the valleys in the evening. This day they didn't wait for the evening, they hit us sporadically all day and night with a frenzy that made me glad we had a 60 lb. CQR plow anchor and an all ⅜" chain rode. I clocked one gust at 27 knots and I was told that 40 knots is not uncommon. With only about 100 yards of fetch off the beach, no waves built up. So, the winds were more mentally distressing than physically uncomfortable, until, that is, we went ashore in the Avon inflatable dinghy. The oarsman was sorely put to hold his ground against the gusts, but, on the other hand, surfing wasn't bad returning to the boat from shore.

The valley of Hana Vave was more lush than any we have seen, and well it should have been since it never quit raining along the sheer 2000-foot walls surrounding it. In fact, it rained so much in the harbor that I had to give up any thoughts of sleeping in the cockpit, my usual spot when at anchor.

Before I proceed further I must describe an economic scenario that affected our two-day stay. During those days four supply ships called at Hana Vave. One was a French LST carrying mostly passengers, but the other three—*Taporro-2, Tamarii Tuamotu-2,* and *Vaiatea*—were all buying copra at 20¢ per lb. and oranges at 14¢ each at the shoreline. Amidst this economic flurry, a yachtsman had little chance of mingling with the local population in the usual relaxed atmosphere.

At one point in our village wanderings we had the genial assistance of a French navy officer, Lt. Pierre Carron, from the LST. I had engaged a Marquesan in a game of charades to learn where one buys tapa cloth. He spoke only Marquesan and I only English. Lt. Carron, sensing our predicament, had his Tahitian partner translate the Marquesan into French and Carron then translated the French into English for us. Through that language chain we learned where to find the tapa cloth makers and we all had a good time with our four-way language conversation.

Hana Vave is noted for its tapa cloth and we bought from one of the local women a roll 2' x 8', which will eventually make beautiful wall hangings. Tapa cloth is made by pounding the bark of the breadfruit tree into a paper-thin layer, which is then sun dried. Patterns are painted on it with a locally made dye. From my observations it must be a rapidly disappearing art in these islands. This is the only place we found tapa cloth made from breadfruit trees. Generally it is made from the bark of the paper mulberry tree.

In most villages we visited there was an individual especially friendly to the yachtsman. Hana Vave was no exception, and Jean Vaitai, a

Tahitian ex-prizefighter, was the self-styled host and interpreter for visiting yachts. Like the rest of the village on this weekend, he applied his interests mostly to selling his twenty 100-pound bags of copra to the supply ships. In fact, even the village baker did not bake bread until Tuesday afternoon since he, too, was wheeling and dealing.

All in all, our Hana Vave visit did not have any of the hospitality we had encountered earlier in the Marquesas. We would have done better one week later. But time kept moving on, so we set our course for Tahiti and Bastille Day. The 780-mile leg to Papeete was made in excellent weather; we logged 150 miles per day in easy sailing. We passed through the Tuamotu Archipelago at high noon on the fourth day, sailing about a quarter-mile off the west shore of Rangiroa atoll. In passing these impressive atolls we had to console ourselves with the thought that maybe we could stop at them next year on the way to Hawaii. Sunday night, July 6, at 1830, we passed through the reef into Papeete harbor and anchored for the night secure in the knowledge that we were in plenty of time for the Bastille Day celebrations during the week of the 14th.

Before I leave the Marquesas story, I would like to give you the result of a poll we took aboard *Horizon* on our way to Tahiti. The question was, which anchorage did each of us enjoy the most and why?

> *Betty*—Tai Oa Bay because of its seclusion, no other yachts, and the wonderful family that lived there
> *Sven*—Taiohae Bay because it was the first anchorage after a long crossing and there were many yachts and friendly people ashore to meet
> *Earl*—Hana Menu Bay because of its exotic setting and the enterprising family that lives there

Our first four weeks in the islands of Polynesia had left us with a variety of impressions, such as:

—The few people remaining in these lush islands
—The paternalistic French colonial government
—The vicious nau-nau flies on the beach
—The large number of cruising boats
—The degrading impact of alcohol on people with little to do
—The eerie feeling of hearing drums in the night
—The young people's longing for the modern society of Europe and America
—The friendliness of the Polynesians toward strangers

5

Sophisticated Tahiti

We were in Papeete, the capital of French Polynesia, in 1970, at the end of a Los Angeles–Papeete yacht race, and so we can now make a few observations based on five years of change. European sophistication is rapidly replacing the traditional South Seas image along the waterfront. Yachts still tie stern-to at the quay, but it is no longer Quai Bir Hakeim, now it is Boulevard Pomare. Gone is the most famous of all South Seas saloons, Quinns, with its two madames, each operating their respective if not respectful halves of the dance floor. Gone, likewise, is the old Vaima's restaurant and bar, not unlike Quinns in reputation. Modern buildings of reinforced concrete are being built in their place with the most modern of French construction equipment operated by bronzed men dressed in swim suits and thong sandals.

The yacht berths along the quay have been extended to the southwest but have also lost some of the best berths near the center of town to commercial and sport fishing interests. The Chinese junk, *Chang Feng* is still at the quay, but it is only a bare hull in place of the interesting former restaurant. Adding to the picturesque scene at the Tahiti waterfront is the former copra schooner *Tamara,* now restored to museum-quality appearance. One of the last surviving sailing copra boats, she has been equipped with diesel auxiliary power and takes tourists on local charter trips. Economic sophistication has also arrived in the form of mooring fees charged all yachts in Papeete harbor. Partially compensating, though, is a bathhouse where yachties can shower in fresh cold water and do their laundry in private rather than on the quay. The fees charged pleasure yachts are an entry fee of 650 Colonial Franc Pacifique regardless of size and a daily mooring fee, which depends on where you are and services used. (In May 1975 the exchange rate was 78 CFP to $1.00 U.S.) Along the natural bank of Boulevard Pomare the daily mooring fee is only 55 CFP. At the Quai the rate jumps to 110 CFP per day, and if you use shore electricity, an additional 15 CFP is tacked onto the daily bill.

While we were disappointed at the diminishing beauty of the waterfront, we were aghast at the automobile traffic. Five years ago bicycles and motor scooters abounded, but today they have been

"Tahiti style" mooring at the Quai Bir Hakeim in Papeete.

replaced by automobiles driven in the mad style of Parisians. Accidents are very common (we saw at least one per day), and the victims are most often cyclists and scooter drivers. From our observations of the number of cars in private yards per capita car ownership must be close to Los Angeles. The noise created by these cars is a real disturbance to the yachts at the old quay location right on the street and even bothered us at the newer mooring area where the street was further away. "Les trucks," the Tahiti bus system, still operates, but automobiles and taxis are making dangerous inroads into it. Tahiti is, I'm afraid, destined to make the same public transportation mistakes as has most of the world.

Papeete is certainly a crossroads of the South Pacific, if commercial harbor activity can be used as a measure. Two or three large ships are usually tied up at the piers each day transferring cargo. One of these is almost certain to be a tanker discharging refined oil products. Copra is the only significant export, but frozen fish is a unique "transfer cargo." Japanese and Korean trawlers bring in catches of tuna, which are placed in a cold-storage pier warehouse. These fish are then reloaded into large refrigerator ships bound for Pago Pago, American Samoa. There they are canned by Starkist or Van Camp and end up on stateside tables.

Papeete is also the distribution center for supplies to all of the French Polynesian islands, which number over 100 and have a total population of about 120,000. No, there are not 1200 persons per island. Tahiti has about 65,000 of them, and Moorea is second with 5,000. Many atolls sustain only 40 to 50 persons, which seems to be the threshold size for a permanent village in the islands. The interisland freighters, generally small—200 to 300 tons—are diesel-powered and have totally replaced the trading schooner of the romantic past. Interisland trading is conducted mainly by two companies—Donalds, which evolved from an earlier European copra trading venture, and Wing Man Hing, which is an aggressive Chinese business of import, export, and local sales. Those companies' trading ships compete in purchasing copra and selling goods throughout the French Polynesian islands. Where neither feels they can make a franc, the French navy sends its LST's to meet the needs of the islanders. The French navy tries not to compete with the local island traders, and we did not hear of any friction.

Papeete harbor is also home port to the French fleet supporting nuclear testing at the Gambier Islands, east southeast of Tahiti. While many South Pacific kingdoms decry these tests, they have greatly expanded the Tahiti economy, and one wonders what the local economy will do when this source of income no longer exists.

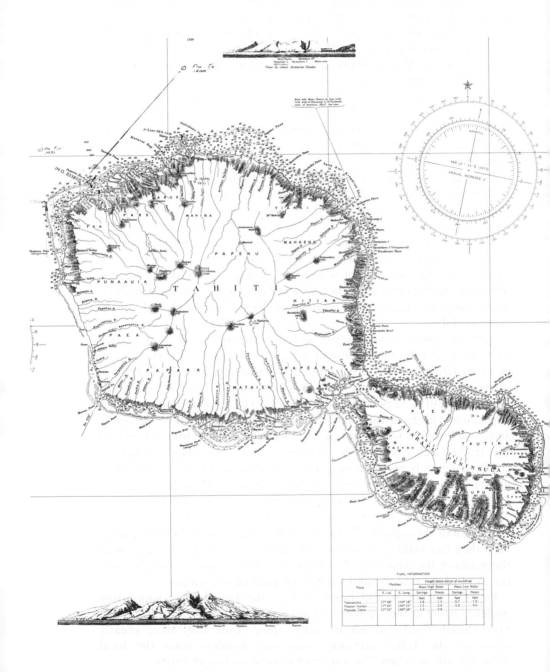

Among the interesting vessels seen in Papeete during our stay was the U.S. tracking ship, *Vanguard,* which stopped for a few days of recreation for the crew just prior to taking up their station west of Tahiti for the *Apollo/Soyuz* space mission. In addition, there were two yachts of unusual character among the forty or so that tied up at the quay. One was the *Curlew* from the Isle of Man, sailed by Tim and Pauline Carr. *Curlew* is a 76-year-old Falmouth Quay Punt formerly used to carry ashore passengers from anchored sailing ships. She has a deck and waterline length of 28 feet and an 8-foot bowsprit, no engine, no head, no electricity, and no gadgets. Propulsion in a harbor is furnished by Tim at the end of a single 20-foot sweep at which he is very expert. The Carrs have been cruising for six years on *Curlew.*

The other yacht of distinction is *Havørn*—one of the last sailing double-ended fishing boats built in Norway (1935). She is 48-feet long and ketch rigged. The really unusual feature of *Havørn* is her 1-cylinder, 70-horsepower, diesel engine, which stands 5 feet high and turns at an amazing 400 rpm. The engine is started by compressed air and a blowtorch and will run in either direction. *Havørn* is the family home for Lee and Greta Ehrheart and son Yance, from San Diego.

Cruising yachts have always made Papeete a port of call, since, beyond its romantic atmosphere, it is also the best place to reprovision after the long haul from Hawaii, North America, or Central America. A climate unparalleled, a people of grace and beauty, and the annual Fete entices the cruising boats here. It is now becoming common to see 50 to 75 cruising boats at one time in Papeete harbor. They come from all over the world carrying crews with a universal love of adventure. While the number of family crews seems to be increasing rapidly, there are also great numbers of friends traveling together. We learned here that it is not discreet to ask about last names when introduced—they rarely match!

Business activity in Papeete, which is the commercial hub for all French Polynesia, runs a hectic pace from 0730 to 1130 and 1400 to 1800. The French say cynically that "Tahitians don't do much but they do it early." (The latter is correct but I doubt the former.) Their marketplace opens daily around 0530 and abounds with fresh fish, flowers, and bread, continuing throughout the day with other types of produce, and, late in the day, the fresh fish reappear from the daytime catch. However colorful the weekday market is, it can't match the great social affair of the Sunday morning market. The Tahitians must spend Saturday night getting the produce ready, for shortly after midnight *les trucks* start to converge on the market loaded with families and food. At 3:00 AM the market officially opens and the islanders buy their food

This most famous of South Seas bars was torn down in 1973 (photo from 1970 TransPac Race).

for the big Sunday feast. But they do not buy simply by the kilogram or piece, each purchase is accompanied with a social dialogue that convinced me that everyone on this island knows everyone else. At 7:00 AM the market closes abruptly as the people return to their homes via *les trucks* and get ready for church. Unlike the La Paz and Mazatlan markets, only fresh foods are sold and the Papeete market is the epitome of cleanliness and orderliness without the sterility of the modern supermarket.

Betty's pursuit of foods for daily consumption as well as to restock *Horizon* brought forth some interesting problems. Our supply of fresh eggs from Mexico was now seriously depleted, and, knowing their scarcity in these islands, she began inquiring around for powdered eggs. One sage Tahitian woman in all seriousness advised her to forget the powdered eggs and take chickens instead!

One of our big disappointments was the almost total absence of any kind of sausage at the meat markets. In our earlier visit we had been able to get good sausages, which now would have gone well with the New Zealand cheese being sold there. Sausage keeps well and gives a welcome change to a diet of canned meats at sea. As in the Marquesas, vegetables are not a common local food, but we were able to get our old friends California carrots and celery at the Magasin Cecile, which specializes in American and European foods.

While there was certainly no shortage of food in Papeete, we found the prices to be the highest of all the islands we visited. Take that universal commodity, beer, as an example. It sold for 48 CFP per 600 ml., which in U.S. money was $0.97 per quart. We considered that high but not as bad as the 49 CFP deposit charged for the bottles, which would make the thrifty individual careful to return empties to the store. But the jovial, beer-liking Tahitians seem not to worry, and after a weekend the harbor beaches were littered with bottles. We thought it strange that there were no enterprising children collecting bottles for return.

The building pace on Tahiti is unbelievable for a South Sea isle. Concrete office buildings, large warehouses, small versions of freeway-type bridges, and of course, traffic lights on the streets. Housing is still built on an individual basis, but the thatched roof hut with dirt floor on the coastal plain has given way to colorfully painted frame or cement-block houses on concrete slabs (termites are a problem) setting on the hillsides like the best of California developments.

There is one English language newspaper, published five days a week—the Tahiti *Bulletin*, established in 1969. Distributed free to all hotels, banks, and travel agencies, it is also delivered by dinghy to each yacht along the quay. Besides the usual world news, it carries the stock market and other business news and some sports news. For the price, it can't be beat.

Three different business cultures exist throughout the islands. There is the traditional Tahitian culture, which is simple, generous, and easy-going. Then there are the Chinese who display great ambition, while showing as low a profile as possible. Newest is the sophisticated European business atmosphere, which is rapidly replacing the other two. The Tahitians take well to sophistication, and, while I personally regret the passage of the old South Seas image, the new Papeete is, except for the automobile traffic, a delightful combination of both ages.

No trip to Tahiti is complete without a visit to the Gauguin Museum. It has been greatly expanded in the last five years. It now tells his life story, but with little reference to the reputation for drunkenness and debauchery that characterized his last years. You can get some idea of Gauguin's life from Somerset Maugham's book *The Moon and Sixpence*—a fictional piece paralleling Gauguin's life. There are no originals of Gauguin's art works in the museum since they reside in public and private collections around the world. The largest number of his works now reside in the United States.

Polynesian history is almost unknown before the advent of the European. There was no written language, and the past was recorded only in the minds of the people. Wtih the great depopulation of the islands following the Europeans' arrival, history and social customs perished, and today only a few stone artifacts exist to tell of their early culture. Most of these are now displayed in overseas museums, but some are still in possession of the Papeete Museum, headed by Aurora Natua. Aurora has spent her sixty-odd years studying Tahitian culture and is probably the local historian in these islands. The most recent filming of the movie *Mutiny on the Bounty* used her as a technical advisor. We met with Aurora to seek information on Raivavae Island. In her enthusiastic manner she told us of her knowledge of the islands to the south but then referred us to overseas institutions for the rest. These turned out to be the Peabody Museum in Salem, Massachusetts, and the Bishop Museum in Honolulu, Hawaii. To us it seemed sad that so much of their history lies on foreign shores.

One of our extra delights in Tahiti was renewing acquaintances with Lt. Pierre Carron of the French navy, whom we had met earlier in Hana Vave. He was leaving his ship to return to school in Paris (chemical engineering), so he had moved ashore to share a beach house with another navy officer, Claude Benown. To our great pleasure they invited us to dinner at their house, and it turned out to be a gastronomical delight! Pierre's uncle is a Paris chef and Pierre learned well the art of preparing and serving in the French style, as he so aptly demonstrated to us. Two locations (patio and dining room), three wines, seven courses, and four hours made a rare evening of relaxed dining. While both Pierre and Claude speak some English, Pierre also speaks German (which Sven understands) and Claude speaks Spanish (which Betty and I understand somewhat). Whenever the conversation got knotted up, we resorted to one of the other languages, creating a virtual Tower of Babel when we got our wires crossed!

Several days later we had Pierre and Claude aboard *Horizon* for cocktails and dinner. Because the dining saloon gets a little crowded with five people in it, we planned serving in the cockpit. Wouldn't you know it started raining in the late afternoon! But by the time they arrived it had quit, so a quick mopping-up allowed us to continue as planned. Anyone who has been buttoned-up in a sailboat cabin in a tropical rain knows the problem we faced at the time. But with the rain over, Betty served one of her typically good *Horizon* two-burner stove dinners, which, preceded by some Cuttysark, made another memorable multilingual evening.

Not far from the sophistication of Papeete, you find the natural beauty of Tahiti.

Always on the lookout for artifacts, we learned from Pierre of the woodcarvers that reside at the Leprosarium a short distance from Papeete. Leprosy in the Society Islands is now nearly nonexistent, and with few new cases appearing, all the leper hospitals in the outer islands have been closed and the few remaining cases transferred to this small picturesque rambling hospital on a hillside. It doesn't look like a hospital and, in fact, it is not because the patients are all stable noncontagious cases and free to move about, although their disfigurements usually prevent them from re-entering society. So they stay here in their own village and keep busy with craft work. We stopped at several private homes displaying crafts as we searched for a different woodcarving and finally ended up at a craft store run by the villagers. Here, there was a great variety and we found several of interest, but our attention focused on one—an intricately carved ceremonial canoe paddle. The carver was one of several patients present and he beamed with delight as we talked to him about it and got a price. This unfortunate fellow, confined to a wheelchair because he had lost his feet, was a 40-year-old Marquesan from Nuku Hiva who knew both Uki and Daniel. While he and the others talked sociably with us as best we could with different languages (they always remained a short

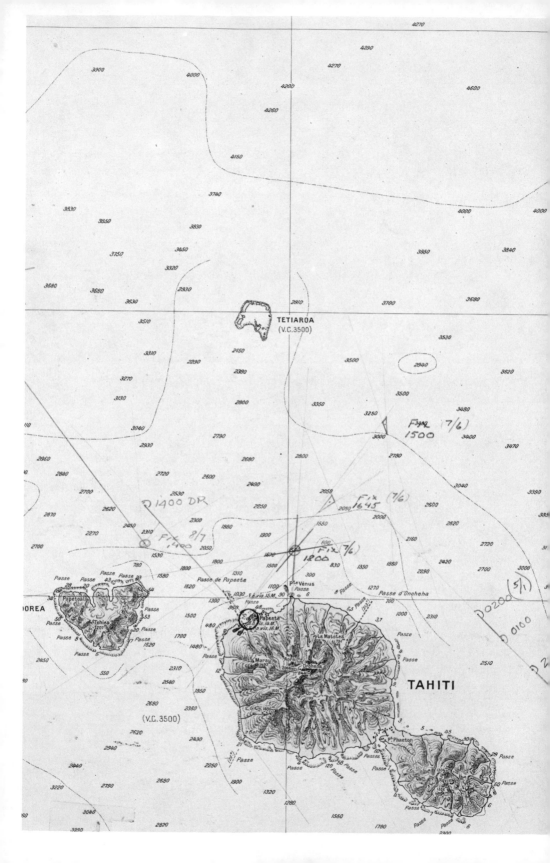

distance away and carefully avoided touching us), the deal was made— 3,000 CFP—and we felt satisfied with our acquisition. Riding back to town on *les trucks* we remarked that these people show great courage in leading active, self-sufficient lives despite being social outcasts.

Our new adventures on Tahiti were not to end here, for we looked longingly at the small end of this figure-eight island called Tahiti-Iti (small Tahiti). A rarely visited place away from the bright lights of Papeete, it had escaped us on our previous visit, and now we were determined to see it. By *les trucks* from Papeete we rode the 54 km. along the north shore of Tahiti, passed the village of Taravao at the isthmus of the island and another 17 km. to Tautira—the end of the line. After checking *les trucks* schedule at the Chinese store and finding out that the last bus back to Papeete left at 1230, we bought some French bread, cheese, and beer and headed to the beach on foot. Our picnic was superb, sitting on a coconut log alongside the peaceful lagoon with the 4300 foot-high peak of Mount Roniu at our back. Noon approached, so we headed back to the bus stop to wait for 1230, it came and went, but still no bus. Inquiring of local people, using our best fractured French, we learned that the next bus was at 0500 the next morning! So, with more fortitude than dignity, we started to hitchhike back to the big city. Our first ride was in the cab of a pickup truck driven by a Tahitian who took us to Taravao. From there we got a ride with a Chinese but had to contend ourselves with the box of the truck, since a little girl was asleep in the front seat. His itinerary was unique. First, an unplanned stop to buy bags of freshly picked drinking coconuts in a coastal grove. Then, a hospital call followed by a stop at his home where he left his daughter off. All this time we communicated with the driver by sign language, fractured French, and pidgin English. Finally we arrived in downtown Papeete at a large import dealer and to our embarrassment found that our benefactor not only spoke good English but had attended school in the U.S.!

Part of the reason for our return to Tahiti in July was a desire to once again see the Fete. Timed to coincide with Bastille Day, it encompasses a week of contests ranging from laborious copra making to exotic traditional dances. Opening day is Bastille Day with much official ceremony by the French Territorial Government, followed by a military parade and an Olympic-style march of Fete participants. As with all activity in Tahiti, the parade started early (0700), and our arrival at 0645 left us fifth row standing room only. One can easily appreciate the early start, because by parade's end at 1000, it was really hot along the wind-blocked parade route. The Tahitians take the Fete seriously; they compete in large numbers and most establishments close

The Queen of the Fete leads the Bastille Day parade through downtown Papeete.

their doors for the first few days so that everyone can see the events. There was something for everyone, including: fruit carriers' race, flower-decorated canoes, horse races (Tahitian style), outrigger canoe races (1, 3, 6, & 16 place—men and women), sailing outriggers, Polynesian coronation ceremony, swimming, javelin throwing, weaving baskets, hats, copra preparation, singing and dancing, and 6 hours of outboard motorboat competition!

Moored as we were along the scenic waterfront, we had front row seats (especially high in the rigging) to all the water events. There were crowds of people at all events, including camera-carrying tourists by the hundreds who were always in my way. But, since I, too, was carrying a camera, I just pushed and shoved with the rest.

One of the major features of the Fete is the *barraque,* which I call a carnival. There are all sorts of games of chance to win kewpie dolls, pareu cloth, or even a squealing piglet, and endless purveyors of good local foods, such as fish, French pastries, and coconut milk. The *barraque* was located on the waterfront about a mile away from us, but those barkers kept us awake until after midnight. The worst part of the *barraque* was that it continued operating for an additional week beyond the end of the Fete. Ah, sleepless Tahitian nights!

While we saw dance practice at Taiohae and later a dance show at Bora Bora, we saw none of the Fete dance contests because of outrageous ticket prices. Seats for the nightly contests sold at $13 each, and admission to the dance exhibitions for camera enthusiasts was $26 each. Many of the dance teams are professional and receive cash prizes. Professional photographers abounded at the Fete so one can assume that the high admission prices are fair if not in keeping with the traditional hospitality.

All of the islands in French Polynesia celebrated the Fete in their communities. Raiatea and Bora Bora were the only others of significant size. It's hard to beat the magic of Tahiti, but having seen the big Fete twice, we would now prefer to get closer to the traditional thing in the

The Tahitian male physique shows well in the copra preparation contest.

outlying islands. All in all, it was a great celebration by a great people.

Our memories of Tahiti abound with pleasant thoughts from two visits there. We recall, in particular:

—The delicate beauty of the Tahitian with combined Anglo-Oriental and Tahitian blood
—The picturesque and efficient public transportation system known as *les trucks*
—The disappearance of the native culture in favor of a modern European society
—That Tahitians are now willing to buy fish at high prices rather than catch them
—The Tahitians' love of beer
—What a great social gathering place the Papeete market is at 0300 on a Sunday morning
—Their enthusiastic participation in the annual Fete
—Sunsets over Moorea

6

Tragedy at Moorea

The story was carried in the *Tahiti Bulletin* of Monday, July 28, 1975:

PAPEETE—A 50-year-old American came to Tahiti to visit friends of 25 years, sailed to Moorea and died there while swimming.

Norman O'Brien of Los Angeles arrived in Tahiti on July 20 to join his friends, Earl and Betty Hinz, on their yacht *Horizon*.

The three sailed to Moorea last Friday. As soon as they anchored in Cook's Bay, O'Brien climbed down the ladder and laid back on top of the water. Then he began swimming the breast stroke.

Mrs. Hinz says she looked just a few seconds later and O'Brien was lying face down in the water. Hinz and a crew member immediately swam to O'Brien and began mouth-to-mouth resuscitation in the water.

Mrs. Hinz brought the dinghy over, O'Brien was placed inside and two Tahitians towed the dinghy to shore with their outrigger canoe.

O'Brien was put into a truck and taken to the Bali Hai Hotel, where a paramedic from San Francisco, assisted in the resuscitation effort.

Hinz said O'Brien was continuously given resuscitation from the moment they reached him in the water until the doctor shook his head and said "no hope" more than 1½ hours later.

O'Brien and the Hinz family had been friends for 25 years. The two had worked together for the Aerospace Corporation in El Segundo, California.

Hinz described O'Brien as "hale and hearty" when he came. He was tired from long hours of work and was looking forward to a three-week vacation with his friends aboard *Horizon*.

The exact cause of death has not been determined, but heart failure is suspected.

Burial plans are incomplete pending notification of next of kin.

Norm had arrived at the Papeete waterfront just after dawn on Sunday, July 20. This was to be a vacation for Norm and a way for him to enjoy some of the fruits of his labor in helping us get *Horizon* ready for the South Seas. Besides his personal interest in getting to these islands of paradise, he brought along some equipment we had ordered and 2½ months of accumulated mail. The most important piece of equipment he was carrying was a quartz chronometer to replace the misguided Bulova Accutron, which could no longer be relied on for celestial navigation timekeeping.

The Fete was over and life in Papeete was slowly returning to normal. Never having been on a South Seas island before, Norm walked the waterfront and nearby roads, always returning with the comment "it's even more beautiful than I thought." Now that Norm had arrived, we rented a Peugeot sedan and all of us took off for a grand day-long tour of the island, including a stop at the impressive Gauguin Museum. It was late in the afternoon before we returned to *Horizon*. The evening was spent reminiscing about the days activities and watching yet another picturebook sunset over Moorea.

It was a tantalizing scene we watched that evening and under its influence we decided that we should visit Moorea as our next order of adventure. The following day, Thursday, in accordance with port procedures, I informed the port captain of our proposed visit to Moorea and gave him and the immigration officer copies of the crew list for the short trip. It is usually such a casual trip to Moorea that many cruising boats overlook this simple administrative step. But on *Horizon* we routinely followed all the official procedures set by the host country, recognizing their prerogative to run their ports as they please. This instance was to prove the value of playing the game right.

Friday morning at 0930 we departed the Papeete reef for Moorea arriving off Motu Iti at the northeast corner about noon and then gliding along the north reef past the airport, Mahana village and the Bali Hai Hotel. At 1330 we entered Avaroa Pass leading into beautiful Pao Pao Bay more popularly known as Cook's Bay. A fringing reef submerged to 4 ft. in spots prevents anchoring close to shore, so we set our bow anchor in the coral sand bottom just off this reef. The bottom drops rapidly away to 15 or more fathoms so Sven in the dinghy hand-set the stern anchor on the reef itself. Taking the captain's prerogative, I personally inspected the set anchors by taking the first swim of the day in this clear refreshing water. I walked armpit-deep in water on the reef to where our stern anchor, a Danforth, lay idly on its flukes side. The holding appeared poor, and we would have to keep watch for a change of wind. It was holding mostly by its own weight, and I wished I had also taken along a Northhill that could bite into the coral crevices and give some real holding power.

Back on *Horizon* I went forward to check the bow anchor chain-grabber. Norm, now in his swim suit, backed down the swim ladder into the water and using the breast stroke started his sightseeing across the coral reef. The rest of us were getting set to join him when Betty shouted that Norm wasn't moving! With common thought, Sven and I dove over the side and reached Norm in seconds. There was no sign of life. While I supported Norm, Sven started mouth-to-mouth resuscitation. Betty brought the dinghy over and we lifted Norm into it while trying hard to maintain a rhythmic air exchange and drain any water from his lungs. The shore seemed far away, so Betty and I first swam the dinghy over to *Horizon* from where we attracted the attention of two Tahitians in an outrigger. They came over and towed the dinghy to the beach while I spelled Sven at the resuscitation effort. On the beach a crowd had gathered including an English-speaking islander who advised us to take Norm's still-inert body to the Bali Hai Hotel where a professional lifeguard might be available to help. A bystander offered us his VW bus and away we went with Sven and I continuing mouth-to-mouth resuscitation. At the Bali Hai, Phil Stubs, a lifeguard from California, took over, but to no avail. He judged the body beyond help, saying that even if breathing could be restored, the brain was now most likely irreparably damaged from lack of oxygen.

The resident doctor on Moorea, a young Frenchman displaying great aloofness, made a cursory examination and declared Norm dead at 1700. With an all-knowing look on his face he told the waiting gendarme (in French, translated for us) that the American had died of hydrocution—heart stoppage due to water shock. Our inability to speak French kept us from learning any more about hydrocution except that another case had happened there a few weeks earlier.

Now it was the gendarme's turn to take over. He first wanted Norm's passport and then a statement. I went back to the boat, got the passport, and returned to the Bali Hai, where Hugh Kelley (one of the three American owners) generously offered us the use of his private hotel quarters and, best of all, a cup of coffee. With Philip Byot, the desk clerk, interpreting, I gave the gendarme a detailed statement, which he slowly wrote in long-hand French in his black notebook. When finished, it was read back to me through Byot, and I was requested to sign it. I hesitated, not wanting to sign anything I hadn't read myself. Now for the first time the impact of being a captain responsible for the crew really struck me. If I didn't sign, the body would be buried on Moorea immediately, since there is a 24-hour limit on holding a corpse above the ground. We found out later that this is commonplace throughout the Pacific islands. I was tempted to have Norm buried there—what nicer place could you end your days in? But civilized thoughts, later of questionable merit, told me to buy time so that Norm's next of kin could advise on their choice. I signed, but the gendarme had already anticipated an American reaction; he had called Papeete in the meantime and a boat was on its way over. It arrived shortly, and Norm's body was taken to Papeete and placed in the morgue at Mamao Hospital.

Philip Byot kindly drove Betty and I back to the boat where we found Sven busily trying to stave off another disaster. The wind had changed direction and *Horizon* was swinging towards the reef edge with no restraint from the stern anchor on the reef. I had no desire to stay in that spot any longer, so we weighed anchor, motored to the head of the bay near Pao Pao village, and reanchored in a better holding ground.

Horizon was quiet that evening as Betty and I discussed what to do next. It was clear that we had to locate the next of kin as soon as possible, but Norm was a bachelor living far from his childhood home in Michigan. We decided at last to enlist the aid of a mutual friend, Larry Selzer, who worked at the same company as Norm had, and from which I had so recently retired. Larry had sailed with us for many years on *Horizon* and her predecessor, *Bald Eagle*. He and his wife, Barbara, had entertained Norm and the crew of *Horizon* just before we departed from Los Angeles. First we thought to send a telegram to Larry but dismissed that in favor of a telephone call, during which we could give more of an understanding of the problem.

Saturday morning Betty and I took the dinghy ashore and walked through the spacious gardens of the Aimeo Hotel (the name of Moorea in Captain Cook's day). Guests were just beginning to appear for breakfast, and we envied them their cheerful early-morning countenances. We introduced ourselves to Louise, the Tahitian desk clerk who spoke English well, having lived several years in the Los Angeles area. Louise placed the call to the Papeete operator, and then we waited while time rolled by. We knew that the direct circuits to the U.S. were turned off at noon on Saturday, and only a limited circuit through Paris was kept open the rest of the time.

Two and one half hours later, with the clock approaching 1145, Louise called us out of the garden where we were taking solace in the grandeur of tropical flora. The connection was made, but Larry was not at home. Would we talk with Mrs. Selzer? We paused—did we want to unload this shock on her? Too late, she already knew we were calling and that something must be up. I picked up the telephone and introduced the situation as easily as I could to Barbara. The connection was poor and I could only hope that my request for next-of-kin information got through. After hanging up, I asked Louise to send a backup wire, but the circuits were already closed and we were isolated once more.

We sat and wondered if we had thrown a bad curve to Barbara, made worse by the poor telephone connection. But we needn't have worried, for we later learned that, although shocked by the news, Barbara had set the necessary wheels in motion.

Monday morning I checked in with the port captain and immigration who were already aware of the tragedy. At this point I was certainly glad that I had properly cleared port on Friday with the harbor officials.

With *Horizon* officially re-entered, I went back to the boat for Betty. Our first move took us up Avenue Bruat past the governor's residence to the Gendarmerie. There we were met with blank looks as we presented our problem. We referred in vain to the Moorea gendarme's admonition for us to check in with the Gendarmerie as soon as we arrived. The French gendarme of the bay rose to the heights of bureaucracy by suggesting that we should go see the Sureté instead. So, back down the street we went to the Sureté headquarters.

Here, in a colonial-like police office, we found friends. Portrayed in the movies as the dreaded French police, the Sureté turned a different side to us and helped in a friendly and sympathetic manner. We were dealing with the Immigration and Investigation Branch, headed by Norm Chave, a handsome Tahitian who spoke excellent English as well as French and Tahitian.

Friendly they were, and inefficient they were not. Soon we had the full picture of the official steps to be taken to bury the body or get it released for transport. In either case we had to have a *Permis d'Inhumer* and the *Acte de Décès* from the Maire de Pao Pao on Moorea. My initial thought was to personally go over there to get the papers, but better sense prevailed as I thought of the problem of tackling bureaucracy in a little village where I could not communicate. Instead, Betty and I visited the office of the Maire de Papeete, where we found an English-speaking Tahitian girl willing to help. With a lengthy telephone call to Moorea, Josette Tumahai persuaded the Pao Pao mayor's clerk to prepare the two papers and send them to her attention. Even with Josette's help from the inside, it took two days to get those papers, and we were thankful that we had not attempted the job by ourselves.

There was little else we could do for the moment until we heard from Norm's next of kin. But suspecting the wrong decision, I also stopped at the Pan American Airways ticket office and talked with manager Georges Sanford. Georges knew both the American and Tahitian requirements for transporting a body to the U.S. and I was given cost estimates as well as a list of papers we would need. But more important, I was given names of persons who would provide some of the local services. It gave me a comfortable feeling talking with Georges and I sensed that Pan Am was to be of considerable personal help to us. We were to conclude later that your country's flag air carrier can, indeed, be your link to home.

Telephone communications from Tahiti were poor at best. Connections were not clear and the daily time slots for calling were limited. If you did not have a local telephone, you placed calls in the lobby of the central post office, talking from an open telephone booth. The gregarious nature of the Tahitian and the noisy demeanor of tourists of all nations made the post-office lobby a bedlam of noise. So, we sought a solution with the receptionist at the tourist office on the Quai. She suggested we contact August, the day desk clerk at the Royal Papeete Hotel. August was most accomodating, placing our calls for us and then letting us talk from the privacy of an unoccupied hotel room. We were beginning to feel the compassion of the Tahitians.

Wednesday morning we received the unwanted telegram from the States—send the mortal remains of Norm O'Brien to Pontiac, Michigan. We looked in dismay across the channel to Moorea, which should have been the last resting place for our friend. A more beautiful spot to turn your body back to nature could not be imagined. But instead, he would lay preserved in the tired earth of a dirty industrial city. It gave Betty and I cause to think of our own final resting places. A shining coffin, draped in silk and placed in a well groomed cemetery? Not on our deaths! We made a pact for burial—where we die, with cremation to hasten the return of the body to nature.

We had only one more item of business to complete—a word of thanks to the Tahitian people—which was sent to the Tahiti Bulletin for publication:

6 August 1975

We wish to express our sincere appreciation to the people of Tahiti and Moorea for their kind, understanding and generous help to us following the recent tragic loss of our dear friend Norman O'Brien. As we continue our westward journey our hearts will remember the Tahitian spirit of goodwill.

Earl & Betty Hinz
Yacht *Horizon*

Now it was all over and Earl had missed his 56th birthday party—for that was the day Norm died.

It took many months for us to dispel the emotional trauma and personal loss we felt in Norm's death. But finally we were able to look back objectively at the events which started on Moorea. In a coconut shell we carry in our memories from Moorea:

—The 10 most difficult days of our cruise
—The compassionate nature of the ever-friendly Tahitians
—The contrast between the commercialized way of death in America and the simple, dignified burial customs of the islanders
—How beautiful an island at which to end your days on earth
—Loss of a friend

7

The Splendor of Bora Bora

Having done all we could for our departed sailing partner, we turned to the task of getting *Horizon* ready to put to sea. Our plan was to visit fabled Bora Bora and then sail on to the Navigator Islands. In doing so we would have to pass up lonely but lovely Suvarov Island, an atoll in the Cook group that we had planned to see but for our unforeseen delay in Tahiti.

One normally tries not to follow a schedule when cruising, but weather conditions often require it. It was now August 5, and with the Southwest Pacific hurricane season beginning in late October, we felt the need to move along if we wanted the opportunity to see the Fiji Islands.

Mainly we needed to put provisions aboard for another month plus an emergency amount. As always, shopping was time consuming, but by Wednesday night we were satisfied that we were ready and turned in for another good night's sleep under clear Tahitian skies.

Thursday, August 7, we departed the Papeete harbor reef at 1100. In a record sail we arrived off the Bora Bora reef 24 hours later, traveling the distance of 172 miles at our hull speed of 7.2 knots under genoa and mizzen sails. While airline distance is only 140 miles, we tacked downwind to safely clear the islands of Huahine and Raiatea during a dark and rainy night. (Currents around these islands are highly unpredictable and not to be trusted.) While our fishing luck has so far been almost nil, we again set a trolling line made of 400-pound test nylon with a ¹⁄₁₆-inch steel cable leader and a 6-inch double hook spoon lure. We don't know what kind of a fish (or shark) we attracted this time, but the steel leader was bitten cleanly through and we lost our last spoon.

The magnificent peak of Bora Bora came into view at 0800 Friday, as we passed a few hundred yards off the neighboring coral atoll of Tubai at 0915 approaching Bora Bora along the north reef. We were securely anchored to a coral sand bottom in the Bora Bora harbor in 13 fathoms of crystal clear water by 1145. *Horizon* had been just as eager to get there as was her crew.

Bora Bora lies totally within an outer coral reef and is also surrounded by an inner coral shelf just awash in many places. Coral reefs generally rise abruptly from the deep bottoms on both their inner and outer edges, so there is no depth warning of their presence. Between these two coral rings was an amazing bed of coral sand at an almost constant depth between 12–15 fathoms. These outer reefs were as dramatic as any we have seen. On many parts of it small islands with vegetation known as motus become established. We spent most of one day on Motu Ahuna adjacent to the only lagoon entrance. Ahuna covers about two acres and is surrounded by knee-deep water over a coral bottom where we went shelling. Shells were few and far between, but mosquitoes bred in the damp underbrush of the motu were plentiful and ravenous. The resulting welts stayed with us in an itchy state for the next 24 hours, and we all agreed, no more motus.

Motus aside, it took us only a short time to conclude that Bora Bora is the most beautiful island we had seen thus far. Even the name has the ring of romantic adventure. Its sharp mountain peaks with many vertical stone faces present a variety of dramatic profiles. The peaceful multihued colors of the waters of the lagoon contrasted sharply with the big Pacific swells breaking in towering white masses on the outer reef. And each mosquitoey motu looks like your dreamed-of private South Sea isle. Add to this the profusion of flowers, the colored foliage, and the fragrance of the Tiare Tahiti and Frangipani flowers, and you can easily understand how we were captivated by this island.

For a bit of recent history, Bora Bora was a large American ship resupply and ferry base for aircraft during World War II. It has the largest natural harbor in French Polynesia, approximately one square mile, and with its good bottom it reportedly held up to 100 ships at a

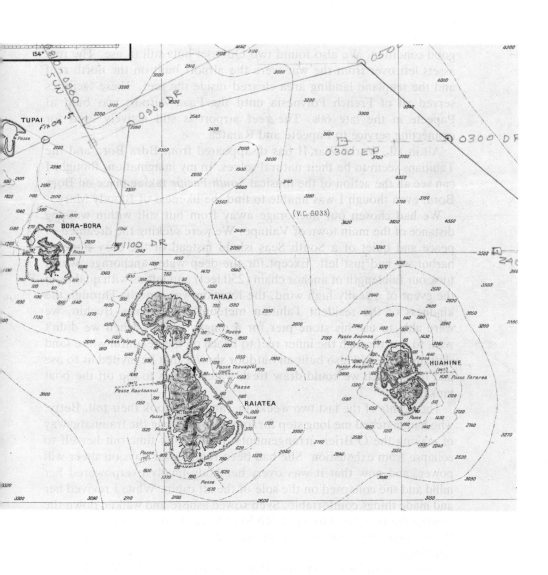

time. The American forces were said to number as many as 6000, which was devastating to the local economy. The present population is 2200 and it was less then. Fortunately, little evidence from the war years remains. There is one pier in Faanui Bay still in use by the interisland trading vessels, and there remain many bare warehouses and concrete slabs around the island. On the top of the hill overlooking Pointe Pahua (near our anchorage) are two 7-inch coastal guns in surprisingly good condition. We also found two Quonset huts still in use. The real assets left over from the war were the airport built on the north reef and the seaplane landing area cleared inside the reef. These facilities served all of French Polynesia until the Faaa Airport was built at Papeete in the late 60s. The reef airport is still actively used for connecting service to Papeete and Raiatea.

All in all, World War II has disappeared from Bora Bora and the Tahitians seem to be their natural selves. In my imagination, though, I can see all the action of the musical *South Pacific* taking place on Bora Bora, even though I was unable to find the likeness of Bloody Mary.

We had chosen our anchorage away from but still within walking distance of the main town of Vaitape. We were seeking the dreamed-of peace and quiet of a South Seas island instead of the busy Papeete harbor we had just left. Except for the deep water anchorage, which took our full length of anchor chain (250 feet) and left us with qualms in the event of a really high wind, the location was superb. Through the kindness of the resident Tahitian meteorologist, James Buchin, we were able to use his stone pier for a dinghy landing when we didn't want to row through the inner reef to beach on the beautiful white sand shoreline. He had also built an outdoor shower that he invited us to use and from which we could draw fresh water in jugs to top off the boat tanks.

The events of the last two weeks in Tahiti now took their toll. Betty, who had matched me long step for long step all along the traumatic way of making the O'Brien arrangements, finally took time out herself to collapse from exhaustion. She had been running for days on sheer will power, and now that it was over, her body finally overpowered her mind and she collapsed on the sole of the aft cabin. While I revived her and made things comfortable, Sven rowed ashore and walked down the road to the taxi stand by the Club Med to get transportation. We took Betty to the dispensary where we were delayed until they could get an interpreter.

If one has to be sick in Bora Bora this dispensary would make it all worth while. Spotlessly clean and situated in a grove of mixed breadfruit, frangipani, and coconut palms, it is the most restful location one can imagine. Even the lagoon at its back door only murmurs as the waves ripple unceasingly over the fringing reef.

The interpreter turned out to be the local postmaster with whom previously I'd had several friendly conversations while mailing letters. With his help the problem was finally diagnosed as lack of iron, and Betty was given a supply of ampules containing liquid iron to restore her system's balance. When we were ready to leave the dispensary, we were pleasantly surprised to find that the taxi was still waiting for us. While in most countries such service demands a tip in recompense, Tahitians consider it below their dignity to accept tips of any kind; they prefer the friendly smile. The taxi soon had us back to the boat and Betty's recovery was rapid—hastened, no doubt, by her eagerness to join Sven and me in seeing the beauty of Bora Bora.

We saw much of this island by our daily hikes along the coastal road made of shoe-destroying coral. The pleasant little business center of Vaitape, where all government functions take place, lay about 3 kilometers to the south of us. It was just recovering from the Fete with a well organized cleanup in progress when we were there. To the north of our anchorage another 3 kilometers was the village of Faanui, without a single store but with an interesting variety of domestic architecture. It ranged from a typical turn-of-the-century European planter's house with rusting corrugated iron roof and veranda, to thatched-roof wood buildings on stilts to protect against termites, to a modern, rambling, cement slab and concrete block house so common to the suburbs of Arizona cities.

Walking about a new island adds a personal perspective to your enjoyment of it. It is typical of these islands that the population all live on the narrow flat coastal plain, so walking the circling road takes you through the heart of the island people. In the afternoon you see the housewives relaxing under beautiful trees, strumming soft music on their guitars. And in the dusk as you walk near the beach you hear a deep, melodious voice coming from the shadows, returning with undeniable sincerity your greeting in their language: "Ia–Ora–na" (pronounced yourana). We grew to look forward to these evening walks when the gentle breezes would carry the smell of frangipani and, more often than not, the pleasant smell of a dying coconut fire in the foot hills.

We never thought of danger. To us the Tahitians were supremely honest and honorable. We felt perfectly at ease walking along the unlighted roads at night. At all of our island stops, there never was a need to lock *Horizon* when we left her.

Since our walking was limited to a few kilometers either way along the coast road, we soon had thoroughly covered that area and decided to rent a car to see the remainder of the island. Which of the two car rental agencies to do business with was quickly settled when we saw that one agency was operated by the two prettiest Tahitian girls (sisters) we had ever laid eyes on. One of the girls spoke some English and the other didn't have to! Tearing ourselves away from lengthy rental negotiations, we sped off at 35 kilometers per hour in a small orange Citroen jeep-like wagon rattling at every joint. At that speed we would cover the island in one hour, but many stops at maraes (ancient temple ruins), reefs, World War II ruins, beaches, and other points of interest made it a half-day trip. Several stops were made at private houses to purchase fresh produce for our coming passage to Samoa, but the only thing we could get was a stalk of bananas and that at only one house. Fruits and vegetables appear to be unusually seasonal here.

Maraes are in particular abundance on this island, but because they are made of natural materials they are difficult to see with an uneducated eye. A map of the island lists 42 of the ancient altars by name and land holding. Most of those we recognized appeared to be family or domestic altars rather than priestly or public altars. The map was the only local information we could get on ancient religious customs, for here as elsewhere in Polynesia there is a reluctance to discuss early religion with strangers.

We made our usual acquaintance with the Chinese merchants in the three *magasins* of Vaitape. Surprisingly well stocked for such a small island, they provided us with many fresh fruits and vegetables plus the ever-fresh and delicious French bread. But it was the ice cream that really tempted us and with which we were again to see the shrewdness of the old merchants. For when we would buy ice cream cones we would get a large scoop if served by the grandchildren but a stingy scoop if served by the patriarch. Either way we found it enjoyable to shop the Chinese markets with modern products displayed amidst a conglomeration of things antique and dusty.

There are three hotels on Bora Bora—the large Bora Bora, which seems to be the choice of Japanese tourists, the Club Med which is a private hotel, and the Hotel Oa Oa. The latter is known as the yacht hotel since it caters to the more civilized yachtsmen who moor their boats stern-to at the dock. This is the closest thing to a yacht club in Bora Bora and the manager, Hans Flesch, has scrapbooks covering the visiting yachts. The bar is adorned with house flags and yacht club burgees from around the world. On behalf of the Cabrillo Beach Yacht Club, I presented one of their burgees to Hans, and we spent the evening as his guests watching the floor show of pulse-enlivening Tahitian dancing. Not a bad exchange!

As all things must, our stay at Bora Bora came to an end on Thursday, August 21, when we departed for Samoa we were wearing new pareus. The *Horizon* crew never looked so good. As we left the anchorage, our new friends waved a long farewell to us from their pier. While many islands may disappear beyond the horizon, Bora Bora will never leave our *Horizon*.

There are other things we will always remember from Bora Bora, such as:

—The housewives relaxing in the afternoon by playing guitars
—The pleasant smell of coconut fires carried on the breeze
—The supreme honesty and humanity of all Tahitians
—The deep, melodious voice coming from the shadows on the beach returning with undeniable sincerity your greeting in their language: "Ia-ora-na."

8

In Search of the Navigator Islands

In 1722 a Dutchman named Roggeveen sighted a new group of islands in mid-Pacific on his way west to Java, but having calculated their position incorrectly, they remained unknown for another 46 years. In 1768 the French navigator, Bouganville, refound Roggeveen's islands. He saw natives paddling outrigger canoes far from shore and, thinking they were far-ranging sailors, called the island group the Navigator Islands. But his assumption turned out false as these sailors in fast outrigger canoes were actually chasing schools of ocean bonito and were close enough to return every night to their villages. Since his basis for the name Navigator Islands was erroneous, the islands eventually became known to the Europeans by their native name, Samoa. Following many years of political struggles between Germany, Britain, and the U.S., the islands were partitioned into Western (German) Samoa and Eastern (American) Samoa. The British withdrew their claims in return for rights in the Tonga Islands to the South.

Although Samoans are really one people, unfortunately, they are still politically divided between Western Samoa, now an independent country, and American Samoa, a U.S. territory. Family members live in both Samoas and they travel freely (if not free) between the islands. Both Samoas are dedicated to "fa'a Samoa," which means the preservation of the Samoan way of life and has proven to be a real headache for foreign rulers trying to Westernize the islands. "Fa'a Samoa" has also resulted in the Samoan reputedly being the purest surviving Polynesian stock.

Life in Samoa appeared to us to be very drab if not downright dull. It is not a very colorful land and the people display a lack of incentive. As an example, many of the handicrafts offered to tourists are made in Tonga or the Fiji's. When I purchased a dress lava-lava, it was suggested that I buy the material (which is made elsewhere) and take it to the Pago Pago Craft Center where the Tongan women would custom sew it for me. Their music, while melodious, is slow and repetitive, tending to make it monotonous after a while. They are at their musical best (and very good, too) when singing church hymns. Dress is in obvious conflict with the weather. Men wear long pants or lava-lavas (long wraparound skirts) with shirts. Women wear almost floor-length skirts and sleeved blouses. None of these are really clean because of the incessant rain, muddy roads, and absence of laundry facilities. Because body cover-up in public is fa'a Samoa (the effect of early missionary influence), visitors are advised to dress accordingly, which made us very warm and uncomfortable. We were always glad to get back to the boat where shorts were our tradition.

Samoans do have a practical side of life as demonstrated by their traditional house (*fale*) and meeting place design. These buildings are oval in shape with steep thatched roofs supported by a peripheral ring of coconut palm posts spaced about 3 feet apart. There are no walls to hinder airflow, but blinds of woven pandanus palm leaves can be lowered on the sides to keep out a driving rain or a low sun. The floor, made of evenly scattered pieces of small coral, is placed higher than the surrounding ground to help keep it dry. Furniture is virtually nonexistent, since Samoans sit, eat, and sleep on pandanus mats on the floor. The construction of the *fales* are usually fine examples of native handwork.

On arriving in Samoa we were struck by the lush tropical growth seen from shoreline to mountain top. The islands are volcanic and have a very fertile soil. Located only 15 degrees south of the equator, they also receive much sunshine. *Horizon*'s cabin temperature, which was normally cool because of its sandwich and floating headliner construction, varied between 78 degrees at night and 85 degrees in the daytime during the period we were there, which was their springtime. What the Samoas have in great excess is rain. Tutuila, easternmost of the 3 big Samoan islands receives 200 inches of rain per year. We were there in the dry season and we had only 3 24-hour periods out of 21 days in which it did not rain. With an average relative humidity of 80%, the boat got pretty stuffy below when buttoned up to keep the rain out.

The Samoan Islands lie 1100 nautical miles WNW from Bora Bora, giving us an almost dead downwind run on ESE winds. We departed Bora Bora on Thursday, August 21, and arrived off the island of Tutuila, American Samoa, at daybreak on Saturday, August 30. Winds were light (6–8 knots) the first few days, but they increased to 15 knots as we neared the islands. On the last night out we shortened sail to storm jib, only reducing our speed to 3½ knots to ensure a no-earlier-than-dawn arrival. We were 1 mile off Aanuu Island at the SE corner of Tutuila at 0500 and entered Pago Pago harbor at 0800.

There is a pecularity in the Samoan language that makes Pago Pago sound like "Pango Pango" when spoken. In their language the "g" is pronounced like the English "ng" as in sing. Hence, the main harbor of American Samoa is called Pa(n)go Pa(n)go. Likewise, the main village, Fagotoga, is pronounced Fa(n)goto(n)ga.

Our harbor chart for this exercise consisted of one I had made on graph paper using information from a Light List, Sailing Directions, and a sketch in the *Pacific Islands Yearbook*. I was unable to get a conventional nautical chart published by the U.S. Defense Mapping Agency because it was restricted for "Official Use Only." Is the government still preparing to fight the Germans and British for possession of the Samoas? Later I discovered that another agency, the Coast and Geodetic Survey, working for the Department of Interior, which administers the territory, publishes a nautical chart that would have made us considerably more confident of our harbor entry, since my chart lacked water-depth references.

Bureaucracy not withstanding, we safely negotiated the Pago Pago harbor reefs and at the west end anchored to a coral sand bottom in 60 feet of water. But sailing never stopped! Pago Pago harbor is a 1-mile long, narrow volcanic crater oriented E–W with the entrance opening to the south. The famous 1700-foot-high Rainmaker Mountain (Mt. Pioa) closing the east end, extracts endless showers from the southeast trades and dumps them in the harbor or, when not doing that, repackages the winds into blustery 15–25 knot gusts that buffet the full length of the harbor.

The Samoas are at the eastern edge of the southwest Pacific hurricane belt. During the summer months in the Southern Hemisphere, November through April, cyclonic disturbances generate between 5 degrees and 20 degrees south latitude and west of 160 degrees west longitude. Each year at least four or five disturbances, and in some years as many as nine or ten, develop into destructive storms of hurricane force. The annual pattern is never the same and prudent yachtsmen usually seek the shelter of hurricane holes for these months. Pago Pago harbor is one of the best. Surrounded by steep mountains over 1000 feet high and with an L-shaped, reef-bordered entrance, it offers about as much protection as possible from high winds and heavy seas.

American Samoa shows all the symptoms of a spoiled child with an almost spoon-fed economy, paid for by the U.S. taxpayer. The island has a wage economy, mostly government, and while the import merchants prosper, agriculture has declined, as evidenced by the small and poorly supplied farmers market. The wage economy is now partly supported by Star Kist and Van Camp from California, companies which have established fish canneries in the former navy buildings on the north harbor shore. While the mechanized canneries operate with the local labor force, the fish have to be supplied by foreign fishing fleets, namely, Korean, Taiwanese and Japanese. There was no evidence of a commercial Samoan fishing fleet even to supply the fresh fish for their own tables. We took advantage of the canneries' presence to add a case of first-quality white tuna to our provisions.

Koreans from the fishing fleet are already beginning to establish themselves on the island. The Korean House, ostensibly built to provide a recreation place for the transient Korean fisherman while ashore, has been opened to the public as a restaurant, grocery store, and duty-free gift shop, much to the passive chagrin of local merchants. Koreans from the fishing fleets are also seen in menial jobs ashore at restaurants and stores. One day we will see them running the Eastern Samoa businesses as the Chinese do in Tahiti and as the Indians do in Fiji.

At the present, though, the main stores are run by descendants of the early South Seas traders, who dealt mostly in copra. Several Max Halleck general stores and services are here while Burns Philp operates the largest and very modern supermarket. It was at Max Halleck's Store No. 3 that we became acquainted with the typical Samoan. One bank of *Horizon*'s batteries were getting weak and we decided to replace them. After scouting the stores for new ones, I settled on a pair of dry-charge batteries at Max Halleck's. The clerk who waited on me was a young, burly Samoan. He was unable to locate battery acid in any of the Halleck enterprises. The woman store manager solved the problem by calling her husband, who was manager of the shipyard, and finding that his electrical shop had an ample supply and could give us some. So without further waiting, the Samoan clerk, pressing the two batteries together, picked them up as easily as I would have two books and carried them to his car. He repeated this several times and I became impressed with his strength. So much so, that when he asked if I was a Christian, I was glad I could truthfully say "yes," knowing that he was also an evangelist. Although husky, he was very pleasant, and we got the batteries filled without problem and back to our side of the harbor.

Pago Pago is considered to be the best harbor in the South Pacific, and although it has a beautiful setting, it is also the dirtiest harbor that we visited. While porcelain fixtures are not new to this area, many Samoans still seem to prefer a more natural life. Add to this an abundance of loose trash and garbage and you have a very uninviting

Burns Philp, South Seas traders since 1883, operate the major store in Neiafu, Vava'u.

area for visiting yachtsmen or cruise ship passengers. These unsanitary conditions were also evident at other parts of the island that we visited. Paradoxically, the worst kept harbor areas seemed to be those administered by the Office of Marine Resources. In fact, on one occasion during our stay, their engine maintenance shop personnel poured gallons of waste oil in the harbor. Unfortunately, the one and only fresh water shower available to yachtsmen was in the Marine Resources building and we had to face this unhealthy area or go dirty. As days went by we resorted more and more to using our precious on-board fresh water supply for sponge baths.

In spite of our aversion to government handouts and environmental carelessness, we found more than enough interesting features in American Samoa to keep us happily occupied for two weeks. One jaunt that tempted us many times each day was the aerial tramway that crosses over the harbor on a 5,400-foot cable climbing at its northern end to the top of 1,600-foot Mt. Alava. Originally built to enable the erection of an antenna for island-wide educational TV coverage, it is now also open to visitors. Finally, on our last day Sven and I overcame our mental barriers and took the opening ride of the day over the harbor. Our appreciation of the magnitude and setting of this beautiful harbor increased with each foot of altitude gained in the crossing. Our faith in the cableway faltered only once. That occurred a hundred yards or so before reaching the upper end, when the car paused for a few long seconds but then continued upward at a slower pace. We later learned that the operator shifts to a lower gear for that last, almost straight-up pull. On solid ground again at 1,600 feet we saw a breath-taking panorama of land, sea, and sky. All of Tutuila can be seen from that one spot, and we are told that on a day without haze the smaller adjacent Manua Islands and even Western Samoa are visible. This cableway has become a magnificent tourist attraction and really booms on cruise ship days.

A very recent addition to Samoan culture and another worthy tourist attraction is the Jean Haydon Museum, recently opened in the old post office building, which was built early in the century when the navy had a coaling station here. Jean Haydon is the wife of a past governor of the territory, and she donated a large number of exhibits besides assembling those which were scattered in various government buildings. The museum fills an important gap in describing Samoan life—past and present—to visitors. The museum also sells a number of interesting books on Samoa and copies of an 1872 harbor chart made by the U.S.S. *Narragansett*, which remains an improvement on my more recent chart.

Social activities for visiting yachtsmen here are self-made, as in most places. While there is a yacht club, it is far removed from the harbor and mostly devoted to Hobie Cat and Sunfish sailing with intraclub regattas and competitions with the Apia, Western Samoa, yacht club. With about 10 cruising yachts in the harbor, a pot-luck dinner evolved for one Sunday evening aboard a near-derelict LCM. Host boats tied up alongside the LCM and set up a buffet, bar, and row of hibachis in the cavernous, partially covered hold of the LCM. The 10-degree list of the LCM kept the collected rainwater to one side, leaving plenty of dry space for socializing by the 40 or so yachtsmen and their guests from Connecticut, Florida, Arkansas, Michigan, California, New Zealand, Switzerland, and Samoa.

The guest from Switzerland, Bob Blaesi, was quickly corralled by Betty when she learned he was a watchmaker. Bulova Watch Company operates a watch sub-assembly plant here that employs about 50 persons. They have similar plants in the Virgin Islands and on Guam. *Horizon*'s stop-watch had been in trouble for some time, having lost its second hand even after the Papeete watchmaker had assured me that it was fixed for all time. Also, my Bulova Accutron, which was to be our primary navigation time piece, had such an erratic rate that we could not depend on it. So Bob, who likes yachtsmen and knows Accutrons, volunteered to help us out. Before adjusting the Accutron, however, we discussed how and where it would be mounted. For precision timekeeping this is a must, since the tuning fork mechanism is sensitive to attitude, vibration, magnetic fields, and temperature variation. The Accutron, when adjusted and permanently installed, kept better time than ever before.

We had one more problem to solve before we left Samoa, and that was the question of hull insurance on *Horizon*. When we bought the boat we had purchased hull insurance with New Zealand Insurance Company, since they were one of the largest in the business and covered the Pacific. Before departure we had the boat and crew surveyed in order to obtain an endorsement on the policy which would cover "the waters of the Pacific Ocean not south of 22 degrees south latitude, not west of 175 degrees west longitude and not north of 38 degrees north latitude." Now we were to leave those waters and our insurance agent in California was to secure a new policy for us, since New Zealand elected not to cover us any further. Having heard nothing from him, I called him on the Ham radio aboard *Betty J*. His earlier optimism about getting coverage had faded away like so many salesmen's promises, and he had come up with only one—Lloyds of

London. The annual premium was to be $2,160, or a hefty 5.5% of the declared value. The premium was too high to consider, so we made the decision to go uninsured the rest of the way.

While we now felt uncomfortable not having insurance, which had been a way of life with us, we also felt a greater confidence in ourselves than the insurance companies did. So we set our minds to self-insurance by keeping the boat ship-shape, watching the weather carefully, and taking no chances with dangerous landfalls. For $2,160 we could be very careful!

Now, with the insurance problem resolved, we had only one problem left and that was with our crewman. Sven, feeling that he had become indispensable, told us that he would have to leave us in Samoa or, if we wanted to have him along to the Fijis, we would have to give him an airline ticket to Australia from there! I had no intention of buying his services at that price. Time, however, was beginning to be a problem, and it did not appear that we could visit the Fijis and still avoid the hurricane season.

As part of our strategy to convince Sven he was not indispensable, Betty and I started the daily handling of *Horizon* by ourselves—like weighing anchor to motor over to the deck for fresh water when Sven was ashore. Soon he began to worry about his professional status and became attentive to his duties once again. Now we discussed our plan with him, and that was to skip Fiji and go to Tonga instead, which fit the weather pattern better and was also more directly on course to New Zealand, our ultimate destination. We had made no attempt to get another crewman because we indeed planned on continuing by ourselves. We had taken his challenge but left him the option to go along to Tonga if he wanted. He decided to stay with the boat, so we patched up ruffled feelings and continued boat life as usual.

As with all of our stops, time passed too quickly for us to do or see everything in the vicinity. So, having replenished our provisions with old familiar brand names from the states and frozen New Zealand beef, we departed Pago Pago harbor at 1400 on September 15, for Apia, Upolu Island, Western Samoa. This should have been a milkrun, but the weatherman refused to cooperate. Winds were light all the way and rain was plentiful. The navigation light on the island of Fanuatapu at the Eastern end of Upolu island was not working, so, with no recognizable landmarks throughout the night, for safety we stood well off the shadowy, misty island. The rain increased in the morning, and at noon, between showers, I got a quick visual bearing on the town of Apia, which was the last we saw of it until, with a failing engine, we motored through the reef at 1400.

Since we bought the boat we have been plagued with air entering the fuel system and stopping the engine. At this critical time it got another case of the burps but did not stop. While we were always concerned about this happening at the wrong time, I became expert at bleeding the air out of the fuel lines, and we also learned to play it safe with as much leeshore distance as possible and sails and anchor ready.

The clearance formalities brought further consternation and confirmed what other yachtsmen have reported on Apia. First, the harbormaster, Captain Evans, a man of distinct British background, welcomed us from his commercial dock, which towered over us. But in his second breath he warned us again about "dinghy borrowing" and outright theft of oars and motors by the locals. Evans suggested that when we went ashore we bring our dinghy alongside his big harbor tug, leaving the oars on the tug for safety. Having paid his respects and given us the do's and don'ts, he returned to his office and informed Immigration, Customs, and Port Health of our arrival. Immigration appeared next on the scene. He was a good looking, efficient local lad who quickly stamped a 2-week visitors pass in our passports and proceeded to warn us of a local confidence man who preys on yachts. After his description of "Jack," Sven remembered him as an ex-pug who had his con game going 5 years ago when Sven previously visited Apia. I suppose we were lucky since we were never approached by Jack-the-Ripoff. On leaving, Immigration strongly suggested that we allow no locals on board.

Next came the Port Health official a bear of a man—typical Samoan physique, soft spoken, and obviously well educated. Quickly convinced that we were in good health, he proceeded to expound on the dangers of Dengue fever, which was mildly epidemic here. This fever carried by mosquitos, of which we were soon to find many, had an incubation period of 10 days, which could find us at sea again if it struck. He suggested that we take along a supply of sulfa tablets and a pain reliever. Since their hospital supply was dangerously low because of the mini-epidemic, he recommended a chemist to us in Apia and said we could get them without prescription. Sure enough, we presented our request to a young clerk who had the chemist measure out and bottle 60 sulfadimidine tablets for which we paid only $1.60 (US). No symptoms of Dengue fever appeared on *Horizon*, and I wonder what other sickness we can ward off with our ever-growing apothecary stock.

The last player in the clearance game was the Customs officer. He did not appear in a reasonable length of time so I tracked him down at the Customs Office just outside the harbor road gate. I had nothing of interest to him on board so he took my departure clearance from

American Samoa and told me to come back when ready to leave. We were free at last to see Samoa.

Western Samoa differed only in minor respects from American Samoa. Litter was still common, but community sanitation was noticeably better. Mud, of course, existed everywhere because rain and Samoa are synonomous. Off the main streets of Apia and out into the countryside the families lived in the same traditional *fales* as on Tutuila, but a greater sense of pride was evident in the maintenance of the *fales* and the cleaner yards. While there was also a great semblance of order in urban building placement, this also tended to make Apia less colorful than Fagotoga, the Pago Pago commercial center, where the helter-skelter layout made walking an interesting game of directions.

Apia, stretched out along the harbor, retains most of its early British colonial atmosphere. The government offices and many houses are frame buildings of early Victorian gingerbread style, painted white with red roofs. Churches abound here as in all Samoa and there were one or two large churches in every block along the waterfront. Their significance to the mariner can be more than religious, since the Sailing Directions describe many harbor entries as for Apia "The Catholic church, a grey-white building with twin towers, serves as a good landmark." And for us it did, since we did not identify the adjacent range markers until we were on land!

Aiding immensely to the local color is the Western Samoa constabulary. Their unique dress includes lava-lavas and British bobby-style helmets. But don't let those lava-lavas fool you. Under them are the same robust Samoans that I would rather have for friends than enemies! The motorcycle police apparently found the lava-lavas a problem, so they have resorted to westernized dress of long blue trousers.

The Samoans love ceremony, so when they execute the morning flag raising in front of the prime minister's office at the harbor, it is a spectacle to behold. Rising extra early (for us) one morning, we went ashore to photograph this very traditional and proud event. To the measured beat of drums the colorful constabulary marches down the sidestreet from their barracks to the harbor-front street where all traffic has been stopped. The flag of independent Western Samoa is slowly raised to the roll of drums and the rigid salute of the guard, and the day is officially begun.

One of the world's better kept literary secrets is that Robert Lewis Stevenson (*Treasure Island, Dr. Jekyll and Mr. Hyde*), spent the last five years of his life here. In ill health, he left Scotland and sailed over much of the Pacific looking for a place in which to heal and to continue his writings. He finally chose the Western Samoa island of Upolu and built a magnificent Victorian-style mansion near the little village of Vailima on the hillside above Apia. There he continued his prolific writing until his death in 1894. Stevenson is buried at the top of Mt. Vaea next to Vailima. The mansion is now the official residence of the head of state for Western Samoa and permission to visit it must be obtained from the prime minister's office. This Betty and I did one hot and sultry afternoon, taking a taxi up the hillside in preference to walking or taking the jitney bus, which runs only every hour. While we could not enter any of the buildings, we were allowed to walk the grounds after showing our pass to the guard. The house sits on a knoll surrounded by a well kept, beautifully landscaped lawn and garden. To the north one sees the Apia harbor and reefs, while to the west looms Mt. Vaea, which in this climate we did not climb. A reverse view from the harbor is equally impressive, with the long red-roofed, white mansion clearly visible above the trees, Mt. Vaea alongside, and in the background, visible only in the morning sun, a high waterfall.

While days were spent seeing all the nearby points of interest on foot and others further away by taxi or jitney bus, nights were spent aboard *Horizon* reading or playing Yahtzee after dinner with a common early-to-bed routine. In Apia, however, we had decided to break with routine and visit Aggie Grey's Hotel for dinner. The hotel has been a South Seas landmark for years, made famous by countless writers of South Sea stories. To quote from Aggie's own brochure, "If Samoa is the heart of Polynesia, then Aggie's bar is the heart of the heart of Polynesia." Betty and I went right to the heart for a fascinating evening in a British colonial atmosphere. Relaxing with us in the wall-less bar were many local people and persons of obvious British connection, whom one would expect to find in these colonial areas. This particular night a formal reception was being held, and we must have seen every foreign dignitary in Apia in their tropical dress as they passed through the adjacent garden.

Dinner was sumptuous. Course after course was brought until we had to give in and retire to the veranda for coffee. The atmosphere and the delectable dinner will make Aggie Grey famous forever in our minds. Unlike Quinn's of Papeete, Aggie Grey's is a South Seas institution destined to survive for many to appreciate.

We left the Samoas with mixed feelings. While "fa'a Samoa" seems right for these people, they cannot avoid the modern world and its standards. In particular, American Samoa, caught between a major world power and a Polynesian heritage, seems to be having the more difficult time. Aside from politics and international affairs, we will always remember Samoa for:

—Our return to an English-speaking society after 6 months of Spanish and French
—The heavy emphasis on nonalcoholic ceremonial kava drinking
—The pathetic sight of persons afflicted with elephantiasis
—The bingo games at the Fagotoga market place on Saturday afternoons
—The tenacity of the kids selling paper shell necklaces
—The hospitable and relaxed way of life in the old British colonial atmosphere of Aggie Grey's hotel

9

On to the Friendly Islands

You may believe whom you would—Captain Cook who named the Tonga Islands the Friendly Islands, or Captain Bligh who, on the Tonga Island of Tofua, suffered his only casualty in his remarkable 3,620 mile trip in an open launch after the mutiny on the *Bounty*. We on *Horizon* found the Tonga Islands beautiful, the customs and climate in contradiction, and the economy poor.

The Kingdom of Tonga consists of three island groups—Vava'u, the northernmost; Ha'apai in the center; and Tongatapu in the south. About two hundred islands spread over 100,000 square miles of ocean area. The two principal islands are Vava'u, for which the northern group is named, and Tongatapu, for which the southern group is named. Tonga with a population of 90,000 is a constitutional monarchy, the last in Polynesia. As a point of royal interest, the present king's mother, Queen Salote, attended the coronation of England's Queen Elizabeth in 1953 and reportedly almost stole the show because of her regal bearing and warm personality. We are told that this event did more to make Tonga known to the world than any political maneuvering could have accomplished.

This monarchy is closely interwoven with religion, and in the following words the constitution specifically sets aside the Sabbath as a day of religious observance, "The Sabbath Day shall be sacred in

Sailboats from Tongatapu's out islands raft in Nuku'alofa's small boat harbor.

Tonga forever and it shall not be lawful to do work or play games or trade on the Sabbath. And any agreement made or documents witnessed on this day shall be counted void and not recognized by the Government." While in principle this guides the people to appropriate Sunday observance, in practice it is not working out well. There is simply too much communication with the outside world, and hotels, restaurants, transportation, and police and fire services find a growing need to operate on Sunday. Like the rest of the modern world, expediency whittles away at principle and now Tonga's Sunday law is being legally challenged in their court system.

Naturally churches abound and church schools are common. The early missionaries' influence has not only hung on in the church but in their conservative way of dress. Except for children, body exposure of any kind in public places by either sex is *tapu* (forbidden). Long sleeve blouses and long skirts (*valas*) for women and lava-lavas or pants for men are standard dress. The climate is so hot and humid that wearing the required clothes was oppressive and we probably spent less time ashore because of it. I unthinkingly stepped off the boat one day without my shirt on and was quickly corrected by a local citizen.

A well-dressed Tongan also wears a unique wrap-around-the-waist mat called a *ta'ovala*, which in western formal dress is called a cummerbund. It is most often a mat woven of pandanus fronds, but sometimes a more ornamental one is made of yarn or plastic. The common *ta'ovala* is 12–16 inches high, but we saw some that reached the ground. The long ta'ovalas were mats about the size of a sleeping mat! These *ta'ovalas* seem to be traditional and not religious, but we were unable to learn anything of their origin. None of the other Polynesian peoples wear them.

The Tongan people, while very similar in physical appearance to the heavyset Samoans, displayed a disposition more like the Tahitians. In the market place one could hear light-hearted laughter as bargaining took place. I came to admire these patient people with their wide, deep brown eyes, who have such great love for their children and their country.

Tonga is also noted for its postage stamps—probably the most unusual and beautiful in the world. The stamps have irregular shapes outlining the particular subject being honored, a banana for instance. The banana stamp is small enough to get on a postcard, but most stamps are so large that they overrun the address space. Furthermore, the Tongan postal clerks took a great delight in giving us the maximum number of small denomination stamps so that our mailings ended up looking like a Tongan public relations billboard.

This intriguing Kingdom of Tonga lies SSW of the rainy Samoas. We departed Apia, Western Samoa, on Saturday, 20 September and arrived at the northern Tonga Islands 3 days later, after sailing a distance of 345 miles. We had some squalls along the way in the early mornings but it was mostly easy tradewind sailing.

This short passage broached the classical navigation dateline problem, but with a unique local twist. We passed into tomorrow when we crossed the International Dateline, but the zone time jumped from 12 hours slow on Greenwich time to 13 hours fast rather than the normal 12 hours fast. This anomaly was created by Tonga, which wanted to be on the same time of day as Samoa (even though a day later) and the same day of the week as New Zealand (even though an hour earlier). The resulting world time position gives Tonga the opportunity to use the motto "Where time begins," which appears on their stamps and most of their publicity handouts. While a timekeeping problem such as this never fails to confuse first-year navigation students, in practice it is necessarily mastered quite rapidly.

We raised Vava'u, the northernmost island, at 0200 on the 23rd (actually the 24th), entered its magnificent channel approach at 0800 and then, under power, motored for 8 miles along one of the most beautiful waterways we have ever seen.

Tonga contains both high and low islands. The Vava'u group is high in the sense they are volcanic and rise to moderate heights of 700 feet, although they turn into reefs further south. With good soil, plenty of rain and sunshine, the hillsides were a lush green. Coconut and banana palms abound and the beautiful beaches are fringed by the ever-present coral reefs. The 8-mile channel was deep water for its full length, in fact, large cruise ships come 7 miles into it before they are stopped by a right-angle turn not negotiable by a vessel longer than a couple hundred feet. At this turn the main town of Neiafu and its large protected harbor with sparkling blue-green water comes into view.

The anchorage at Neiafu was in 16 feet of water so clear that the bottom sand was visible. Taking advantage of this we searched out an open sand area between gigantic coral heads and carefully lowered the anchor to lie peacefully on its side on the sand. It never did dig its way into the bottom in this calm, well protected anchorage, but the grating of the anchor chain across the coral heads occasionally produced monstrous noises. Incidentally, this harbor at Neiafu is one of the few hurricane holes in the South Pacific. Surrounded by hills 400 to 600 feet high with a narrow reach to its south (closed) end, small boats can find haven there from the tropical cyclones that generate between November and April. While not as good as Pago Pago, it did seem adequate, and, in fact, it is the only other hole available short of New Zealand.

Customs and agriculture officials arrived on the scene in a common fishing skiff with outboard motor handled by a young Tongan. The custom's official was obviously the more important individual and he sat with an air of dignified authority as the skiff was brought alongside. He was first aboard *Horizon* and after brief introductions went below and took over the dinette for his office. The customs officer felt right at home with us since he served with the Los Angeles police force at one time in what I took to be the Narcotics Detail, which also was his concern on Vava'u. Both officials were pleasant Tongans and we chatted about a variety of things Tongan. Customs was perfunctory and the agriculture office had but one task—to help control the rhinoceros beetle infection. While I have never seen a rhinoceros beetle, it was described to me as about 2½ inches long with a large horn on its head from which it gets its name. It has a voracious appetite for coconut palm fronds, causing stunted growth of the trees and poor coconut crops. Truly a serious problem in a land where the coconut is the basis for their largest export product, copra.

To our knowledge only the Vava'u group was infected, and we

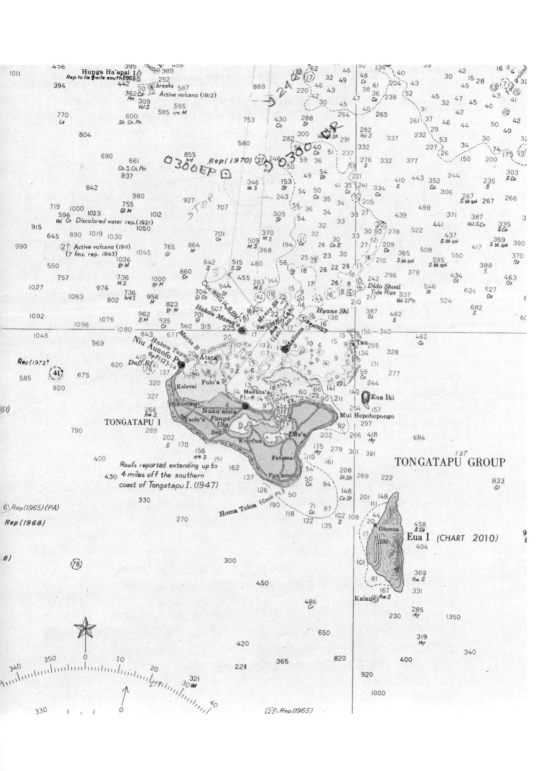

weren't certain that we could later visit the Tongatapu group since we had spent several weeks in the Samoas where the beetle was already a raging menace. We were to learn however, that Tongatapu was already infected, so we would be allowed to go there without special treatment. But not the Ha'apai group. It is still free of the beetle, and we would have needed special inspection and permission to visit it if we had desired.

Formalities over, we all relaxed with a bit of brandy and chatted mostly about things non-Tongan. The agriculture man was an avid reader of *Time* Magazine, but we had traded all of ours off at Pago Pago so we were unable to improve our image here, beyond a *Reader's Digest*. The customs official, on the other hand, was an avid fisherman, unable to get heavy-duty swivels in Neiafu. From our well-equipped fishing-tackle box we produced a couple of large brass swivels, which we were glad to offer him; we hoped he would have more luck with them than we had been having. I have previously mentioned how the "yachtie-help-yachtie" policy works to the benefit of all in keeping the cruising boats going. One can also say that "yachtie help local" and vice versa is also useful in working your way through the islands. But beware that you don't attempt bribes or other tricks of sophisticated business, since the Polynesians would be greatly offended. A small gift, however, gives a warm feeling to both giver and receiver.

As soon as the Customs and Agriculture officials departed (we handled Immigration later on shore) the local friends of the yachtsmen started to appear. Con men par excellence! They would paddle their skiffs, one at a time, up to your boat, offering to give you fresh fruits and vegetables. Laying them on your deck, they would then ask to come aboard. All too smooth in our estimation—so we immediately shooed them off. Other yachtsmen later told us that we did the right thing since the gifts were neither free nor reasonable, being about twice the price that was charged at the Saturday market. These peddlers were continuing pests to all yachtsmen, and one boat that let a local on board had the fellow lay down on deck and go to sleep like he was at home in his *fale*! This was a far cry from the spontaneous on-board welcome we had received at Haka Maii, but with so many yachts now cruising these waters, I think we will see more and more commercialism develop in the islands. While we generally go out of our way to be friendly with the local people, we drew a hard line on the Neiafu con artists.

Ashore at Neiafu, we were greatly impressed by the orderliness of the little hillside town. It was laid out with straight roads and rectangular blocks as far as the topography would allow. On inquiry we found this due to the kingdom's unusual land-ownership policy. All land remains vested in the crown, but a male on reaching the age of 16 is given 8 acres of rural land for farming and ⅔ acre of city land for living. This parceling of land has forced the Tongans to do some elementary land-use planning and to make careful surveys of lot boundaries to avoid ownership disputes. The result was pleasing to our eyes, and with the Tongans' better sense of public sanitation (compared to the Samoans), we found Neiafu (and later Nuku'alofa) a pleasant tropical village.

With 200 islands to tie together into one kingdom, Tonga depends heavily on its interisland trading vessels. It has set up its own national fleet, Pacific Navigation Company, which not only runs between islands but connects with New Zealand, Fiji, and Western Samoa. Both the flagship of the fleet, the 1000-ton *Olovaha*, and one of their trawler-size traders, *Pakiene*, were at the Neiafu wharf during our stay. We noted that the *Olovaha* is particularly well maintained since she is also the royal yacht used by the king on his visits to the islands.

We remained a week at Neiafu, which, like all our other stops, was too short a time. One of those days was taken up shelling on the eastern side of Vava'u. At low tide, acres and acres of a flat reef shelf became exposed, and, with suitable foot protection, we scoured the nooks and crannies of the coral bottom finding all sorts of tropical marine life—some weird, some pretty, all interesting. We were joined in our search by a number of wading birds who found the reef life also very tasty. A large number of new shells were added to our Pacific collection from this reef.

Our last day at Neiafu was a Saturday, which is also the weekly open-air market day. People come by small boat, from all the surrounding islands arriving at daybreak to sell and to buy fruits and vegetables. The market was set up on the ground in the harbor wharf backup area, and it buzzed with activity until about mid-morning, when everybody packed up and left. Yams, watermelons, taro roots weighing up to 30 pounds, papaya, bananas and plantains, carrots, and corn were in evidence. We got stung on a stalk of bananas we bought, which apparently was cut too green, since the bananas would not ripen and we had to deep-six it two weeks later half way to New Zealand. As a matter of interest, we hang banana stalks for ripening at the aft end of the main boom just behind the helmsman, which sometimes produces amusing reactions in heavy seas as it swings into the unsuspecting person on watch.

Our next port of call, Tongatapu ("sacred Tonga"—capital of the Kingdom), lay 170 miles to the South with most of the other 148 islands stretched out along the way. We have a great respect for reefs, so we carefully studied alternative route possibilities. It appeared to be a 36-hour passage, so we had our choice of two days and one night or two nights and one day. We chose the later because we preferred daylight sailing during the middle of the passage when we had to pass between Tofua and Kao (high) islands and the Ha'apai group of atolls. This plan also gave us a morning approach to Tongatapu island with a reserve of daylight in case of adverse weather or other difficulties.

Departing Neiafu at 1540, we sailed the beautiful 9-mile western passage out to the open sea and turned SSW on gentle tradewinds and a setting sun. Mid-morning the next day, Tofua island (scene of the *Bounty* mutiny) came into view on our starboard bow and all day long atolls of the Ha'apai group slid by on our port side. At nightfall we were able to turn directly south, and, if our dead reckoning was correct, we would be able to see Tongatapu in the morning before we hit it. At 0500 we picked up the principal navigation light on Malinoa islet, which turned out to be the only navaid recognizable from the British Admiralty chart. All the rest had been changed since the chart and the U.S. Sailing Directions were issued. Having learned in Mexican waters not to put implicit faith in any navaids, I sent Sven up the ratlines to the main spreaders to direct us through the reefs, which make up the whole north side of the island. Rain showers added to the challenge but the wind remained steady from the east, and we tacked our way through the reefs up to the small boat harbor at the capital city of Nuku'alofa, which was to be our home for the next week. We were to learn later that our arrival at Nuku'alofa was witnessed by royal eyes. In our visit to the palace grounds during the week, the sergeant of the Royal Guards told us that the king had followed our entry through a telescope. He might also have been interested in my thoughts concerning his navaids and charts! We shared the small boat harbor with only one other overseas cruising boat, *Babalachi*, a ferrocement ketch from Vancouver. Few cruising boats visit Tonga and fewer still visit Nuku'alofa. We found it pleasant not to be in the midst of a lot of cruising boats, but we also felt that others were missing a fine port of call.

Life in the small boat harbor was a fascinating view of Tongan life. It started daily with the predawn arrival of the small interisland ferry boats, which discharged people and farm products onto the wharf. While patiently awaiting daylight and their local transportation, these people would spontaneously sing the well-known church hymns. Like the Samoans, their voices were clear and mellow—a most pleasant way to be awakened. The next arrivals were the fishermen in Sea Gull

A well-dressed Tongan wearing the ta'ovala in the Nuku'alofa market.

outboard-motor-propelled skiffs who had fished by lantern light throughout the night. They would announce their arrival at the street wharf with policelike whistles, and the early rising city dwellers would come over to buy their string of beautiful reef fish for dinner. The fishermen, while waiting, would doff their oilskins and enjoy a breakfast of the cool milk and soft, sweet meat of the young coconut.

Arriving at almost any time of the day or night and usually in the early part of the week, were the working sailboats from the out islands surrounding Tongatapu. About 35 feet long, they were strongly built, gaff-rigged, bowsprit sloops, using only sailpower; all colorfully painted and well maintained. They would bring families to the big city to shop and visit. They also were ladened with farm products such as copra, taro, yams, young banana plants, and squealing piglets, and sea turtles destined for the table. Throughout the week the return cargo would gradually appear at the wharf—lumber, iron roofing, cement blocks, store-bought provisions, and finally, the families and friends to see them off. By this time the boats were well overloaded—up to one foot over their waterlines! But no one in these gay crowds seemed to mind. With the towing help of the pilot boat, *Unga*, they departed the small boat harbor and were seen for hours endlessly tacking away towards their home islands.

In addition to being a small shipping terminal, the harbor also had an industrial face. Across the road a new 80-foot personnel ferry was under construction, and the rhythmic beat of caulking hammers was heard all day, interspersed with the staccato scream of chain saws shaping timbers for the interior. At the closed end of the harbor was the marine railway with a trimaran on the ways, and alongside in the water was the harbor tug undergoing a major renovation.

Evening was the fun time in this small boat harbor. That was the time the local children came for a swim. While we didn't think the water was very clean, they couldn't have cared less. Older kids in swim trunks, younger ones in their birthday suits—jumping and diving off the harbor walls, swinging on the mooring lines and thoroughly enjoying themselves. And such was the day's life in the most active small boat harbor we had yet seen.

Facilities for yachtsmen outside of the well-protected small boat harbor were nonexistent. We took our showers in a hut behind a *fale* about one block away. To get there, one traversed several backyards scattering chickens, pigs, and dogs, while being amiably greeted by a host of smiling children. On the honor system, you simply took your shower and then left 10 seniti (100 seniti equals one pa'anga, so 10 seniti is about ten cents) with the owner living in the *fale*. Water was available at a small motel across the street but had to be carried in jugs to the boat. The nearest available trash cans were three blocks away at the Nuku'alofa Yacht & Boat Club. By now none of this was a hardship to us, since we have learned to consolidate our trips ashore to accomplish the maximum number of functions with the minimum number of steps.

Although the Nuku'alofa Yacht & Boat Club turned out to be more of a social than nautical group, we were able to solve our engine problem there one night. By coincidence we were talking to the Gardner (Australia) diesel engine representative—a wiry little Scotsman living in Tonga by way of Australia and New Zealand. Posing our problem to him, he advised replacing the fuel lift pump (which we had in our engine spares inventory). Two days out of Tonga on our passage to New Zealand, I made the change, and we have had no trouble since.

The town of Nuku'alofa stretched for a mile along a shoreline which was protected from northerly seas by a continuous coral block wall. The palace and royal church, both built in Victorian frame construction, lay on this waterfront amidst a stand of beautiful Norfolk pines. The town business area stood one block back from the waterfront and it had a very clean and orderly people's market at its center, which also served as the terminus of the island buses. Both of the big South Seas merchandisers carrying mostly New Zealand products were represented here—Burns Philp and Morris Hedstrom. Delight of delights to us was the frozen beef and fresh apples, to say nothing of the excellent New Zealand ice cream. Incidently, you may wonder what we do with the local money left over when we leave a foreign country. In the case of Western Samoa and Tonga we used it to buy New Zealand apples, which were a real treat on our night watches at sea.

The generosity of all Polynesians is inherent in the Tongans. Outside the fish market wharf near the palace was a group of snack vendors catering to the passersby. We stopped at the green coconut stand to enjoy the milk of the nut before continuing our tour of the palace area. Several days later this same vendor appeared at the small boat harbor to board one of the out island sailboats. He saw us and, obviously remembering our enjoyment of the earlier drinking nuts, threw us several more, which we took along to New Zealand. While business is business, a gift is greatly appreciated.

On the subject of public eating, we also learned of another Tongan custom attesting to the dignity of these people. One does not eat or drink walking along the streets. Our introduction to this was through the ice cream cone, a confection of delicious passion fruit ice cream from New Zealand put into the usual cracker cone. After ordering ours in a small ice cream store, we noticed that other people who had also ordered were standing about eating them inside. This seemed wise to me in view of the hot sun outside. But it aroused Betty's curiosity, and she asked a Tongan, who simply stated that it is not their custom to eat on the street. Gum chewing, however, appeared to be an exception.

Nuku'alofa has not always been the capital of Tonga. In pre-Christian times the town of Mu'a was the home of the kings. It is located inland from the sea on a very large lagoon surrounded by dense tropical vegetation. We visited Mu'a by bus on a rainy day. Because most early Tongan buildings were build of biodegradable materials, little is left to see of the earlier civilization. The royal families wanted to be remembered in death, however, so they built large terraced tombs (100 feet square) rising up to 20 feet and faced with huge coral blocks weighing tens of tons. There are supposed to be 40 of these terraced tombs (*langi*), although we saw only a half dozen in our short tour. The practice of above-ground burial continues to this day (in a more conservative manner) because the topsoil is shallow and below it is made up of hard coral.

Tongans are noted for their handicrafts. They are not only sold outside the kingdom, but Tongans themselves use their own handbags in shopping and tapa cloth for bedding. Near Mu'a we saw a piece of tapa cloth being dried, which we estimated to be 10 feet wide and 150 feet long! Although tapa cloth making is a disappearing art in most of Polynesia, the Tongans continue to make it and also cultivate the mulberry tree as a source of bark. At Vava'u, as well as Tongatapu, we saw women at work matting the bark fiber together by pounding them over coconut logs with a special mallet. The rhythmic tap-tap-tap resounds softly through the village, reminding you that here is a people who remain proud of their heritage.

By the close of the 18th century ships of the English East India Company as well as Yankee Traders had built up a commerce with China for their silk, tea, and fine porcelain. In trade for these exotic products of the Far East they delivered to China shiploads of fur pelts from the coast of North America—sea otter, ermine, bear, and seals. When these animals were driven to near extinction, the traders turned to sweet-smelling sandalwood as a medium of exchange. Highly prized by the Chinese for its fragrance, sandalwood was made into furniture and chests and an oil extracted from it was used in incense, perfumes, and medicines.

While the principal species of the tree is native to India, other species were found on high islands throughout the Pacific from New Guinea to Hawaii. It took only thirty years at the beginning of the 19th century for the traders using and abusing native populations to decimate the sandalwood forests of the Pacific islands. The wood is now rare, but we learned in Neiafu that some still grows in Tonga and small pieces are obtainable. One of the local Vava'uans, who conduct their sales business with yachties from fishing skiffs, "had a brother on the other side of Vava'u who could take his horse into the mountains and bring back a piece of sandalwood." This long story of difficulty in getting the wood simply led up to a high price—10 pa'anga (the pa'anga is equal at this time to $ US 1.26) for a piece about 20 inches long (measured by the spread of hands) of unknown diameter and quality. We thought this to be too uncertain and turned our thoughts to getting a wood carving made of sandalwood when we reached Nuku'alofa.

Woodcarving is a craft at which the men excel but which is now mostly souvenir oriented. We, however, wanted a different carving made, so we negotiated with a woodcarver along the waterfront to carve a turtle out of sandalwood. The turtle we wanted was to symbolize Tu'i Molilo (Chief Molilo), the giant land tortoise brought to the islands by Captain Cook in 1777, which lived in the various palace grounds until it died in 1966. Our woodcarver did not disappoint us and in a couple of days we had our Tu'i Molilo artfully carved in sweet-smelling sandlewood.

Our Tonga stay was now at an end and New Zealand beckoned. But we had stored up memories of this unusual little kingdom such as:

—The patient nature of these people with the wide, deep-brown eyes
—Their lighthearted laughter in business as in pleasure
—The early morning hymn singing at the harbor
—The rhythmic tapping sounds from backyards where tapa cloth was being made
—The incompatibility of the weather and the style of dress
—The big sea turtles lying on their backs in the hot sun—waiting for the market.
—The con artists of Vava'u
—Stamps of Tonga
—The great pride the Tongans have for their country

10

Interlude in Kiwi Land

New Zealand's land area is made up principally of two large islands—North and South Islands—with a total land area about equal to the state of Colorado, but it stretches north and south for 1,100 miles with no inland point more remote from the sea than 68 miles. It lies at latitudes south of the equator similar to California's position north of the equator and has a similar climate. The northern end of North Island is subtropical, enabling the growing of citrus fruits, while the south end of South Island has cold and snowy winters. On its rugged southwestern rim South Island has spectacular fjords and glaciers. It is this jagged and indented coastline that gives New Zealand a coastline length that approximates that of the contiguous 48 United States. Westerly winds are the rule, and rain, while seasonal, is well spread over the two islands, giving lush natural pastures, "bush" that is impenetrable in spots, and trees of magnificent stature.

Besides good summer weather yachtsmen are attracted to the highly indented coastline, which provides innumerable harbors for exploration, isolation, or a sanctuary from a local storm. In particular, the northeast coast of North Island is favored by the Kiwi yachtsman and has also become the overwhelming favorite of overseas yachts. South of East Cape to Bluff there are only a handful of snug harbors, while even

The pleasant little town of Russell, Bay of Islands, was once a haven for whaling ships.

fewer exist along the entire west coast of both islands facing the Tasman Sea. Separating the two islands is Cook Strait, noted for its violent winds. Here the prevailing westerlies are funneled between mountain ranges forming the strait and the resultant winds and currents make the notorious Alenuihaha Channel of Hawaii look like a millpond.

There is some evidence that the first New Zealand natives were lost Polynesians who arrived here by accident and not intent. Possibly they were out fishing or in small canoes voyaging between the islands far to the north and east and had been blown south to ultimately land on these islands. These first inhabitants arrived about A.D. 500, and they found the islands to have insufficient vegetable growth to sustain them. They turned to hunting the giant flightless and now extinct Moa bird. Their nomadic, isolated existence lasted until about A.D. 1100, when adventuresome Polynesians from Hawaiiki (believed to be Raiatea Island in the Society group) started migrating throughout the vast triangular area of the Pacific formed by Easter Island, the Hawaiian Islands, and New Zealand. These later Polynesian arrivals—now called Maoris—eventually eliminated the earlier race of Moa hunters and established their own society based on independent tribes but having a common culture.

The Maoris were the fiercest of all Polynesians; they constantly engaged in warfare in which the loser would expect to be eaten. While wars were usually fought for the purpose of conquering neighboring tribes or for revenge, it was also a sport with chivalrous periods. Halts in battle were frequently called to return the wounded. After the arrival of the European guns, battles were sometimes extended by one side giving additional ammunition to the other side. It was the guns in the hands of warring tribes together with disease which reduced the Maori population from an estimated 200 thousand to 400 thousand in 1780 to a low of 42,000 in 1896. Today they number about 250,000.

The first European explorers to see these islands were the Dutch under Abel Tasman in 1642, and, subsequently, the islands were named after a Dutch province—Sea Land. It was, however, the English explorer, Captain Cook, who in 1769–77 thoroughly explored and charted New Zealand for the first time. We have obtained from the Alexander Trumbull Library in Wellington a copy of his remarkably accurate 1777 chart of New Zealand.

Following closely on the heels of the explorers were the exploiters of the period—sealers, whalers, and traders. By 1830 sealers managed to virtually exterminate the seal population, found principally off the South Island, and then they turned to whaling. It was the humpback whale that became the new hunting target. The humpbacks migrated south along the New Zealand coast in October through November to spend the summer months in the Antarctic and returned north in June through July to winter in the tropics. Their shoreline migration at slow speeds (4 knots) and their huge bulk (40 to 50 tons) was their undoing.

New Zealand whaling reached its peak in 1838. Whalers sought their R & R (resupply and ribaldry) in a little Bay of Islands settlement called Kororareka, which could boast of 30 grog shops. At one time in 1836 there were 36 whaling ships from around the world anchored at Kororareka. While whaling greatly diminished in these waters in the following years, the town of Kororareka survived. Today it has but one pub and carries the respectable name of Russell.

Serious colonization of New Zealand began after the Treaty of Waitangi was signed in 1840 between the Maoris and the British. Traders, missionaries, and farmers from England flocked to the islands, which proved to be fertile grounds for the work of all three. While many settlements arose, some were deliberately planned like the bit of Scotland developed on South Island's Otago Harbor, now known as Dunedin, currently New Zealand's fourth largest city, with a popula-

tion of 110,000. Christchurch on the Canterbury Plain of the South Island was a planned Church of England settlement. It is more familiar today as the jumping-off place for Antarctic expeditions. Wellington, New Zealand's capital, was sited by the New Zealand Company on the north side of Cook Strait which separates the North and South Islands. The land for Wellington was bought by the New Zealand Company in 1839 from a Maori tribe who supposedly owned it. But, like Spanish land grants in early California, the true ownership is very confused and even today poses a problem for land courts. New Zealand's largest city, Auckland (750,000 population) is a bustling, cosmopolitan seaport on the North Island.

The flora and fauna of New Zealand are unique in their abundance— much of the flora and little of the fauna. This is the land of the giant kauri tree, found also in limited numbers on islands to the north and west as far as Malaysia. A slow-growing tree living over 1000 years, the kauri reaches heights of over 150 feet with the lowest limbs over 60 feet above the ground and a girth of up to 50 feet. Once growing in great stands, it started to disappear rapidly after the arrival of the Europeans since it was first used as masts for English warships, then by settlers for buildings and export to Australia. Now it is protected and its uses limited to applications such as boat building, which need its fine qualities. Gum for varnish was a much sought by-product in the 1800s and gum diggers scoured North Island for buried chunks of fossilized resin left from ancient stands of the trees. To help save the remaining kauris, faster-growing pines are now farmed to supply New Zealand's timber needs, and for export.

There are some other unusual trees in this unusual country such as the punga, which is a tree fern reaching heights of 50 feet and the cabbage palm (inedible) similar to the pandanus palm of tropical islands. But our favorite was the pahutukawa tree—a massive, gnarled, many-limbed tree as big as the largest oak or Brazilian pepper tree. It grows in the most improbable spots on steep hills, rocky bluffs, and at the ocean's edge. Covered most of the year with conservative grey-green leaves, it bursts forth in summer (December and January) with brilliant crimson powder puff flowers. The pahutukawa trees form dramatic red splotches in the bush covering much of the hilly land.

Geologically speaking, New Zealand as it exists today is only about 5 million years old. Its hills and mountains are still jagged, and conversion by erosion has not progressed far. Other than the Canterbury Plains of the South Island, there is little level land in this country, and, consequently, crop farming has not developed. On the other hand, the hillsides of both islands, covered with lush grasses interspersed between the valleys of inpenetrable bush, make it ideal grazing ground for sheep and cattle.

It was at this land of milk and honey that *Horizon* had been pointed for the last nine months and which we were now about to see.

The southwestern Pacific hurricane season occurs during the Southern Hemisphere summer months of November through March. An average year generates 11 tropical storms with winds from 35 to 64 knots and four hurricanes (called cyclones in this area) with winds in excess of 64 knots. While most of these storms originate and move well north and west of New Zealand, some move east posing threats to Fiji, Tonga, Samoa, and the sailing routes to New Zealand. For this reason the prudent yachtsman intending to summer in New Zealand starts his passage south at least by the first of November.

Being very prudent, we departed Nuku'alofa, Tonga, on October 5 for the 1060 mile rhumb-line passage to the Bay of Islands, New Zealand. This would become our longest run since departing Mazatlan for the Marquesas. The rhumb-line course lies SSW, initially traversing a poorly charted area of coral reefs. Alternatively, by traveling due south you can visit New Zealand's Kermadec Islands enroute, but you are then faced with beating into the westerlies at the more southern latitudes. After a careful study of the weather patterns on the Pilot Charts, we elected to first go SW, staying to the north of the Minerva Reefs until we met up with the westerlies and then head south. Our planning turned out to be correct, since we had one of the fastest passages of all the boats making the Fiji–Tonga to New Zealand run that season. Even so, it took 13 days for us to sail 1125 miles compared to the 9-day passage we had made earlier for the 1100 miles from Bora Bora to Pago Pago.

Now we were departing the tradewind belt and had to face the variables again. They were mostly light winds from the east with NE and SE winds and, occasionally, no wind at all. We made our westing on these variable winds for the first 9 days. By the tenth day we were due north of the Bay of Islands with still no west winds, so we turned south only to run into two days of southerly (head) winds—the strongest about force 5 (20 knots). Only on the last two days did the expected westerlies develop, giving us a good turn of speed directly to our destination.

Our best day's distance-made-good was 120 miles and our slowest day yielded only 51 miles. Overall, this passage averaged 92 miles per day, which was the lowest average of all passages since leaving the U.S.

Like the passage, our navigation proved to be routine. We were able to get morning celestial position fixes from stars and planets on 8 of the

13 days. The four navigation planets, Mars, Venus, Saturn, and Jupiter, were all visible, and on two mornings I took 3-planet position fixes. Of the other five days, overcast prevented morning star sights completely, but I was able to get midday sun lines twice to supplement the dead reckoning.

On our thirteenth day out, broad-reaching south at 5 knots on gentle west winds, we raised New Zealand at 1240 in clear weather. By 1835, when we passed Cape Brett, the entrance to the Bay of Islands, we were being pummeled by wild, wet squalls. As darkness descended and visibility further deteriorated, we sailed into the bay as far as cautious judgement would allow. Then, as the lights of Russell came into view around the headland, we lowered sails and motored into the anchorage dropping our hook at 2030. Thus ended our nine-month, 8200-mile outbound trip from the U.S.

Ruins of fishing camp once used by Zane Grey at Deep Water Cove, Bay of Islands.

Our introduction to the typical New Zealander took place early the next morning when a large ferry boat (without passengers) put out from the Russell wharf and came directly to *Horizon*. The operator, who turned out to be the town policeman, welcomed us and volunteered to alert the customs and other officials at Whangarei (about 40 miles south) so they could drive up to Opua, the Bay of Islands entry port, to clear us into New Zealand. He made his call as we motored the 5 miles to Opua surviving on the way a hail storm that left our decks covered with ice. Truly, we were now out of the tropics.

After clearing customs and agriculture we returned to Russell, anchoring at nearby Matauwhi Bay along with many other local and overseas yachts. Our first few days were spent getting acquainted with the Kiwi way of life, which was not hard to do or hard to take. We located a do-it-yourself laundry at a camp ground on the hillside above Russell so Betty gathered all our clothes and bedding, which hadn't seen a real wash since La Paz, and, putting them in a sail bag, we carried the lot to the laundry for an all-morning wash session.

What we hadn't considered in this wash day plan was the greater weight of the wet clothes after washing, which had to be carried back to the boat for drying. We gamely started out, one at each end of the sail bag carrying our clean wash down the hill. It was necessary to stop every block to rest and get a new grip on the sail bag. At one stop a local resident observing our labored progress remarked that none of us are getting any younger so why don't we put the bag in his pickup truck and he would take it to the dock for us. We did, and he did, and our aching hands and arms were much relieved. Our benefactor was Don Johnson, a retired shipwright, who with his wife, Nona, became fast friends with us during our stay in New Zealand.

Now that we were settling into Kiwi land for six months, our crewman decided to go off on his own. Sven bid us a final farewell one day and to our disappointment, we never heard from him again.

Most cruising yachts arriving from the tropics make the Bay of Islands their first landfall. Besides being the most northerly port of entry, it is a yachtsman's paradise. There are over 50 smaller bays or inlets having good holding ground and providing good protection. In addition, the 100 or more islands provide a variety of scenery, good beaches, and many more sheltered coves for anchoring. Several rivers, some navigable at high tide like the famous Kerikeri River, flow into the bay. The principal population centers of Russell, Kerikeri, and Paihia and their suburbs, have a total population of about 2500 persons.

Nowhere have we met people who were as warm or offered us such hospitable treatment as here in New Zealand. And it seems that people from all countries now residing here adopt the same outgoing, friendly New Zealander attitude. Take, for instance, Kelley, a retired British Royal Air Force officer, who, according to his entry in our guest log was "just roaming around." We met Kelley at Waitangi while trying to find a place to dispose of old oil just drained from the engine. He came along on his bike and offered to haul it to a garage where they collect waste oil for recycling. After disposing of the oil he returned to continue our chat, and soon Kelley was insisting that we use his car while we were moored here. We could hardly refuse such generosity, so with his wheels we also got to see the island citrus-growing region and the colorful town of Kerikeri.

And then there were Blue and Sue Wilson who ran a dairy store in Paihai—our favorite stop for tea or ice cream while out walking. Their interest in our adventures led to an offer to provide for us at cost any food supplies we needed. Before we left Paihai for Whangarei we had obtained through them cases of canned cream and butter and 70 pounds of American-grind coffee for those lonely night watches some months ahead.

While at Paihai Betty located a dentist to repair her tooth broken prior to our arrival in the Marquesas. He was a yachtie himself, and Betty was able to get an early appointment. He temporarily repaired the fracture adequately to get through another year of cruising.

Yes, even Americans living in New Zealand get the friendly Kiwi spirit as proven by Margaret and Bob Croft from Denver, Colorado, who had built a beautiful house overlooking Tutukaka Harbor. Bob, a retired Air Micronesia pilot, invited us up for cocktails one evening when we were anchored at Tutukaka, and through him we met several Kiwis from the surrounding area. One cannot help but feel at home in Kiwi land.

It is usual to think of New Zealand in the context of its European population, since the *pakehas* (those of European origin) represent 93% of the country's inhabitants. In all the other islands of Polynesia that we have visited the native Polynesians were the dominant inhabitants. While one would no longer expect New Zealand to drastically change its racial mix, they are facing new problems with the additional immigration of Polynesians from Niue, Cook, Western Samoa, Tonga, and Tokelau Islands. As an example, Niue Island has a current population of 3600 persons, but Auckland has a Niuean population of 6500 persons. These islanders come to Auckland primarily to seek work, and it is said that Auckland has the largest Polynesian population of any city in the world. Unfortunately, Auckland cannot socially or economically assimilate the rapid influx of island peoples and integration difficulties are apparent.

The cost of New Zealand-produced foods and products made of local raw materials, milk, bread, beef, lamb, wood, paper products, and the like, is generally lower than in the U.S. Imported products or products made of imported raw materials are high in price—plastics, metals, petroleum, etc. Gasoline was about $1.25 per gallon, automobiles 50–100% higher than in the U.S., color TVs near $1,000. Because of the higher costs of manufactured articles, Kiwis tend to do more maintenance on hard goods to extend their useful lifetime. This in turn has created an extensive service industry of small repair shops, which are very handy for the visiting yachtsman.

In 1969 New Zealand took the big step to convert to the metric system. It had earlier converted its money from pounds–shillings–pence to decimal dollars. Most products are now sold by the kilogram or meter, but package markings are often conveniently in both kilograms and pounds or meters and feet. The metric system of measurement is being fully applied to all navigation publications, replacing everything but the nautical mile. Water depths and heights of objects are shown on New Zealand charts in meters and tenths of a meter. With *Horizon*'s depth sounder graduated in feet and fathoms, we did a lot of mental gymnastics when moving about in shoal waters.

Combine, if you will, the holidays of Christmas, New Year, and summer vacation on wheels or water and you have New Zealand's hectic holiday, which starts mid-December and runs through January. Seasonally, this is summer in the Southern Hemisphere, so school is out and much of the work force takes its vacation. New Zealanders are great travelers and vacation-time finds them boating, camping, and generally roaming their islands from one end to the other. Northland, the northern end of North Island, is the summer domain of Aucklanders, and the Bay of Islands, even as big as it is, filled with yachts, while the usually sleepy little towns of Paihia, Waitangi, and Russell swell to three to five times their normal population. It's like Catalina Island or Long Island Sound on the Fourth of July.

But this year the weather didn't cooperate and the coldest summer weather in 27 years slowed down the exodus. Can you imagine snow on the Fourth of July in California? They had it on the South Island in the dead of their summer, while here at the North Island we had rain and winds to 30 knots. White caps rolled through the anchorage with the barometer hanging at an even 1000 millibars for days. To top it off, a series of earthquakes traversed the Fiji–Kermadec Island area with one particularly heavy jolt occurring in the Tongas, which caused the New

Zealand Civil Defense to issue a Tsunami ("tidal wave") alert. We waited on board *Horizon* listening intently to the radio for verification of an approaching wave, but none developed and we breathed easier. Curiously, while Radio New Zealand alerted the listening public in houses and cars, the national marine weather broadcast being made precisely at that time made no mention of it.

When we first arrived in Whangarei I did some library research on New Zealand weather patterns. This is a region of westerlies with high pressure cells (anticyclones) generated over Australia marching with regularity across the North Island every 6 to 10 days, normally moving eastwards at a speed of 300 to 400 miles per day. When the high pressure (1020–1025 millibars on the barometer) is over the North Island, the weather is fine. But between the successive high pressure cells are troughs of low pressure (1000–1010 mb) usually containing a cold front from the south and with some rain.

What happened to the usually predictable cyclic weather pattern this January was that the air masses failed to continue moving east. Instead, they stagnated with the low pressure trough covering the North Island while warm moist air was fed into it by NE winds from the tropics, which caused the heavy rains. This warm front instead of the normal cold front was occasioned by the generation of tropical cyclone David to the north in the New Hebrides Islands. This cyclonic disturbance overpowered the usual weather pattern of southerlies in a low and induced strong NE winds to carry the moist air of the tropics over New Zealand. Cyclone David continued to strengthen and reached a low of 975 mb with hurricane force winds near New Caledonia. It continued to move slowly westward and died over Australia after causing considerable damage in Queensland. It is these tropical cyclones occurring from November through March in the southwest Pacific that bring so many of the cruising yachts out of the tropics to see beautiful New Zealand.

On a final weather note, New Zealand area weather forecasts of use to yachtsmen are broadcast every six hours from New Zealand Marine Radio (ZLD) at Auckland. In addition, the early morning broadcast (0318) gives detailed weather coverage between 25 to 40 degrees south latitude and 160 degrees east to 170 degrees west longitude which nicely supplements the WWVH (Hawaii) coverage of the Pacific Ocean area.

This year had its unusual Christmas Day dinner—a yachties' barbeque ashore, hosted by Roger and Evelyn Miles from Vancouver, B.C., who sailed here last year in *Rainbow*, a 28-foot converted British Royal Navy pinnace built in 1888. Overseas yachts that had been hanging out in other coves, started appearing Christmas morning, and altogether there must have been 25–30 boats in attendance. They were from such distant ports as Germany, England, Scotland, Canada, and both coasts of the U.S. As a point of interest, there are 70–100 overseas yachts that annually sit out the hurricane season in New Zealand.

It should come as no surprise that Kiwis are an enthusiastic boating people. Aucklanders claim to have more boats per capita than any other city in the world, and, since it appears plausible, I'm glad that Auckland isn't any bigger than it is. The general run of boats tend to be one-of-a-kind designs built of wood. Only recently has fiberglass been introduced for production models and they are quite expensive. Many old wood boats with classic lines are to be seen and the owners obviously take a great pride in their maintenance. But not all wood boats are classics and New Zealand is producing its share of sailboat racing winners. Here their craftsmanship and the good kauri wood pays off handsomely in custom construction. Most recently their *Prospect of Pansonby*, a 36-foot long one ton class wood design won the Southern Cross series against competition from Australia, Britain, Papua New Guinea, U.S. and Japan. Most famous, certainly, is *Ragtime*, a 62-foot wood sloop, which has, under U.S. ownership, won the Los Angeles to Honolulu race the last two runnings against the finest of ocean racing competition.

Blue water cruising is also a Kiwi forte and we have seen New Zealand yachts throughout our Pacific travels. New Zealand, in fact, lies in one of the great cruising areas of the world. Within easy grasp of a three-month cruise are Samoa, Tonga, Fiji, New Hebrides, and Solomon Islands in various combinations. For six months you can throw in French Polynesia and the Cook Group. More than one overseas yacht has made New Zealand its base for seasonal cruising in the South Pacific.

Lest our personal interest lead you to believe that there are only sailboats or power cruisers here, let me assure you that "fizz" boats far outnumber both. A fizz boat is any outboard-powered craft and their popularity is evident at the holiday season when every bay, river, campground, and road is alive with them afloat and awheel.

This great interest in boats also makes New Zealand a good place to accomplish whatever maintenance is required in preparation for another year of cruising. While Auckland may have the most boatyards and chandleries, visiting yachts find it more convenient to accomplish their maintenance work at Whangarei where everything is within walking distance of the yacht basin at the city center.

Whangarei is an inland city of 35,000 inhabitants connected to the

Whangamumu Harbor, total peace and tranquility.

ocean by tidal waters, which snake for 12 miles across mud flats and sand banks to eventually meet the outflow of the Hatea River at the city center. The headquarters of the Northland Harbour Board, which administers all Northland harbors, is here, and it is their harbor pilot staff who, in addition to their pilot's duties, oversee the small boat activities. It would be hard put to find a friendlier group of crusty sea captains than these fellows, who, in between piloting supertankers into the harbor, help the yachtsman in his stay.

The Whangarei harbor is not only a waterway but a thriving industrial community. It includes a major petroleum refinery, a cement works, shipbuilding facilities, general cargo wharfs, and numerous small industries. All of this is stretched along a 12-mile tidewater channel providing the yachtsman a thrill a minute as he makes his inland transit for the first time.

The approach to this harbor is beneath the towering (1600 ft.) Bream Head and local seafaring knowledge suggests that the yachtsman furl his sails under Bream Head and motor into the harbor entrance to save the time and trouble caused by alternating violent gusts and patches of calm. Beyond Bream Head are the lower reaches of the long harbor, which have a quarter-mile width and 50-foot depth channel for the supertankers. But, before arriving at the Town Basin the channel shrinks to a few feet deep and a hundred-foot width shared with mangroves and shorebirds. Tidal flow is an important consideration in the lower reaches where ebb currents reach 3 knots while draining miles of mud flats on both shores. If the tidal set is unfavorable, the yachtsman can duck into Urquhart Bay, a comfortable little anchorage just off the main channel, and there await the turn of the tide. The two-hour trip upstream is best started no later than one half of flood tide so that if you are unfortunate enough to go aground, you can still be floated off on the rising tide.

Leaving Urquhart Bay at mile 0 the channel upstream leads between mud flats and drying banks that extend over one mile on each side of the channel until you reach the narrows at the Marsden Point supertanker terminal and oil refinery at mile 2. Beyond Marsden Point the mud flats broaden even further. At mile 3½ you can, with care, traverse the shoals on the north side into shallow and sheltered Parua Bay with its snug anchorage called "The Nook." The main shipping channel continues to be well marked with lateral marker pairs spaced every ½ mile and at mile 7 you negotiate a long S-turn, sweeping around the community of Onerahi on one side and Limestone Island with its now abandoned cement works on the other. Small boats easily maneuver through this maze, but freighters are literally turned-in-place to make the sharper bends. Further along at Mile 9 are the general cargo wharfs, which extend for one mile to the end of the 26-foot-deep-dredged ship channel. One half mile beyond the wharfs brings a melancholy sight in *Nam Sang,* the veteran U.S. transpac racing boat of the '50s, now a moored hulk involved in complex insurance litigation. Masts down, partially stripped, and covered with torn and flapping canvas, she bears little resemblance to the sleek white-hulled racer we used to see at Newport Beach.

Next is the raw tidal channel with low water soundings of 3 feet in spots. Proceeding on the flood tide there is 8 to 10 feet in channel center but less if you carelessly cut across the inside of the bends. "Round all turns generously, keeping the red pipe markers about a boat length on your port side," says local knowledge. At mile 11 is Orams Marina and Boatyard and the town basin lies ahead at mile 12.

Resident yachts in the Town Basin are moored between end pilings like floating hammocks, at the unbelievably low charge of $55.00 per year. A few jetty side ties are available at $85.00 per year. Transient yachts generally raft up alongside the now unused city wharf where they pay $5.00 per week for water, electricity, and hot showers. Laundry facilities are also available.

The first raft *Horizon* joined included *Windjob* from Portland,

Life was never dull at the Whangarei City Wharf.

Oregon, *Moana* (a single hander) from San Diego, and *Rabbit* from Palm Beach, which was the "host boat." The host boat along the wharf comes in for a lot of worries, like scraping vertically along 10 feet of cement pilings as the tide changes four times a day and having foot traffic from the other boats passing across its deck to the wharf at all times of day and night. Generous fenderboards and careful attention to the dock lines minimize the scraping problems, but the foot traffic you just endure. At high tide you can almost step across to the dock, but at low tide it requires a precarious climb on a crude ladder. Low tide also brings an unhealthy smell and a repugnant view of the underside of the wharf with its years of accumulation of jetsam and flotsam.

Whangarei has three boatyards capable of hauling boats up to 100 tons and a complete line of supporting services from sailmaking to engine overhaul to electronic repair. Haulouts ("slipping") are made on conventional marine railways, and the owner can do his own work without limit. Moderate size boats (to about 40 feet) can also be hoisted onto cradles on the "hard" for extended work or dry storage. Most Kiwis and some cruising boats take advantage of the 10 foot tidal range, resting their boat's keel on a water's-edge wood grid, which allows several hours of work to be done while the tide is out. By far the most popular spot for cruising yacht maintenance is Allen Orams Marine Ltd. Orams designs and builds wood, fiberglass, and ferrocement boats so they have all the skills for any job. Orams and Cater's Chandlery (near the city wharf) is able to satisfy virtually all marine hardware needs from their stocks, and, where they can't, they get it in one day from Auckland distributors.

Labor costs run about two-thirds of U.S. costs, locally made marine hardware is about three-fourths of U.S. costs, and petroleum and chemical products run from 50 to 100 percent higher than U.S. costs.

While we were able to accomplish all our maintenance with no difficulty, restocking of some mechanical and electrical spares posed a problem. The U.S., with its extensive market, produces a broad variety of competing hardware lines—some very sophisticated. If you choose the wrong line, you're in trouble overseas. As one example, *Horizon* has installed a Fram combination dirt and water separator diesel fuel filter, which is the most widely used and advertised in the U.S. It is, however, not made by Fram (NZ), nor are there any equivalents to this efficient filter imported, so we had to get replacement from the U.S. by air. Direct current electrical components are conventional 12-volt car and marine types, but the New Zealand A.C. electricity is 240 volts, 50 cycle, so boats with stateside 120-volt, 60-cycle equipment need to carry a full complement of spares. My candid advice to a cruising boat is to carry two to three years of critical spares since the need for any one may show up at the wrong time. We saved the morale of the crew of *Sweet Thing*, a Morgan 54, in Papeete by giving them our spare refrigerator compressor shaft seal, which was needed to get their ice maker back in operation.

Our days at Whangarei were busy with refurbishing *Horizon*, including a haulout at Orams for bottom work. Now we were ready to see the rest of New Zealand. Eric joined us for this trip flying on an Air New Zealand DC-10 taking only 18 hours for the trip as compared to the 84 days of sailing time it had taken us. After a brief look at the Whangarei area we proceeded south for a whirlwind tour of the rest of New Zealand.

By car we drove to Wellington, stopping for a couple of nights at Rotorua, which is the center of Maori culture. It is also a volcanic plateau that has been active within the memory of European man. The volcanoes are now dormant, but thermal energy abounds in mud pots, geysers, and steaming fissures. It is no wonder the Maoris were attracted to this region, for the natural heat is welcome in winter and the sulphur pools therapeutic at all times.

Bess from South Africa shares moorings at Whangarei with a decrepit Nam Sang *of ocean racing fame.*

Our arrival at Rotorua preceded by a few days the Second South Pacific Festival of Arts which was to run for eight days. Participants were already arriving from 22 countries of the South Pacific and 1200 performers were to participate in proud displays of native culture as shown in dance, music, drama, artifacts and handicrafts, games, and languages. Our schedule would not allow time to see any of the Festival so we settled for visits to points of local interest and attendance at a Maori dance show one evening. Polynesian dancing and singing is colorful to say the least, and the Maoris were unique in that their dress was made of beautifully colored flax and reeds. We were not to miss all of the Festival though, for at Russell we saw a touring group of Cook Islanders and at Whangarei a touring group of Fijians.

Our whirlwind tour of New Zealand continued as we drove south to Wellington, the capital of the country. Although situated on Cook Strait between the North and South Islands and with its own large harbor, Wellington does not have a large yachting activity because the weather is said to be generally too boisterous. We couldn't prove that since it was very mild on our stops there.

By jet plane we flew on to Dunedin where we continued by car again to Invercargil and Bluff, the southernmost city in New Zealand at 46

Taiaroa Head, Otago Peninsula, is the nesting ground of the Royal Albatross.

degrees 36 minutes south latitude. Bluff is famous for its succulent oysters, which are shipped the length of New Zealand to please the palates of seafood lovers.

The real attraction here is Fjordland on the southwest coast, a rugged, indented coastline reminiscent of the fjords of Norway. It is all a National Park left in its natural state and with no access roads. One gets in and out only by sea or air. We were told that parts of it are still unexplored and that the best chart of Dusky Bay is still the one made by Captain Cook in 1773. This can also be taken as a tribute to the cartographic and surveying skill of Cook.

We were defeated in our attempt to see Fjordland. In the brief time we had, our plan was to fly over the area in a charter plane. But, alas, the winds were too strong and the air too turbulent for flying, so we settled, not unwillingly, for sightseeing at Queenstown.

Our return car trip took us back to Dunedin, which is a city of Scottish descent. Eric left us here to fly back to the U.S. via Auckland. Betty and I now embarked on New Zealand's fine public transportation system for the rest of our tour. By bus we went up the east coast to Christchurch, a truly English city with an extensive array of well landscaped parks and the River Avon flowing serenely through its center. Christchurch is probably better known as the jumping-off place for Antarctic exploration.

The next leg of our journey was by overnight ferryboat to Wellington. We are among the last to ride the picturesque ship, *Rangatira*, for it was soon to be discontinued for economy reasons. Another victim of the automobile.

At Wellington we boarded the daylight train to Auckland known as the Silver Fern. In a rare bit of transportation planning, the train station was located only a few steps away from the ferry terminal. While waiting for the Silver Fern to depart we had breakfast and were entertained by a bagpipe band in its daily morning ceremony at the train station.

The Silver Fern diesel-electric train covered the 430 miles to

The southernmost tip of New Zealand—next stop, Antarctica.

Auckland in 11 hours. It traversed spectacular bush country as it wended its way over the mountains, passing through tunnels and across viaducts. We found the clean and comfortable Silver Fern an excellent way to see the countryside and mingle with more Kiwis.

This interlude in Kiwi land has covered most of the six months allowed us by our visa. During this time we had refurbished *Horizon* and ourselves so that we are ready for another interesting 8000 miles of travel. We saw much and we would like to have seen more, but neither New Zealand's immigration laws nor our own wandering spirits would permit us to remain longer. So, with only the final fresh food provisioning to do, we were looking forward to our return trip and other interesting ports of call to the east and north.

New Zealand has left some lasting impressions on us, like:

—The peaceful rolling green hills of the countryside
—A sincerely friendly people
—The attractiveness of the Maoris in their native dress adapted to the cooler Polynesian climate
—Being told we have an accent
—The interest Kiwis have in the people and activities of the U.S.
—Keep left whether walking or driving
—Evenings at the Town Basin watching the diving birds (shags) catch and swallow eels
—Tea rooms serving delicate and delicious sandwiches and sweets for tea (lunch)
—Being persuaded to use butter in place of margerine because of lower price
—The copious consumption of beer
—The home-spun wool yarn made into family apparel

11

Raivavae

Few people have ever heard of Raivavae Island (ry-va-vy) and even fewer have ever visited it. On the chart of the South Pacific it is but a dot located at 27°52′ S. latitude and 147°35′ W. longitude—360 miles south southeast of Tahiti. It is a high island of considerable geologic age surrounded by a well-developed barrier reef, which is just awash in most places but which also has some of the familiar wooded islets known as motus. While the oval barrier reef measures 5 miles north-south and 8 miles east-west, the 1400-foot high volcanic mountains that form the island proper cover an area of only 2 by 5 miles. The intervening annular space is a beautiful lagoon with a coral sand and mud bottom, uncounted coral heads, with many rising close to the surface, and a fringing reef along the shoreline making dinghy landing difficult. The blue-green lagoon, the lush green growth of the coastal plains, and the spectacularly eroded mountains give it a beauty rivaling Bora Bora in the Society Islands.

Raivavae today is a quiet, almost subdued island with little of the gaiety and love for pleasure that we found on the other islands of French Polynesia. But it was not always so. In the 18th and 19th centuries Raivavae was alive with 3000 people in a social order said to rival that of Tahiti. These early people were daring seafarers who not only voyaged to neighboring islands but north to Tahiti and Raiatea

Horizon *on the grid at Orams for a final bottom cleaning before heading for the Austral Islands.*

and, reputedly, even to the shores of New Zealand. Fishing was then an important part of their daily life although little is done now and, in fact, they no longer seem to have an affinity for the sea. Their early civilization developed agriculture to a fine art using terracing techniques for growing taro—the universal food of the Pacific high islands. Warfare between the districts of the island was a way of life, and the mountainous backbone of the island was in many parts made a fortress. But disaster came to Raivavae in 1826 when a very contagious, malignant fever was brought from the neighboring island of Tubuai. The disease decimated the population, reducing their numbers to an estimated 120 persons. Unable to sustain their culture any longer, it vanished into the underbrush and the Raivavaeans today preserve no more of their heritage.

Raivavae is one of five inhabited islands comprising the Austral Group, which extend over 800 miles of ocean in a northwest–southeast direction. The other inhabited islands of this group are Rimatura, Rurutu, Tubuai, and lonely Rapa, 290 miles southeast of Raivavae. The Australs are considered geologically to be the southeast extremity of the same sunken mountain chain making up the Cook Islands, which lie 600 miles further to the northwest. The Australs, part of French

Polynesia since Pomare II of Tahiti visited there in the early 1820s and converted them to Christianity, have a total land area of only 63 square miles which supports a current population of about 5,000 persons. Isolated as they are, off the beaten path of both tourist and cruising yacht, we set our minds to visit them on our way east from New Zealand to Tahiti.

Our interlude in New Zealand was to end at the termination of our six-month visas in April. But as the hurricane season east of New Zealand was safely over by the end of March we began to look forward to an earlier departure. Again we thought in terms of taking along a third crewman since the coming passage to French Polynesia would again be one of over 2000 miles and sailed in those pesky variable winds. So we put the word out along the Whangarei waterfront, but it

Raivavae's beltline highway.

was hardly necessary because there were already many seeking passages on small boats. We interviewed all comers, looking for some experience but knowing now that we didn't need a professional. The applicant pool was varied, and after eliminating twosomes wanting to travel together, individuals of an obviously unstable nature, and girls, we looked favorably on a 17-year-old Australian, Roger from Sydney. He had graduated earlier that year from high school and was headed around the world before going on to college. He was an athletic and self-assured individual with a Cockney English accent that often gave us difficulty in conversations. His experience was weekend sailing out of Sydney and a recent passage from Hobart, Tasmania, to Auckland on a race boat. On the surface he looked OK and a check with the skipper of the Hobart boat verified some of his background, so we shook hands and set a date for his joining *Horizon*. In the meantime he was to go to Wellington to get his U.S. visa. While he did go to Auckland and got an Australian passport, he frittered away his time so that he did not get a U.S. visa before our departure date, and this was to cause me considerable embarrassment later with the U.S. Immigration authorities in Honolulu.

Provisioning *Horizon* for the return passage was not difficult nor expensive in New Zealand. With the exchange rate at $1.00US equal $.97NZ, we made our inflated U.S. dollars go a long way. Canned foods were plentiful, with the exception of meats. Because their meat export trade is based on frozen processing, they have not developed a line of canned meats except for corned beef, of which we finally bought a case. From a wholesale produce house we purchased a case each of apples and oranges which we later agreed was a very wise move. Nothing tastes better at sea than a piece of fresh fruit. While the apples were Kiwi grown, the oranges had come from our home state of California and were bought at 10¢ per lb.—far less than we would have paid for them in Los Angeles. We procured 12 dozen unrefrigerated eggs from a local egg packing plant and, again, Betty greased them with petroleum jelly and the last one, still fresh, was eaten in Hilo, Hawaii, three months later. Sea stores of beer, wine, liquor, and cigarettes were ordered for delivery to Orams marina the morning of our departure. Sea stores are simply tax-free purchases to be consumed outside the country of purchase. In this we realized a saving of 50 percent. Not all countries permit sea store sales to pleasure boats, but where permissible, it's a worthwhile saving.

Departure day from Whangarei, Friday March 26, was ominous— rain and an easterly wind. The nature of New Zealand weather is sufficiently repetitive that the Kiwis will tell you when an easter sets in,

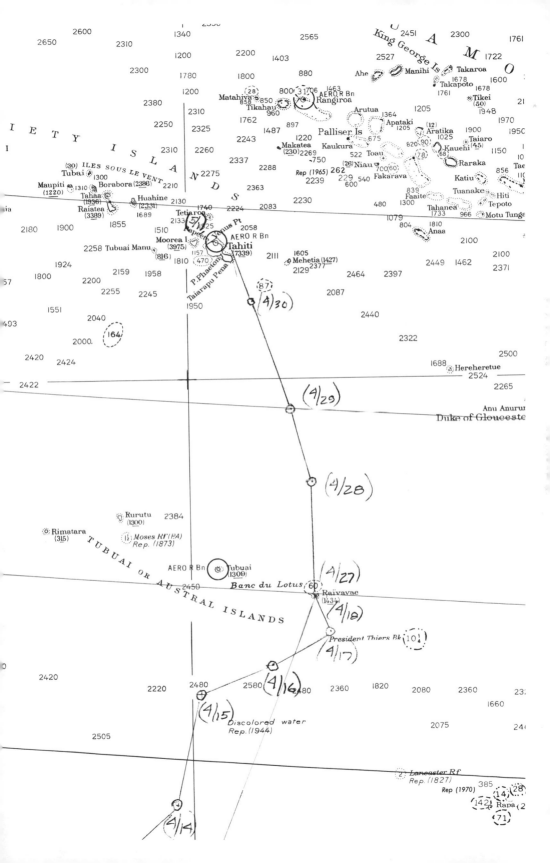

it will blow for three days. Ted Hayes, our Kiwi slip mate at Orams brought this to our attention, but having already cleared customs we decided to at least leave Whangarei, so we motored the 12 miles down channel to Whangarei Heads and ducked into Urquhart Bay to wait them out. Dawn, Monday, found the wind from the north and we cleared the fairway buoy at 0650 heading into what was to be our most difficult passage so far. We were at Latitude 36° S.—near the southern edge of the variable wind belt. Further to the south was the recommended route for sailing ships—the "roaring forties" where the westerly gales would drive the square riggers at 20 knots homeward bound around Cape Horn. While westerly winds would be most welcome, gales were not, so we set our southerly course limit of 40° S. planning to challenge the variable winds all the way. The elements took up the challenge and made us work for every mile gained east.

Excepting the first couple of days out of New Zealand, we held hard on a starboard tack against Force 3 to 4 winds from the southeast. Initially, warm pleasant days were experienced, but then they gave way to cold, wet ones and we continued our mizzen genoa concept for more efficient windward sailing. At midnight on day 5 we encountered our first gale of the voyage at 36° S. latitude and 176° W. longitude. In quick succession we dropped the mizzen genoa, replaced the genoa with a working jib, dropped the mizzen, and finally came about to run downwind with the gale taking in our last sail at the same time. *Horizon* ran comfortably west under bare poles for seven hours losing 23 miles of hard earned easting. At 0800 the following morning, the wind had abated sufficiently to put the storm jib and mizzen up whereupon we also tacked back to an easterly heading and continued our drive to the Australs. While our route kept us to the north of the Great Southern Sea, reputed to be the loneliest stretch of water in the world, we were still able to sense a feeling of that loneliness. Few vessels traverse this area since sail gave way to power. Some Japanese fishing boats, presumably working in the same fleet because of their coordinated maneuvering, were seen four days east of New Zealand on April 1—the first of our two April Fool's days occasioned by the fact we crossed the International Dateline on April 1st in the eastern hemisphere and the next day was also April 1st in the western hemisphere! The only other vessel we saw enroute was the freighter *Badenstein* out of Bremen. The *Badenstein* truly startled us on day 9 when it topped a swell just 200 yards away from us! They obviously had changed course to come over and see what made the big radar blip on their screen and, after they were satisfied, they resumed their westerly heading. This phenomenon of not seeing another vessel because either you or he are alternately in swell troughs can be most disturbing.

On our fifteenth night out we were sailing along easily in force 3 winds with Betty on watch and the rest of the crew soundly asleep. At 2150 the starboard main backstay broke with a report that figuratively lifted me out of my bunk and into the cockpit without touching the companion ladder. Poor Betty, it seemed like she was catching more than her share of problems. But the failure was not of her doing nor of the winds but was an international conspiracy of nonstandardization of rigging. Orams boatyard in Whangarei had installed a new section of 1 x 19 wire cable below the lower insulator of the starboard main backstay. It wasn't until after the failure that we found out that they had spliced a right-hand lay cable to the original upper sections which were left-hand lays. After fifteen days of dynamic tension loadings (well below the working strength of the cable), the new wire broke at its lower swaged fitting. On examination the break appeared to be simple torsional fatigue failure of the wire. I had earlier seen the small rotational oscillations of the lower antenna insulator, but could not understand their origin until it was too late.

We made temporary repairs that night by splicing a spare cable in place below the lower-insulator. In the morning the seas were calm enough for Roger to ascend the mast on the bosun's chair. He removed the broken stay and we installed in its place an equivalent (but uninsulated) plow steel-wire cable taken from our spares inventory. The initial stretching of the cable to ensure final tightening with the existing turnbuckle posed a problem until we remembered our handy-billy tackle. With a 4:1 mechanical advantage it brought coil kinks right out of the new cable, and we were able to easily tune it up with the turnbuckle.

Our easting was now going well enough that we hoped to ease off on our last few days out and then reach north to Raivavae on the seasonally young southeast tradewinds. Disappointment set in as a belt of thunderstorms developed stretching across French Polynesia and the Cook Islands to the west. These thunderstorms swung the wind into the northwest on day 19 and we were forced to continue hard against the wind but now on port tack. Finally, 21 days and 4 hours after leaving New Zealand, on Easter morning, we entered the well-marked Teavarua Pass at Raivavae, having traveled 2200 miles—just slightly more than the minimum distance of great circle route. We were pleased with ourselves for having attained our goal in spite of

—having had to sail hard against the wind for 19 days
—encountering 14 days of rain, squalls, and thunderstorms
—giving in to one easterly gale in which we retreated westward losing 23 hard-earned miles

—breaking a mainmast backstay in a freak failure

—netting only 104 miles per day (55 slowest and 147 fastest).

Twenty yachts called at Raivavae in 1975 but *Horizon* was only the second yacht to call this year. We found out later in Papeete that by late May only two others had been able to make the New Zealand–Raivavae passage because of the persistent easterly winds. Many tried but could do no better than Tahiti direct or the Cook Islands. Others simply went north to the Samoas delaying the inevitable easting to Hawaii.

While we were happy to be at anchor in Rairua Bay, our troubles were not yet over. Tropical thunderstorms persisted for four more days. Strong northwest winds blew across the exposed anchorage to the extent that one night we even stood an anchor watch as we swung perilously close to the inner fringing reef. Business ashore—checking in with the gendarme and getting fresh foods—was done in rain jackets and swim suits. Morale was beginning to sag a bit, but then on Thursday the rain ceased and the sun came out in a clear sky. We were elated at the brilliance of the island—jagged mountain peaks with many waterfalls, valleys of intense greenery, coastal plains covered with flourishing crops, and a barrier reef breaking the big ocean swells in booming cascades of white spray. The hard passage and thunderstorms were quickly forgotten. We set to drying out *Horizon*, washing salt-ladened clothes in fresh water, refilling water tanks, doing minor maintenance work, and generally trying to complete the essential boatwork so that we were free to visit ashore.

The one item of boatwork which had me baffled and which wasn't to be completed until we were in Papeete, was getting the engine running. It had failed to start on our second day at Raivavae and no amount of air bleeding of fuel lines would help it. Even freshly charged batteries through the kind assistance of the gendarme were to no avail. After several days I resigned myself to *Horizon* being a true sailboat for the next passage and set about to enjoy the island.

Raivavae has a population of about 1000 persons, most of whom live in the three villages of Rairua, Mahanatoa, and Anatonu along the north shore, which is protected from the prevailing winds. A fourth village, Vaiuru, is located on the windward side of the island and is accessible by taking the coastal road in either direction or, as the kids do, shortcut across the saddle in the mountain range. I found the view from that saddle to be magnificent.

Rairua is the administrative center for the island and the location of the Gendarmerie Nationale, which, besides being immigration and military headquarters for the island, is also the post office. Rairua has always been the commercial center of activity because of better protection from the tradewinds. It is, however, exposed to the northwest, and its low wharf has been awash on more than one occasion as attested to by the solidified cement sacks stored in the wharf warehouse.

As we have come to expect, the island merchants are Chinese. A few years ago there were four *magasins* (general stores), but now there are only two and they share the commerce of the island. Afa runs the *magasin* in Rairua located at the head of the wharf. He is much involved with island exports and is also the banker. We had arrived at Raivavae without French Polynesia currency, and we were told by the gendarme that Afa was the only person on the island who could cash a travelers check. Afa would only give us 74 Pacific francs for a U.S. dollar, while at that time Papeete banks were giving 82 francs; but we were at his mercy. With that exchange rate we decided that $20US converted to francs was to be our limited contribution to the Raivavaen economy. So, armed with 1480 francs, we plunged into the purchase of French bread, pomplemousse, papaya, and a can of Planters peanuts for a special happy hour. Afa also wanted to buy our leftover New Zealand money, but his best offer of 15 francs to the dollar left us carefully hoarding it for a Papeete exchange.

Amoe's *magasin* was located about a mile east in the village of Mahanatoa, and, while larger and neater, it carried the same stock but lacked the waterfront character of Afa's *magasin*. Amoe was also the baker, and, if nothing got in the way like the breakdown of his truck, arrival of a supply ship, or a shortage of flour, you could get his delicious fresh-baked French bread three times a week. At 16 francs a loaf, it was a real delight.

Traditional Tahitian generosity showed itself during the week when we were given a stalk of green bananas that ripened beautifully and lasted us all the way to Papeete.

While fresh food may have been our first priority, we also had our hearts set on seeing some of their ancient civilization and obtaining some examples of local crafts. We were sadly disappointed in not finding anyone who could show us to a *marae* (pagan temple), but we later learned at the Papeete museum that they no longer exist. All the stone *tikis* have been removed from the island in spite of taboos. One *tiki* is now at the Gauguin Museum on Tahiti. Except for the stone foundations of the *maraes*, which are now overgrown, all other materials were biodegradable and have long since returned to nature. The curator of the Papeete Museum, Aurora Natua, later suggested

The "craft" family of Anatonu headed by matriarch "Mama Rua."

that we visit the Bishop Museum in Honolulu to learn more about early Raivavae, since the Bishop Museum has become the recognized authority on Polynesian history in general.

Giving up our historical researches we turned to the pursuit of local crafts with considerably more success. Leaving Rairua on foot Saturday morning, we headed east along the coastal road leading to Mahanatoa and Anatonu, asking persons along the way where we could get an outrigger canoe paddle—talking first in pidgin English, then limited Tahitian and French with the aid of dictionaries. It was afternoon when we came upon a woodcutter who understood our wants and repeated them to a passing girl carrying a shoulder load of bamboo poles. With the aid of our French–English phrase book, we understood that she would take us where we could buy many crafts. Riding the back of a VW truck loaded now with bamboo and firewood, we arrived after a couple of miles at Anatonu, which was the end of the VW line, and set off again on foot following our bamboo-carrying guide. We followed a side path to her family commune where we met everyone from the family matriarch to a suckling babe—24 persons in all gathered around us. We were delighted that the traditional Polynesian social interchange would precede any business talk so we made ourselves comfortable on the two chrome chairs brought to us while the others sat around us on mats. Grandma brought oranges and bananas and we talked as best we could for a while in the shade of the frangipani trees and the towering breadfruit trees. Eventually the conversation turned to our craft wants, and out came the woven hats, bags, beads, and an outrigger paddle! Since these crafts are all supplied to the Tahiti souvenir market, prices were set with no chance of bargaining, but I got my working canoe paddle. As for ceremonial wood carvings, they apparently are no longer made.

While we were with the craft family we took a Polaroid picture of the group and gave it to the grandmother amidst much clamoring to see it. With a long way to go back to the boat, we took leave and the matriarch presented us with native green-skinned oranges, strings of shell beads, and warm hugs. Arriving back at the Anatonu soccer field we saw intense preparations being made for the Sunday visit of dignitaries from Papeete. Best of all, we were offered a ride back to the wharf.

Sunday was the big day in Raivavae. Representatives of the French Polynesia Conseil de Gouvernement in Papeete had arrived in the morning from neighboring Tubuai Island aboard the supply ship *Tahaa Pae* ("naked five"). They were meeting with the island people to discuss health, economic, administrative and other issues of common cause. But of more interest to the islanders (and to us) was the soccer game to be played in the afternoon at Anatonu. We left *Horizon* at noon hoping to catch a ride to Anatonu, but, alas, we had underestimated the Polynesian's interest in the day's program and everyone was already at Anatonu. Left on our own, it was walk or else, so we walked the three miles along the coastal road and, happily, arrived while the official welcome was still in progress.

Again we were surrounded by the curious children who were much more interested in these strange talking people from *le bateau* than in official speeches. As time went on, one of our acquaintances of the previous day introduced us to the "headmaster" of the Raivavae schools, Mademoiselle Celestine Tetaronia. Celestine, about age 22 and a tall island beauty with a winning smile, had been schooled on the main (although smaller) island of Tubuai and now directed the education of the 200 Raivavae school age children. Sensing our need for an English-speaking friend, Celestine stayed with us much of the afternoon and answered many of the questions concerning this beautiful little island and its friendly, but somewhat somber, people.

But the day was to be more than speeches and soccer—there was also to be a feast showing the generosity of the people to their guests. As the officials moved from the offices of the Maire de Anatonu (Mayor of Anatonu village) to the long tables under the corrugated iron roof, to our surprise and delight, we also received an invitation through Celestine to join in the feast. One cannot refuse Polynesian hospitality, and we quickly found ourselves escorted to near the center of the long table seating 100 island dignitaries and guests. Celestine and Betty were among the few women to be seated at the first serving.

Conversation lagged as foods were passed and wine was poured. The wine needed no explanation, but Celestine identified many of the foods served. The meat course was roast turtle and pork, the baked fish was a favorite reef fish, which was also served raw in another dish. Vegetables were the taro root sliced and baked and also served mashed (their form of poi). There was also baked papaya and the *pièce de résistance*

Betty discusses the feast with Raivavae's "schoolmaster," Celestine Tetaronia.

was banana crepes. Taking a hint from the islanders, we dispensed with forks finding that the foods were really prepared for finger eating. Like the Biblical seven loaves, the serving platters were never emptied, and soon, with appetites satisfied, we listened to the inevitable after-dinner speeches of welcome and acceptance (in Tahitian) and then left the tables so that the women and young people could eat. Nobody went hungry that day.

The soccer match was to pit the Tubuai team against the Raivavae team, but a logistics problem apparently had forced the guest team to stay home so the two teams that memorable day were made up of the local players plus several of the visitors who came prepared for sport. The teams took to the field at 1500 for a bruising two-hour match. Bruises, we saw, were more from the graded coral-playing surface than from body contact, but the players didn't seem to mind. Our ignorance of the game was alleviated by a member of the Council of Governments standing near us, who introduced himself (in excellent English) as Maco Tevane. Maco's principal interest was island health and he proudly told us that the people of Raivavae had the best teeth in French Polynesia because of their steady diet of taro. We had to admit that the teeth of most Polynesians are very poor, but these, indeed, did look better. Remembering our 3-mile hike out, we hastened back to the parking lot when the final whistle blew and got a much welcomed ride back to the wharf.

After that memorable Sunday, anything else we could do on Raivavae would be an anticlimax, so we set our sailing date for Tuesday. We passed Monday watching the bustling activity at the wharf and on the *Tahaa Pae*. While the unloading of the processed foods, fuels, and building materials took place, the islanders were selling their goods to the ship's purser. On this day the island exports were bananas, plantains, taro root, oranges, piglets, and craft work. Passengers to Tubuai and the other Austral islands and Tahiti were spreading out their sleeping mats and making themselves comfortable under the huge awning covering the aft top deck. The *Tahaa Pae* left that evening for Tubuai 100 miles to the west, carrying the representatives of the Conseil de Gouvernement, who would later fly to Tahiti from Tubuai.

Horizon's departure the following day was the most ignominious of our cruise. I had hoped that the young trades would hold their southeasterly direction or even shift more southerly, so we could sail off our anchor and work our way through the maze of coral heads that bound the channel. But no, they shifted to the east on departure day, and I had no thought of beating out against them through the 3-mile-long twisting fairway. So I swallowed my pride and paid another visit to the gendarme to ask for a tow out. The Tahitian deputy seemed delighted with the challenge, but the French gendarme chose to explore the problem in great detail. This was all done in French while I patiently stood by looking first at one then the other hoping for a positive answer. When the discussion centered on my chart of the harbor, I knew the Tahitian had won over his boss, and I breathed easier. At 1000 both gendarmes, looking very official in swim trunks, appeared with their 16-foot, twin Mercury-powered fizz boat and at a conservative throttle setting to avoid overheating they towed *Horizon* about 2½ miles to windward. Once around Point Ahieiteraau we cleared our wind on a starboard reach and sailed out the rest of the channel bound north to Tahiti.

Four days of easy sailing on light but steady southeast tradewinds followed. We sailed dark at night to conserve our remaining electricity for the compass light, occasional lights needed below decks, and for lighting-up, regulation style, should we see another vessel. We carried kerosene running lights but they were unmounted, and we didn't think that their poor illumination capability would help our safety, so we did not try to attach them. At this point I reformed my thoughts regarding a backup lighting system and in the future it will be an independent electric source instead of kerosene.

We rounded the east end of Tahiti known at Tahiti Iti in the first rays of dawn and ghosted west along the leeward reef until we arrived off the Papeete breakwater in mid-morning. Vagaries of the coastal wind, however, prevented us from sailing into the Papeete harbor so we thankfully accepted a tow offered by a French navy recreational fishing boat. He brought us to a clear anchorage in front of Temple Paofai, and we dropped our anchor into the murky waters of Papeete Harbor.

Raivavae has a special place in our memories because of:

—the successful completion of a cold, wet, and trying passage from New Zealand

—a friendly Gendarmerie Nationale staff who made us feel most welcome

—its green beauty and majestic mountains surrounded by a blue-green lagoon

—its people, none friendlier or more unspoiled in the Pacific

—the generous invitation to a sumptuous Sunday feast of native island foods

—learning that we really had a sail boat

12

Sailing the Polynesian Migration Route

Papeete, the crossroads of the Pacific, was once again a port of call for *Horizon*. This time to heal our wounds after the turbulent passage from New Zealand and to reprovision for our forthcoming passage north along the legendary Polynesian migration route to Hawaii. This work absorbed an undue amount of time because of the language barrier and depressed our spirits more than once. But in retrospect our problems were minimal compared to the wild experiences of others leaving New Zealand that year. Broken rudders, spreaders, shrouds, and stays were common and sailmakers had a field day. The worst hit was *Gypsy Soul*, a Canadian trimaran, which had to be abandoned after 12 days of drifting off the North Island, but its crew was rescued. So even being able to get to Papeete this year from New Zealand was an accomplishment.

For most of the first week I labored in the engine room trying to clear the fuel system of the engine, which I believed to be at fault for our engine failure at Raivavae. Then one day I noticed that the asbestos on the dry section of the engine exhaust was moist and I immediately realized that the water-cooled standpipe muffler was leaking and water was running back into the engine. I unbolted the exhaust manifold connection and, sure enough, there was water in it. By turning the flywheel with a large screwdriver on the ring gear I ascertained that the cylinders were not completely full of water nor were the pistons frozen in place. But the starter still would not turn the engine over in spite of fully charged batteries, which we had taken care of at a local gasoline station. Replacing the starter and solenoid did no good nor did cleaning and tightening all electrical terminals. Finally, I short circuited the master switch and, voilà, we had starting power! With the exhaust pipe uncoupled, Betty went through the engine starting procedure with me, observing things in the engine room. First water black with carbon spewed forth and then the engine caught and clouds of black smoke filled the engine room. I signaled to shut down, then bolted back the exhaust pipe, and cleaned up the mess. Betty then made a normal start and all was well. Our problem had been an unexpected double failure—exhaust and electrical systems.

We had spotted an opening at the quay, to which we had intended to move as a more convenient place to work. However, our anchor refused to budge off the bottom. We were fouled on an unmarked wreck. One of the yachties from a San Diego trimaran volunteered to put on his scuba gear and give us a hand. Three hours and one tank of air later we were free and moved up to the quay at last.

I went back to see our benefactor to pay him for his services, but he would not accept money for his help, saying we should return the favor to another boat when we could. I did get him to take the price of an air bottle recharge though.

Now at the quay I removed the old muffler and took it to a local boat yard for rebuilding. While it was being fixed I went to a rigger to get a new backstay made and ran into a metric problem. All their cable and fittings (of French origin) are made in metric sizes, but after a little discussion the rigger offered to remachine the end fittings to adapt the metric cable to my English turnbuckles. It worked and our new permanent backstay was soon in place.

The repaired muffler was soon also back in place and, having rebuilt the master switch myself, we now had a functioning engine once again. But one problem kept haunting me and that was the small but continual amount of air leaking into the diesel-fuel system. I decided to replumb the whole suction side of the fuel system with copper tubing, replacing all the suspect flexible hose. It took several days of scouring stores and car garages to find about half of the fittings and tubing needed. The remaining fittings I got from other yachties after passing the word along the quay that I needed some help. Lyle Chase of *Copy Cat,* an ex-boat builder from Vancouver, Canada, gave me a hand to make the new installation and that ended the saga of air bubbles in the fuel line.

While all this mechanical refurbishment took place, Betty scoured the stores for provisions for the next two months of travel. As this was our third visit to Papeete she knew where to go for the best selection and prices. Our friendly Chinese merchant, who last year supplied us with Algerian red wine, did equally well this year with a dry Spanish burgundy. Fresh foods were, as usual, put on board the day before departure, but this year there was a bonus. Jan Prince of Papeete, an American writer, was to join us for the 3-week cruise of the Tuamotu Archipelago, and she brought along bags of delicious pomplemousse, limes and avocadoes from her garden.

We stayed only three weeks in Papeete because we were eager to see the Tuamotus, but we mildly regretted not seeing another Fete and missing the arrival of the Polynesian voyaging canoe, the *Hokule'a* from Hawaii. Our path north was to take us along the historic migration route that was used by Polynesians many years ago in traveling from what is now French Polynesia to the Hawaiian Islands. Anthropologists say with reasonable certainty that the Hawaiian Islands were first visited by the Marquesans in A.D. 500–700 and that significant migrations from Raiatea in the Society Islands were taking place by A.D. 1100–1300. These trips were made in large voyaging canoes propelled by sail and paddles; guided by ancient noninstrument navigation techniques; and provisioned with native foods such as dried fish, salt pork, dried breadfruit and bananas, hard poi, sweet potatoes, and coconuts. To test this hypothesis, the Polynesian Voyaging Society of Hawaii sponsored as part of the United States Bicentennial observance the building and outfitting of an 800-year-old design Polynesian voyaging canoe, the *Hokule'a*, meaning Star of Gladness, the Hawaiian name for the star Arcturus.

The *Hokule'a* is a 60-foot-long, double-hull sailing canoe whose design follows as closely as research could determine the size, shape, and general construction techniques of the early Polynesian voyaging canoes. Manned by 17 persons, it set forth on May 1 headed for Tahiti, stocked with indigenous island foods and using the ancient navigation techniques. It arrived 34 days later and was received by an ecstatic Papeete crowd in a welcome unsurpassed in their history. On July 4 it set forth again on the return trip, taking only 22 days, but this time using modern navigation methods.

By coincidence, *Horizon* was sailing the same waters and winds as *Hokule'a* and some interesting comparisons of sailing craft of two eras can be made. If we adjust our time enroute to account for the stopovers in the Tuamotus Archipelago and the windward Hawaiian Islands, it took us an equivalent 22 days between Papeete and Honolulu. Both

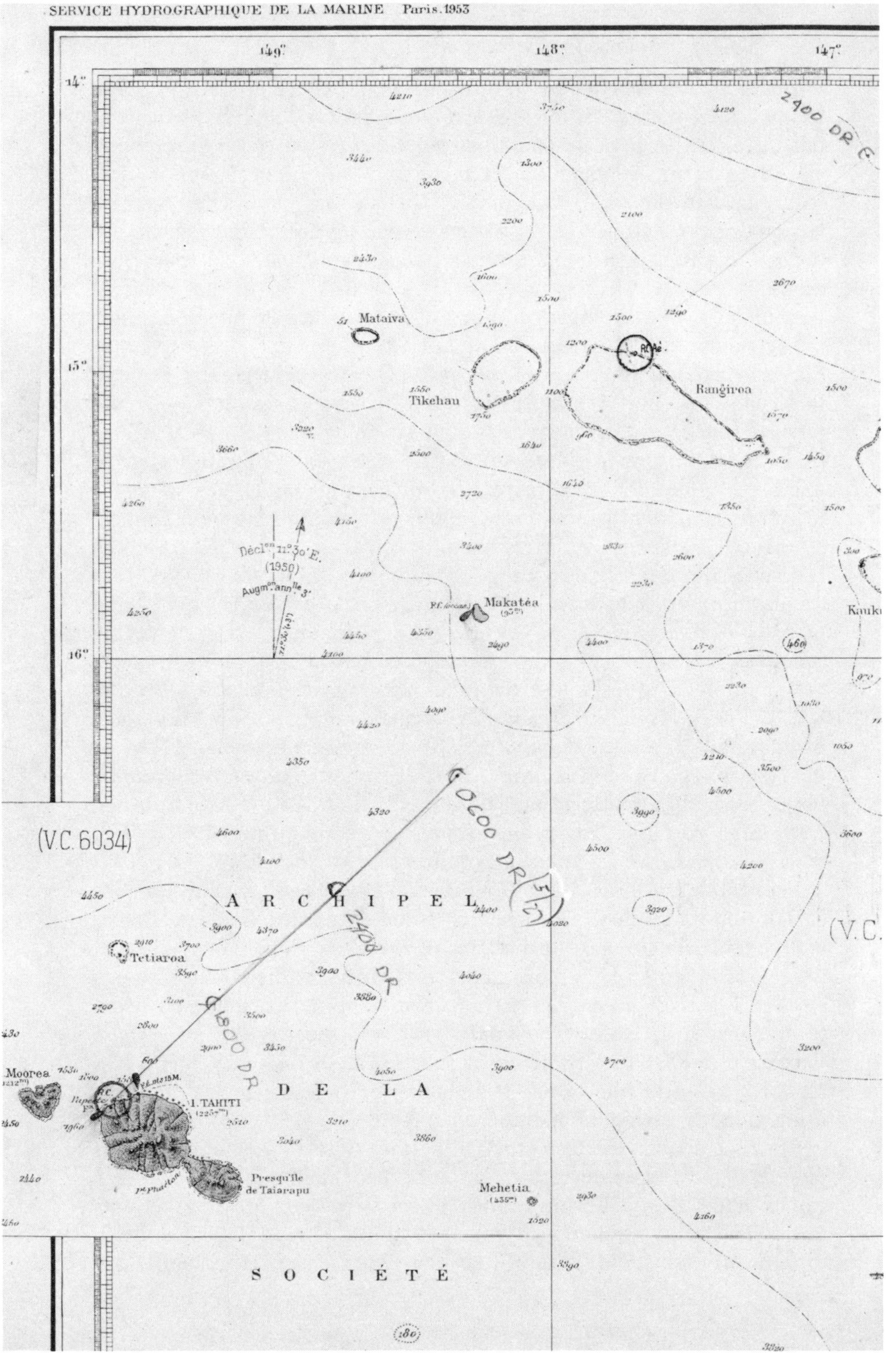

149° 148° 147°

14°

2400 DR E

Mataiva

Tikehau

Rangîroa

RC

Décl¹ᵉⁿ 11°3o'E.
(1950)
Augm¹ᵉⁿ ann¹ˡᵉ 3'

Makatêa
(955)
P.f.lumen

Kauk

15°

16°

(V.C. 6034)

A R C H I P E L

Tetiaroa

0600 DR

2400 DR

4800 DR

Moorea

I. TAHITI
(2237)

Papeete

Presqu'île
de Taiarapu

Presqu'île

D E   L A

Mehetia
(435?)

S O C I É T É

(186)

(V.C.

Horizon and *Hokule'a* produced 160-mile-plus days on the northward voyage. Sailing off the wind, the ancient voyaging canoe appeared to be equally as efficient as the modern cruising boat, although crew sizes to sail them were drastically different. The 32 days it took *Hokule'a* to reach Tahiti going south showed a poor windward performance for this type of craft with plaited pandanus sails. In that context one must admire the early voyaging Polynesians for their perseverence in migrating steadily eastward from the Western Pacific against the prevailing tradewinds.

After three weeks in Papeete at the old Quai Bir Hackiem, we set our course on May 26 for the Tuamotu Archipelago, whose western end lay 180 miles northeast of Tahiti. Departing Papeete at noon, we were soon in 15-knot east-southeast tradewinds. The following morning we sighted Makatea Island and sailed close-in to look at the now abandoned and wave-battered phosphate loading piers. The Pacific Islands Pilot says that landing on this 360 foot high raised coral atoll is "always very difficult." To us it appeared to be impossible and with no secure anchorage for *Horizon*, we continued on towards Rangiroa atoll. Afternoon winds climbed to 20–25 knots with rain but diminished to very light winds during the night. Feeling uncomfortable about approaching an atoll at night and especially about trying to go between two of them (Tikihau and Rangiroa), we altered course at dusk, sailing south for 7 hours away from Rangiroa's west end. At 0200 in the morning we turned again to a northerly course calculated to put us between Tikihau and Rangiroa atolls at daybreak using ocean current estimates from the previous day.

At dawn visibility was still restricted by rain, but at 0725 we got our first wet glimpse of the southwest corner of Rangiroa—barely one mile distant on our starboard bow. Thirty minutes later as visibility improved, Tikihau showed the tops of its coconut palms about 6 miles distant to the west, and we knew we were in the pass between atolls. From there on it was visual navigation as we held close to the breaker line around the west end of Rangiroa. Our entry into the lagoon through Avatoru Pass fortuitously coincided with the ingoing stream which was flowing about 3–4 knots. All was smooth as we motored through the neck of the pass, but when we hit the race where the rushing ingoing stream meets the quiet lagoon waters, we pitched like a bucking bronco for about a hundred yards on steep standing waves. After that we could relax, for we had reached the inside of the magnificent 42-mile-long and 17-mile-wide Rangiroa lagoon, the largest in the archipelago. We continued eastward inside the lagoon for four miles and anchored to a coral-studded bottom in the lee of Reporepo motu sheltered from the tradewinds. Nearby was Tiputa Pass, the second and only other entry to this huge lagoon.

The Tuamotu Archipelago is made up principally of dry forested atolls, with rain as the only source of fresh water. The 76 islands comprising the archipelago have a land area of 343 square miles and range from unbroken circles of coral surrounding a lagoon to glistening chains of coral islets with one or two navigable passes into the lagoon. As with most Pacific archipelagos, the Tuamotu chain stretches along a line northwest to southeast spanning a distance of 1000 miles. At the southeast end are the Gambier Islands, where France conducts her nuclear testing.

Only 30 atolls are permanently uninhabited while the rest support small populations limited by food, water, and space. In bygone days atoll populations were balanced by infanticide and migration, but today big city attractions for youth is the prime balancing factor. An estimated 7,000 persons live throughout the 46 inhabited islands subsisting principally on a fishing and copra economy. In the late 1800s, pearls and mother-of-pearl shells were the major source of income, with divers descending 50–100 feet to gather the valuable molluscs off the bottom. Soon, however, overgathering all but eliminated this income source, and today only experimental black pearl cultivating remains.

Atolls of the Tuamotus were first seen by European eyes in 1615. Jacob LeMaire, a Dutchman, had sailed near the northwestern end in a passage from Cape Horn (which he had named) to Batavia, now part of Indonesia. So many other ships have since accidentally and disastrously discovered the archipelago that it is also known as the Dangerous Archipelago. In recent years many carelessly navigated yachts have added further emphasis to this gloomy name—one only weeks before our arrival. Of all the Tuamotu atolls, Raroia is probably the best known. It was here that the raft *Kon Tiki*, captained by Thor Heyerdahl, landed in 1947 after its epic 4300 mile, 3½ month drift from Peru.

Atolls are composed of the skeletal remains of countless marine plants and animals, which affixed themselves to the warm water shorelines of volcanic lands thrust up eons ago from the ocean floor. The coral polyps, each smaller than a pin head, built their limestone houses on the periphery of the then existing land, never rising completely above the surface of the warm waters nor growing down-ward below 150-foot depths. In time, the volcanic lands, often hollow cones, eroded away and submerged. This proceeded at such a slow rate, however, that the prolific coral polyps managed to keep their upper domain alive near the water's surface, even though their host land disappeared into the depths. The accumulating coral growth, a combination of skeletons and living polyps, formed the reefs hundreds oc feet above the surrounding ocean floor supported by their own living structure.

On the windward side of the atoll, coral growth is most prolific, as the ocean currents bring abundant nutrients to the polyps. On the leetard side gaps in the reef appear as death locally outpaces life among the coral polyp colony. Some gaps attain depths suitable for smalr boat passages into the lagoon. At all edges of the reef wind, wave, marine life, and vegetable growth together wear away at the dead surface layers to produce sand, humus, and islandlike patches above water called motus. Unlike other land masses, the atoll is alive and ever changing, but at a miniscule pace.

The lagoon-encircling reef is continuous in a few instances, but mostly atolls are made up of a series of motus which appear from the air as sparkling beads of a necklace. Motus vary in length from a few hundred yards to ten miles, but they rarely exceed 300 to 400 yards in width.

To the unwary sailor the atolls represent danger. At best in clear weather, they are visible for 7–10 miles, but in rain or at night the visible range can be reduced to hundreds of yards. Reefs rising steeply from thz bottom may be awash; motu land level rarely rises to 10 feet above thl surrounding sea; while the stately coconut tree adds only another 50–75 feet in height. Inside, the lagoon is an aquarium of marine life not sustainable in the deep, turbulent, open ocean. Tropical fish abound in a rainbow of colors and a fantasy of shapes, varied coral "plants" grow with delicate forms and pastel hues, huge coral heads of ugly, threatening brown rise abruptly to the surface, and a coral sand bottom reflects the jade-green rays of the sun to the quiet surface.

Vegetable life on the motus is dominated by coconut palms whose tolerance to a salt environment and poor sandy soil is beyond belief. Coconuts are the wanderers of the Pacific. Floating for thousands of miles until cast up on a shore, they have distributed themselves the world over and have made barren islets into lovely motus. Lying quiescent on its side in the warm tropical sun, the coconut soon sprouts into life, sending roots out through two of its eyes to seek water and food, while simultaneously spikes of fronds shoot skyward through the third eye seeking the life giving sunlight. In five to six years it has matured to the well-known graceful palm tree whose fronds rustle musically in the gentle tradewinds.

But the coconut palm is also the key to life for the islanders who inhabit the atolls. The fibrous trunk is prime building material, while the giant fronds are hand woven into roof thatches of geometric beauty with lifetimes of three years. Carefully stripped, the fronds yield materials for structural lashings, baskets, mats, and essential handicraft items of all kinds. The husk of the coconut forms a cushion to protect the inner nut in the fall to the ground, and it also produces fibers for rope called sennit. It is the nut itself, however, that is the secret to life on the atoll.

A coconut takes a year to develop from a flower to a ripe nut. After reaching its mature size, but long before fully ripening, the green nut is at the drinking stage providing more than a pint of sweet, nourishing coconut milk. Not to be confused with the rancid fluid of the hard ripe nut sold in the supermarkets, the drinking nut furnishes the island substitute for cows' milk, soda pop, and even fresh water. As the nut begins to ripen, a thin white pulp layer begins to form inside the hardening shell. This layer has the consistency and appearance of boiled egg white, and, eaten with fingers or spoon, it makes a rare dessert treat. Left longer on the tree to ripen, the soft white pulp further hardens into a thick layer, while the milk turns to a tasteless water. Shredded, this mature pulp ends up on cake frostings. Removed from the shell in chunks and dried in the sun, it becomes copra, from which coconut oil is extracted, to be used in such widely and varied items as soap, margarine, and nitroglycerine.

A coconut that is allowed to tree-ripen and fall onto the proper surface environment (moisture, soil, light and warmth), will start the amazing process of germination. But in doing so it passes through a fourth and last food phase. Germination causes the formation of a white spongelike substance within the nut, which totally absorbs the liquid and the hard meat. This sponge has the qualities of sweet cotton candy to be eaten with the fingers. But, beware, as the life-giving sponge deteriorates, the juices become poisonous to the human system. The young crewman of *Horizon* found this out at our equator crossing and a painful afternoon ensued.

Besides its vegetarian contribution, the coconut palm fosters the life of the coconut crab. Fully grown he is a big fellow with a two-to-three foot leg span and a body the size of a loaf of San Francisco sourdough bread. They are nocturnal creatures and have a vicious pair of claws. Islanders consider hunting them a real sport. These crabs are prepared for eating simply by boiling, and then they can be eaten with the fingers and a nut cracker (pliers!).

The atoll of Rangiroa subsists on a coconut and fish economy. The valuable nuts grow with little assistance on nearly all of the 150 motus covering 75 percent of the circumference of the atoll. Native workers visit the coconut growing motus for the purpose of making copra out of the coconuts as they ripen. The outboard motorboat is used for conveyance of the workers to the motus and transporting burlap-bagged copra back to the collection points.

Fish exporting is rapidly becoming the economic mainstay of this atoll. The Tahiti islanders' traditional diet of fish can no longer be satisfied by the Tahitian fisherman, since they are rapidly abandoning the sea in favor of 9-to-5 work in the new economy. Commercial fishing in the rest of French Polynesia has, therefore, taken on a new importance. One enterprising operator flies a small airplane daily into several Tuamotu atolls, picking up freshly caught fish for the Tahitians' table that night. But it is the frozen fish business that is giving an economic uplift to the islands.

Adjacent to the pass at Avatoru lies a new frozen fish processing plant, which is on its way to becoming a financial success. The two navigable passes of Rangiroa—Avatoru and Tiputa—abound in fish of all sizes from baitfish through table size. When choice fish are running, dozens of outboards can be seen anchored in the swift-flowing current of the passes, while the islanders using traditional handlines haul aboard hundreds of pounds of filleting-size fish. At the factory, women fillet fish with dexterity and minimum waste. Records are kept of input/output weights and fillets for freezing account for about 60 percent of the wet weight of the fish delivered over the wharf. Offal is returned to the sea, but someday it may be converted to much needed fertilizer for local agricultural uses.

Life at Rangiroa is centered in the towns of Avatoru and Tiputa, situated alongside the passes of the same names. The permanent native settlement of 900 persons is about equally divided between the two villages with atoll administration (Maire de Rangiroa), post office, and the gendarmerie at Tiputa. The usual efficient and intriguing Chinese-operated stores exist in both villages. Bread is baked daily at Tiputa, but orders have to be placed a day ahead, which for transient yachts can be a problem. Five motus comprise the five-mile-long reef between Avatoru and Tiputa passes. On these, modern society is represented in the form of a new hospital, an all-weather airport, and the modern Kia Ora Hotel featuring thatched roof cottages. Air Polynesia flies a five-day-a-week schedule between Rangiroa and Papeete with stops at other atolls and connections to the Marquesas. Anyone can now vacation in the romantic South Seas with comfort, convenience, and an atmosphere that only a palm-studded atoll can offer.

We stayed an altogether too short seven days at Rangiroa, swim-

Fish caught in Avatoru Pass, Rangiroa, are freeze-processed for the tables of Papeete.

ming, hiking, and beach-combing but with little success at shelling, although we collected some pretty sea urchin spines on the jagged ôuter coral reef. While always friendly, the people of Rangiroa have seen so many yachts and have so much contact with Papeete that the casual and spontaneous socializing of yachtie and native was minimal.

Anchored near us in front of the Kia Ora Hotel was a 30-foot boat named *Jeanie* from San Diego. Her skipper, Bill, had a most unusual story to tell. He was approaching the Tuamotus at night from the Marquesas, intending to pass between Rangiroa and Tikehau and go on direct to Papeete. Bill had not judged the currents correctly and, like most single handers, was short of sleep. At 0430 he was thrown from his bunk as *Jeanie* went aground, not on a reef, but on a sand bar inside Tiputa Pass. An amazing bit of luck had saved him, for a combination of open-water currents and a strong in-flow into the lagoon at flood tide had kept him clear of the reefs and almost brought him totally through the pass. What a surprised individual he would have been had he awakened inside the lagoon. As it was, he was thankful to have grounded on a sandbar in the pass with only a broken rudder as evidence of a lapse in alertness.

While Rangiroa appeared indifferent to the visiting yachtsmen, Ahe, our next atoll of call, took them to its bosom and Tuamotuan hospitality overflowed. Ahe is a small atoll 13 miles long and 6 miles wide, lying 80 miles ENE of Rangiroa. It supports one village, Tenukupara, having an estimated population of 250 persons. Ahe's one navigable pass lies at the northwest corner of the atoll while the village is on one of the motus forming the south reef. An entering yacht traverses 5 miles of beautiful lagoon mostly in water depths of 100 feet, but with occasional perilous coralheads breaking the surface. Most but not all were marked with pipes driven into the coral or at worst with a tree limb stuck between arms of coral.

A yacht anchorage lies within a small inner fringing reef at Tenukupara, and the town wharf can accommodate four boats unless the copra ship is present. If you want solitude you anchor out, but if you want to join in the lively atoll life, take the wharf—you will assuredly lose some sleep but you'll go away with beautiful memories of a fine people.

Island life here appears to follow the more traditional patterns of a self-contained Polynesian community without local French administration. "Papa" Toa, a robust 73 year old Tuamotuan is the titular head, or chief of the community. His staff is his wife "Mama" Fana, who speaks and writes French.

Papa Toa was a jocular individual whose favorite gesture was a right thumb pointed up, followed by the island words "mai tai" meaning good. And good indeed was the dinner prepared for us one evening by Mama Fana as she did for all visiting yachties. Betty, Jan, Roger, and I arrived on time in our best pareus and dignified shorts and shirts. Papa Toa saw us coming up the path and whisked off the cloth covering the table to expose a neatly arranged ready-prepared dinner. We were greeted by both and sat and chatted on the porch looking at their guest books and admiring the crafts they displayed. Dinner was sumptuous, with several kinds of fish, taro, chicken, rice, and many sincere "mai tai's" which we gave as expressions of a pleasurable meal.

Ahe has become the favorite atoll of call for yachts traveling the Tuamotu Archipelago due to the warm hospitality of Papa Toa and Mama Fana and the friendliness of each islander from the bare-as-the-day-born toddler to the dignified church elders. During our stay at Ahe there were yachts from England, Sweden, France, Tahiti, Oregon, and California present at the wharf.

Life on an atoll is quite spartan. Poor soil limits food production to coconuts, breadfruit, and some papaya, limes, and bananas. Pigs raised on coconut and chickens scratching for themselves add variety to the menu, but they never grow very large because of too many feasts! While the lagoon abounds in fish, the men of the village prefer to spear larger fish along the outer reef. Drinking water is collected off the roofs of the community buildings and stored in above-ground cisterns for communal use. Except for coconuts and fish, yachts cannot expect much in the way of provisions from an atoll.

Ahe, surprisingly, has two stores that are both small and run by the Tuamotuans themselves. We found the stores usually closed necessitating a search for the owner, who may be washing clothes along the lagoon, tending a small garden, or plaiting fronds to repair a leaking roof. The stores were lean-to sheds and carried a small stock of tinned food products, dried foods, and miscellaneous small hardware and notions. They obviously were not large enough to generate any interest by a Chinese entrepreneur. As an example of the Tuamotuan's generosity and lack of business acumen, we asked (in French) if we could buy some citron (limes). The store owner took us outside to her lime tree and proceeded to pick them until we asked her to stop. She would accept no money for them saying that her home-grown foods are for friends. We thought back to Raivavae and Afa who tried to take us for everything he could. Afa made more francs, but I wonder if he had as much fun as the Tuamotuans.

The atoll's communication center, two-way radio and post office, is run by pretty 18-year-old Emily Mariterangi, who is also the village nurse. Most villagers, however, still practice the art of folk medicine using native plant dressings. Between Rangiroa and Ahe I had developed a tropical ulcer on my shin where the skin had been broken in a careless collision of the shinbone against the companionway ladder. The sore was raw and the ankle and foot swollen, so I sought help from the village nurse. I received treatment daily from Emily, who used French antibiotics on the sore, and, sure enough it improved. Emily, speaking in French with Jan interpreting, explained that such ulcers are common and mine the size of a quarter, was small. We did observe some large scars on some of the islanders' legs, which we suspect might have been a result of their folk medicine treatment. Betty having been taught all the sterile procedures of big city hospitals in her nurses' training, shuddered a bit at the field medical practices used on Ahe.

While at Ahe we tested their postal service, the epitome of simplicity. You hand Emily your letter with the proper postage money and she stamps an Ahe postmark on it and drops it in a box—no stamp involved. We never did find out where it went from there without a stamp, but all of our letters did arrive at their destination.

Island transportation is accomplished by foot, wheelbarrow, outrigger, or outboard motorboat. There is one small truck to use the beltline road around the village, and it can also cross over to other motus at low tide to haul copra back to the wharf. Transportation to other atolls nearby is by copra boat or outboard motorboat with airplane connections to Papeete from Manihi, an atoll just 18 miles east of Ahe pass.

Social life at Ahe centered around the church. In addition to several religious services during the week in Tuamotuan, they held village feasts, cake socials, and fund-raising auctions. The islanders made a particular effort to invite yacht crews to all their functions and, in spite of a language difference, everyone had a great time. Following the evening church activities the youth of the village would collect at the wharf and guitar playing and singing would ensue, with the inevitable tamure being danced vigorously by the islanders and somewhat

Yacht club burgees are presented to Papa Toa and Mama Fana at Ahe.

Pretty Emily Mariterangi, Ahe's nurse, postmaster, and radio communicator.

raggedly by the visitors. While superstition of adversity from being under a full moon still dampens the older islanders' nightly forays, it did not slow down the wharf discotheque, which often continued past midnight. When the evening entertainment ended, we found ourselves at ease within a world of rustling coconut fronds intermingled with the muted roar of the ocean breaking on the rugged outer reef.

Our sojourn on Ahe lasted a brief nine days. Leaving our guest, Jan Prince, with the friendly villagers (she later returned to Papeete on another yacht), we departed Tiareroa pass, June 15, at 1015 on a rushing outflowing current and set our course for Hawaii 2150 great circle miles away. Our passage became a delightful tradewind-sail-first on southeast trades to the equator and then on northeast trades after passing through the intertropical convergence zone better known as the Doldrums. The Doldrums, extended between 1°N and 5° N (about 240 miles), were good to us again. Winds were light but steady and we kept moving at about 90 miles per day. Almost continuous overcast and rain clearly defined the Doldrums limits. As we sailed out of them into tradewind cloud-studded skies, we could look back and see the violent cloud formations, which mark the Doldrum edge. Boat speed again picked up on the northeast trades and we saw consistent 140 to 160 mile days.

Morning skies were clear in both the southeast and northeast trades with star and planet celestial navigation fixes made on 13 mornings. The sun was used on four other days and on only one day in the eighteen-day passage were we completely blanked and had to run on dead reckoning. Life at sea wasn't all idyllic, though. On our seventh day out, while in the Doldrums, our forestay parted at the upper end, due to metal fatigue of the cable. It seems that the rigger at commissioning four years earlier had neglected to put a toggle fitting at the upper end of the stay to allow lateral movement under jib loads. It took several trips by Roger up the bosun's chair to properly affix a

An Ahe housing project on Pora Pora motu.

temporary headstay to carry us the remaining 1700 miles to Hawaii. Attaching a shroud or stay to the masthead 55 feet above a turbulent sea is a real challenge at best, but ours was made considerably easier through a series of photographs of the masthead assembly that I had taken before departing San Pedro. By studying the photographs from all angles, we were able to collect on deck the proper tools and parts for the needed fix. I now limited our headsail to the working jib but even with the sail limitation, our average day's run for the whole passage was 129 miles per day while covering a total distance of 2375 miles. Our additional easting to 143 degrees 38 minutes west longitude to pick up a more favorable slant of winds was well worth the additional 225 miles covered.

Crossing the equator we had to once again pay our respect to Neptunis Rex. This time it was Betty and I as old Shellbacks who initiated Pollywog Roger into the court. Roger met the prerequisites of joining the court by searching for the "line" from the spreaders, posting a letter at the mail buoy, and determining the time and place of crossing which was 0700 on June 22, 1976 at 142 degrees 38 minutes West longitude. Betty decided to bake a cake for the occasion and, in addition, made a special sponge cake for Roger—a real sponge frosted with chocolate. Even Roger laughed at his inability to bite a piece out of the cake. But the hilarity took a solemn turn a few minutes later when Roger decided to eat his sprouted coconut, which he had taken along from Ahe for this occasion. After breaking it open he observed that it didn't look the same as the others. But he tasted a small amount anyway and immediately his throat burned and breathing became difficult. He was obviously being poisoned by the deteriorated coconut meat. We got him to vomit as much as possible and all afternoon Betty fed him milk, milk, and more milk. By nightfall the worst was over, but he was in no condition to stand a night watch so we had him turn in while Betty and I kept *Horizon* going. Since sprouted coconuts are normally good eating, we could only blame his close call on the fact that he had cut off the roots and stem of the coconut before putting it in the ice chest and the normally tasty spongelike interior had deteriorated. That call was too close for comfort.

On July 3 we arrived at our beautiful fiftieth state in time for the National Bicentennial observance but, alas, having come from a foreign country we were quarantined until Tuesday, the 6th, when the entry clearance could be obtained. Not having a detailed chart of Hilo Bay, we entered on knowledge read from the Coast Pilot. No danger involved but the Coast Pilot said that there was an anchorage off Coconut Island so we headed there. No other yachts were present, but the bottom looked good and we anchored for the night, glad to be in port after an 18-day passage. In the morning of July 4 we were visited by the Coast Guard and a harbor representative, who told us we could not stay there but would have to go into Radio Bay around the corner of the Matson pier. And so we did to wait out our quarantine. But it was not a lonely wait as Hilo harbor and shoreline brimmed with holiday activity, and we had at least a partial view over the Matson Lines warehouse of the fireworks display at Coconut Island.

Our travels along the Polynesian migration route left us with new thoughts of people and memories of unusual interest such as:

—The immense Rangiroa lagoon surrounded by its shining ribbon of motus

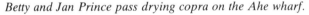

Betty and Jan Prince pass drying copra on the Ahe wharf.

—The islanders' handline fishing methods which adequately supply a modern frozen fish processing plant

—The huge, aggressive coconut crabs, which were so delicately delicious when cooked

—The islanders' continued confidence in folk medicine treatment

—The traditional island dinner served to us by Mama Fana while at Ahe

—Nightly singing at the Ahe wharf accompanied by guitars shared by many musicians

—How wonderfully tuned to nature were the early Polynesian voyagers

—Playful porpoise riding *Horizon*'s bow wave for hours at a time as we sailed north on the tradewinds

13

Polynesia, USA

As the northern crossroads of the Pacific, Hawaii plays host to dozens of overseas yachts every year coming from and going to North American west coast ports. Every odd numbered year it also receives 70 to 75 racing yachts that depart from San Pedro on July 4 for the race ending at Diamond Head. Cruising yachts from California also take advantage of the summer months when both mainland and island weather are quiescent for three-month round trip cruises. Others, like ourselves, include it in a far-reaching itinerary into the southwest Pacific from whence the original Hawaiians also came.

We had deliberated in our early cruise planning whether or not to make Hawaii our first westward port of call from California. It would be a shorter first passage than is the Marquesas Islands from either California or Mexico, but there appeared to be two disadvantages. First, we would see it on the return passage from the South Pacific inasmuch as it makes a natural resupply point in the Tahiti–California passage, and further, it makes better use of the tradewinds than does sailing direct to California. The second reason for not making Hawaii a west-bound port of call is that you then face a long beat to weather from Hawaii to the Marquesas, first on the northeast trades (which are more easterly than northeasterly) in order to get your easting and then

167

on the southeast trades. As it turned out we were right considering the experiences of those yachts who made the passage south from Hawaii, for they found it a long hard beat to weather—some not able to make adequate easting to visit the Marquesas Islands.

The Hawaiian Islands anchor the northern apex of the vast Polynesian triangle through which we had sailed while visiting seven of the eleven groups of islands comprising it. Now we were at the eighth group within the triangle and the only one in the northern hemisphere. This was the grand climax to years of planning and preparing, and we were set to enjoy it to the fullest.

Hawaii is a unique chain of islands that stretches for 1600 miles across the middle of the blue Pacific in a characteristic northwest to southeast direction. It is the longest and most distinctly formed archipelago in Polynesia, made up of 132 shoals, reefs, and islands. In

Porpoise provide hours of entertainment on the long passage to Hawaii.

geologic history the chain began its life at the western end with, in all probability, the appearance of Kure island, now reduced by time to atoll stature. Kure marks the start of a fissure in the ocean floor, which continued to spread southeastward creating additional seamounts whose tops surfaced to form islands. While the origin of Kure and the leeward islands of the group goes back possibly 10 million years, the chain is still growing, as evidenced by the easternmost island, Hawaii, which today continues a robust volcanic growth.

Between Kure and Hawaii lies an almost complete history of land formation in the Pacific ocean. The older leeward islands have now been reduced to shoals and atolls by the irresistible weathering forces of sun and wind and erosion by rain and wave. In the middle of the chain are the last vestiges of volcanic rock such as Gardner Pinnacles, which may be a mere five million years old. But it is the eight major islands at the eastern end of the chain that form the bulk of our fiftieth state. In decreasing order of size there is Hawaii, Maui, Oahu, Kauai, Molokai, Lanai, Niihau, and Kahoolawe. They, together with the lesser leeward shoals and atolls, comprise a total land area of 6,400 square miles, slightly less than that of the state of New Jersey.

But their significance to the yachtsman is not their size, but their location in the balmy tropics, blessed with the northeast tradewinds tempering the climate and making sailing a true delight. The trades are strongest and steadiest during the summer months, blowing from the east northeast up to 90 percent of the time. They are only spasmodically interrupted during the winter seasons when the Kona winds blow from the south. Then the weather turns hot and humid as the islands are blanketed by tropical moisture. The oppressive atmosphere is finally broken by the appearance of squalls, which drop up to 25 inches of rain per year over the entire archipelago. However, the mountainous windward islands receive 200 inches or more of rain each year as the tradewinds are lifted over their summits, dropping their moisture as they rise. From the dry uninhabited atolls of the west to the lush green islands on the east, the chain has a full variety of weather, including snow at the mountain summits of Hawaii.

Violent weather in the islands is rare. Hurricanes are unknown, although the tag ends of spent eastern Pacific hurricanes occasionally pass close bringing winds to 60 knots.

It is not the winds, however, which have caused Hawaii's most significant damage, but tsunamis, those massive swells, caused by violent undersea earthquakes, usually generated thousands of miles away. Of no concern to the mariner at sea, they grow to immense waves in shoal waters battering shorelines and harbors. In past years,

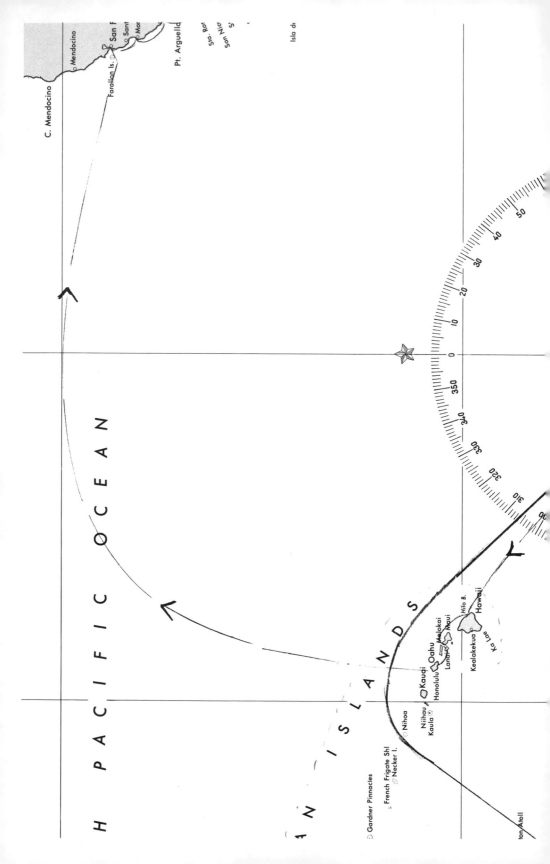

C. Mendocino
Mendocino
Farallon Is.
San F
Sant
Mar
Pt. Arguello
Sta. Ro
San Nic
S
Isla d

H PACIFIC OCEAN

I S L A N D S

Gardner Pinnacles
French Frigate Shl
Necker I.
Nihoa
Niihau
Kaula
Kauai
Honolulu
Oahu
Molokai
Lanai
Maui
Hilo B.
Kealakekua
Ka Lae
Hawaii
on Atoll

50
40
30
20
10
0
350
340
330
320
310
9

damage and loss of life was so great that an extensive tsunami warning system has been built in the Pacific Basin to warn the dwellers of tsunamis anywhere in the Pacific. This system brought us word of the Fiji earthquake in December while we were at the Bay of Islands, New Zealand. Tsunamis, like their parent earthquakes, are unpredictable, but unlike earthquakes there may be a few hours of warning time, since the wave does take a finite time to traverse the broad ocean even at its great speed of up to 400 knots.

Probably the only consistent sailing problem in Hawaiian waters is the roughness of the channels between the major islands. Straddling the trade winds and prevailing currents, the islands form a barrier to normal surface flows, with the result that the winds and currents funnel at accelerated speed through the channels. The channel waters develop steep waves, which make cross-channel sailing real work when the trades are blowing strong. Quieter night passages are generally chosen.

Night passages do bring some problems, such as barge tows of several hundred yards in length. Most island cargo is transshipped through Honolulu and distributed to the other islands by barges, which also seem to prefer traveling at night. With usually good visibility, the danger of collision is small.

More spectacular than barges are the hydrofoil passenger-carrying craft that ply the waters from Honolulu to the other islands. These flying machines on water move at over 50 knots, creating a trail of spray that is more visible than the craft itself.

Hilo Harbor on the island of Hawaii is but a large triangular indentation in the shoreline. It is made tenable for ships and boats by virtue of a natural inside reef on which was built a raised breakwater. Behind the Blonde Reef breakwater lie the cargo docks and the yacht harbor known as Radio Bay—a snug spot reasonably well sheltered from the prevailing northeast trades, but not without some surge. While anchoring space is available in the central harbor area, most boats prefer to moor Tahiti-style to the seawall, which is what we did. There is a small difference, though, in Tahiti-style mooring at Hilo versus mooring at Papeete. Hilo has a higher tidal range, which, together with the harbor surge, mandates good clearance with the sea wall, so it is impossible to use gangplanks to shore for convenience. Instead, dinghies are fitted out as ferries to cover the 10- to 15-foot intervening gap. While the small boat harbor is generally peaceful, it has one day and night a week of hectic activity when the Matson containerships are in port. Then the parking lot area bordering the sea wall roars with diesel engines as trucks shuttle massive containers off and onto the ships.

Overseas yachts at anchor in Hilo's Radio Bay.

We were moored between two boats who were cruising Hawaiian waters from the Mainland—*Lady Lee* from San Diego and *Kalana* from Los Angeles. In fact, the majority of boats at Hilo were from the mainland for a three-month summer cruise, but some were having misgivings about the simple downwind run to paradise. With so many boats making this cruise, a disturbing element of casualness has appeared. A passage to Hawaii can be as difficult as any in the Pacific, with wind and wave challenging you all the way; ill-prepared boats and inept crews flirt with disaster in attempting the crossing just because the Jones are doing it. Later, when we arrived at Honolulu, we were to find many boats either for sale or being ferried back to the mainland because boat and crew were not in harmony with the ocean. While it is disappointing to abort a dream vacation, it is tragedy to be lost at sea. With 15,000 cruising miles behind us we felt sorry for the fledgling trying his wings only to find he really wasn't made to fly.

Hilo is one of four ports of entry for the Hawaiian Islands. All boats arriving from foreign ports just clear through immigration, customs, and state agriculture while boats arriving directly from the U.S. only clear through agriculture. We got the full treatment with two complications. First, we had arrived on Saturday July 3, so this was a three-day holiday weekend and we had to wait until Tuesday to check in. But the time was usefully spent in cleaning up *Horizon* and putting her in order after the long passage. Second, our Aussie crewman had not obtained his U.S. visa in New Zealand so he was paroled in my charge for one month, by which time we would have to appear at immigration in Honolulu. Roger now became my ward and his status would also limit our stay on the windward islands to one month, which was less than we desired.

But we were not to be denied our enjoyment of Hawaii, so we set to work to refurbish and resupply *Horizon*. Except for stores supplying outboards and small fishing boats, there were virtually no marine supplies available on the island and absolutely no chance of replacing the temporary forestay. I went aloft in the bo'sun's chair to check both mastheads and rigging. Since everything appeared sound, I elected to wait until Honolulu for the rigging repairs. With minor repairs made, we sent Roger off with his pack for one week to see the island while Betty and I, at last, relaxed in the privacy of our boat. We took short walks and bus rides into Hilo to see the tourist sights and buy what food we needed to carry us to Honolulu within the month. While Hilo has developed a lush tourist paradise along its harbor, it is the back street area of the old town that is the most colorful. Unfortunately, these back-street stores selling unusual oriental foods and traditional oriental goods of all sorts are rapidly giving way to supermarkets. We enjoyed exploring the confused and dusty counters, broadening our education on another passing way of life.

Hawaii is a big island, 71 miles long north to south and 70 miles wide east to west covering about 3,500 square miles. It has the highest mountains in the archipelago—Mauna Kea and Mauna Loa—both over 13,500 feet high. With so much land and so few harbors along its 325 mile-long shoreline we elected to see the island by road and rental car. Hawaii has a dichotomy of weather caused by its high mountains. The windward side, particularly the northeast coast, has generous rainfall, as it intercepts the moisture laden tradewinds. We traveled for miles through lush forests many bright with flowers and emblazoned with the magnificent orange poinciana trees. Along the steep cliffs, waterfalls abounded, crowned by the magnificent Akaka Falls, 420 feet high in a setting of arboreal splendor. Above the cliffs along the Hamakua Coast grows the sugar cane. It requires much water and Hawaii's windward coast has become the biggest sugar producing area in the islands. Not a day goes by but you see smoke arising from a mature cane field as the leaves are burned off to facilitate harvesting and processing.

At the northern and southern extremities of the windward coast we found other tropical crops. Near the village of Pahoa, papaya trees are planted in precise rows with fruit of such even quality as to not need grading. To the north at Honokaa is the island's largest macadamia nut orchard and packing plant. Macademias are native to Australia where it is called the kindel-kindel. The Aussies, to our amazement, bother little to cultivate these nuts. Still further north is Waipio Valley, which was the bread basket for the early Hawaiian peoples, with its valley floor planted in taro, and coconuts abounding on the sloping valley walls.

As we crossed the north end of the island through groves of trees we entered the grounds of the almost boundless Parker Ranch—350 square miles of land for cattle grazing. At ranch headquarters at Kamuela, one dines in the elegance of Texas cattle barons with beef in a dozen different forms the specialty of the house. Adjacent to the restaurant is the Ranch museum replete with memorabilia of almost 200 years of history of the ranch. There is nothing like a ranch to take a sailor's mind off the sea.

The west coast of Hawaii presents the other face of island weather— warm and dry. It is called the Kona Coast after the westerly Kona winds, which blow when a winter weather front crosses the region causing a temporary cessation in the steady northeast trades. Little grows on the Kona coast except the tourists who flock here from Hilo to enjoy the climate. There are no natural harbors on this coast, only open bays or roadsteads, so we were satisfied in having left *Horizon* at Radio Bay.

A cruise to the South Pacific could be subtitled "In the Wake of Captain Cook," for in his three voyages of exploration he touched most of the islands of interest to yachtsmen. Hawaii was one, and it was here on the Kona coast at Kealakekua Bay where Cook met his death in 1779. An underwater monument to Cook was placed in these crystal clear waters, and it is the British navy which annually maintains it. Kealekekua Bay is designated as a marine park and abounds in protected sea life. For those who sail their boats here, there is only a limited open anchorage.

Another area of prime interest is the City of Refuge National Historical Park. It is a rocky promontory on Honaunau Bay, which in early Hawaii was a sacred place of refuge for defeated warriors. Those who reached here ahead of their pursuers were assured safety as long as they stayed. This park is one of the better displays of old Hawaii.

The high point in our circumnavigation of the island of Hawaii was a day long tour of the Hawaii Volcanoes National Park. Here at an elevation of 4000 feet, we saw the birth of island land masses. Volcanic cones upthrust from the sea, lava flows stretching out to the shoreline, and craters, which in millions of years could become harbors. From basalt to atoll is a long period of time, but we had now seen and better understood the geologic history of the Pacific.

Seventeen days of my thirty-day wardship of Roger had now passed, so we reluctantly decided to leave the island of Hawaii and continue our sail to leeward. Northwest lay Maui, an island named after the mythical Polynesian who supposedly pulled most of the islands from the sea while fishing. Maui like Hawaii is bereft of secure harbors, but sailors have found the roads off Lahaina to be a safe, if temporary, anchorage when the normal tradewinds blow and the social life ashore to be a welcome change from shipboard life. So it was that whalers earlier flocked to Lahaina, and today the yachtie follows in their wake.

We once again elected to make an overnight passage from Hilo to Lahaina. Staying on the windward side of both islands would give us fair winds, and we would avoid the rough Alenuihaha Channel. Departing Hilo at 0800 on July 20 we sailed the 130-mile distance to Lahaina in an even 24 hours. Mostly it was clear weather with steady 10-knot trade winds, but heavy rain showers appeared in the early morning as we passed through Pailolo Channel separating Molokai and Maui. Then, as we approached Lahaina the skies cleared for we were now on the leeward side of the island where the weather is always pleasant.

Horizon was not the only boat headed for Lahaina. Out of the rainy Pailolo channel appeared others who were finishing the biennial Victoria, British Columbia, to Maui Yacht Race—a two-week pines-to-palms contest.

We knew that the small boat harbor would be full of race boats by now, so we sought a good anchorage in the roads outside of Lahaina. Because of the summer popularity of Lahaina as well as the yacht race, there were many boats here. We counted 35 boats in the roadstead, racers and cruisers, and the closest we could anchor was about half a mile out—requiring a long dinghy ride to shore. But it was not a dull ride, for the channel into the small, inadequate harbor sliced narrowly between breaking waves abounding with surfers.

The weather at Lahaina is nearly perfect, as the Hawaiians also knew when they established their royal capital here in earlier years. Yachties took advantage of the sun and semiprivacy of their boats by nude sun bathing—one of the small personal pleasures in boating.

Life ashore probably has not changed much since the days of the whalers. Merchants are still selling to seamen and grog shops have the most business. It had only one blight as far as we could tell, and that was the carefree, and careless individual known a few years ago as a hippie. Because of the good weather they have flocked here and become in some cases a nuisance, living off the land and the local people's generosity.

From the deck of *Horizon* we had a panoramic view of the leeward side of Maui. At the higher elevation the tradewind clouds would collect, and we could see rain descending into the valleys to later irrigate the extensive sugar cane fields. Everyday one or more of the cane fields would be burned preparatory to harvesting, and the soft, silvery ashes would drift lightly down on the water. In the far distance lay cloud-shrouded 7,000-foot high Haleakala mountain, an extinct volcano and now a national park.

But the center of our attention was Lahaina—partly old, partly restored, and much new. The old, however, was not very old, going back only as far as the arrival of the first Europeans and Americans. Most of the true Hawaiian history, as in all Polynesia, has been lost because of the lack of a written language and the use of biodegradable materials for their daily living. Today's history starts with Captain Cook's arrival in 1779 but doesn't gain momentum until the arrival of the missionaries and whalers in 1850. From that era there remain standing the missionary Baldwin's house, the Pioneer Inn for travelers, and the old prison, which housed many an overactive sailor. Around these has grown up a restored Lahaina, shops of all kinds catering to the tourist needing food, drink, or souvenirs.

Because of its climate, this leeward side of Maui has become the scene of extensive building of high rise condominium apartments. While architecturally attractive, they mar the natural beauty of the shoreline, making it resemble another Miami Beach.

Condominiums aside, there is still some local color in the form of the old narrow-gauge sugar cane trains kept in operation for carrying tourist passengers. Known as the Kaanapali and Lahaina Railway, it operates between the old whaling port of Lahaina and the modern condominium complex at Kaanapali. Even if you are not a train buff the ride through the cane fields can be a lot of fun.

We were now getting restless to get to Honolulu where we could do our major boat refurbishment and replenish our provisions. Besides, there is much to see there and my wardship of Roger was wearing at my conscience. But as we relaxed on *Horizon* and looked across the water we saw yet three more islands of this group—Molokai, Lanai, and Kahoolawe. Our decision was to stop at Lanai on the way to Oahu.

On the morning of July 24 we departed Lahaina, and with some motoring and much slow sailing we crossed the almost windless Auau Channel in four hours and anchored in Hulopoe Bay on the south side of the island. While this is a picturesque half-moon bay with a sweeping sand beach, it also had a heavy surge due to hurricane action between Mexico and Hawaii.

While we sat pondering the security of this bay, a lone swimmer approached us through the breaking surf. It was George Stickney from the *Lauree Sue,* whom we hadn't seen since Whangarei. *Lauree Sue* was docked at adjacent Manele Bay, and George convinced us that it was a better spot, so we weighed anchor as he swam back to the beach. A few minutes of motoring took us around the point to Manele Bay, which is Lanai's only small boat harbor. Fortunately, *Horizon* has a shallow draft, for this is not a deep harbor, and we entered it gingerly watching our depth sounder and following the pole markers lining the channel. With help from George's all-girl crew we were soon tied bow-to at a dock finger with stern anchor set in a reverse Tahiti-style mooring.

Horizon at Lanai, Hawaii.

Lanai is a small island of 120 square miles rising to an altitude of 3,400 feet. Near its summit is the one populated area, Lanai City, surrounded by the stately Norfolk pines, which had their beginning on Norfolk Island between Australia and New Zealand. There is no public transportation on Lanai, so hiking and hitch-hiking are the only means to get about. The local people seem to have a soft spot in their heart for yachties, for they generously offer rides to the city.

The whole island is owned by the Dole Pineapple Company. They bought it in 1922 for a price slightly in excess of one million dollars. Twenty-four square miles are planted in pineapples, but they are not for public picking, and sharp-eyed guards roam the area protecting the crop. The only other harbor for the island is Kaumalapau on the west side, at which the barges are loaded with pineapple for shipment to the canning plant at Honolulu.

Sunday is a day at the beach for the outdoor-loving Hawaiians who flocked to Hulopoe Bay for a day in the sun and surf. Their cars, mostly jeeps or junkers, raised a snaking column of dust from Lanai City to the ocean. We joined them on foot spending most of the day hiking about the low peninsula separating the two bays. Walking off the beaten path brings with it certain perils in the form of thorns from the Kiawe tree. Up to ¾ inch in length, these heavy spikes protect the scraggly trees, which are one of the few durable plants on the dry leeward sides of these islands. The spikes are quite dangerous to hikers as they can easily penetrate the common soft-soled sandal. Hiking boots and shorts were the uniform of the day on this hot and windless lee side of Lanai.

Evening brought a party on *Horizon* as the crew of *Lauree Sue* came over to celebrate my birthday. Laureen and Susan made birthday cards, and Betty had baked a cake, so with friends of long miles acquaintance we had a simple and satisfying party.

While not within sight, the island of Oahu was still pulling hard at us and Monday noon we departed the small boat harbor. We anchored outside in the open Manele Bay to spend some time cleaning growth off of *Horizon*'s bottom. It was our last opportunity to do so, for Honolulu's harbor would be too dirty for swimming and after that we would be out of the warm and comfortable tropical waters. Bottom scrubbing was followed by picture taking and *Horizon* sat in placid sunlit waters while her portrait was taken from many angles—after all, this was almost her fourth birthday!

An overnight sail on steady trade winds took us to Honolulu in a mere eleven hours, and we arrived under the silhouette of the extinct volcanic crater Diamond Head at 0300. Then followed three hours of sailing in circles awaiting daybreak before entering the reef. As soon as there was enough light to identify the narrow entrance to Ala Wai harbor, we furled the sails and motored through the reef, avoiding the early morning surfers who used the same channel to reach breaking surf. With a major rigging repair to be made, we headed directly for the boatyard where, luckily, we found a large slip open. There we stepped ashore into a maelstrom of modern society—automobiles, noise, stores and high rise buildings, people hurrying to their daily jobs. We were truly back in the United States.

As with every other port of call most of the first day was absorbed in finding our way around the local area. We had little trouble in locating marine hardware and services, since Ala Wai boat harbor is the focal point of small boat activities in Hawaii. Within walking distance was the necessary chandlery, rigging shop, radio store and boat yard, all adequate for our maintenance needs. But not so stores for reprovisioning and a laundry.

Ala Wai boat harbor is at one end of Honolulu's fabulous tourist paradise. Waikiki is at the other end about one mile away. Along with tourist facilities are many apartments and condominiums and in such an area it is difficult to find the fundamental living needs for the yachtie. Restaurants, souvenir shops, and entertainment abound for the satisfaction of the tourist, and prices are usually higher than the yachtie can afford. But to our rescue came Carol Stratford, a young friend from our days in Riverside, California. When we first met Carol, she was a high school classmate of our son, Eric. It was her father's boat, *Vision* on which I crewed in the Los Angeles–Tahiti race of 1970, and probably more than any other event that was the inspiration for our present travels. Now a grown woman married to a Navy officer assigned to Pearl Harbor, Carol gave us a traditional welcome to Polynesia, U.S.A. Knowing of our plans from a telephone call I had made to her from Lahaina, she had kept her eye on Ala Wai for our arrival. At the right time, namely Happy Hour, Carol arrived with a pitcher of Mai Tais, fragrant flower leis, and her bubbling enthusiasm for life. The evening passed quickly with chatter about her new married life and her work in marine biology at the University of Hawaii. She topped it all off with an offer to loan us one of their cars "for the duration" so that we could get about Oahu more easily. Our hearts were warmed by this friendliness and generosity and we knew our stay would be fun.

But before the fun there was one more piece of business to be tended to, and that was to settle Roger's immigration status. The two of us sought out the Office of Immigration and Naturalization, located about two miles from the harbor. It was a busy place with dozens of Oriental people seeking help on visits and immigration problems. We waited our turn and eventually Roger got his audience with an immigration officer. Soon I was also called in and informed that I was guilty of an illegal procedure in bringing an alien into the U.S. who did not have the proper papers. It was now my honesty in personally bringing Roger to Immigration which paid off, for the officer acknowledged it as an innocent mistake on my part. To Roger's chagrin he could not get a visa but instead received a four-month business visitor's permit. This resolved the problem and took Roger off my hands at last.

Boat work proceeded rapidly and we soon had *Horizon* refurbished so that we could move away from the yard and over to a slip assigned to us for our stay. This was far more suitable to us than the Tahiti-style mooring at the Hawaii Yacht Club, which, while cheaper, was crowded and inconvenient.

Now began pleasant days of seeing Honolulu and Oahu. I sought out the Bishop Museum to study early Polynesia and research some areas in question from our travels. My interest got me a special pass to their library and meetings with several of their staff members. One in particular was most interesting and informative in providing me with information for this book. He was Edwin Bryan, Jr., a man in his late sixties who has spent his entire life studying the geography of the Pacific islands. With his help I resolved most of my immediate questions on Polynesia and learned a great deal more in the process.

Other areas of Honolulu also beckoned us and daylight hours were spent on the move. There was the Foster Botanical Garden which has a most amazing variety of tropical flora growing on its grounds. All of our old friends from the Pacific were there: kauri trees, pandanus palms, the fragrant frangipani, sandalwood, and many others topped off with gorgeous Hawaiian orchids in seemingly hundreds of varieties.

And then there was the Chinese Cultural Center, a blockful of new buildings surrounding a plaza area created to enlighten travelers on the culture and contributions of the Chinese to Hawaiian life. Like so many created displays it lacked the character of the real thing. We found in the remains of the old Chinese quarter of Honolulu a truer picture of Chinese industriousness. There in old wooden stores and shops we saw the Chinese and their descendants plying their trades in much the same way as we had seen all across the Pacific.

It is tragic for future generations that colorful old Honolulu is being demolished under the guise of progress. While other cities like Atlanta, St. Louis, Seattle, and San Francisco are struggling to keep a portion of their heritage intact, Honolulu proceeds in haste to destroy her colorful past. I had spent three earlier years in Hawaii, 1941 to 1943, and recall the narrow streets of old Honolulu with their pleasing mixture of oriental, tropical, and New England architecture. There was character in those buildings that concrete can only dream of.

But other changes are also happening on Oahu as economic pressures reshape the lives of most people. My earlier acquaintance with Hawaii was a result of the war years. I see now that I was fortunate to have been there the year before World War II, when it was possible to enjoy a territorial culture without the political and economic pressures brought on by becoming the fiftieth state. At that time the sugar growers still maintained independent mills, and towns like Ewa grew up around them. The small Japanese stores furnished us with souvenirs, silk shirts, and sukiyaki. Few of them remain, for the closing of the Ewa sugar mill and the building of a freeway in another area has shifted the population and changed their lifestyle.

The old dirigible base at Ewa where I was serving with the marines when Pearl Harbor became headlines has been gobbled up by adjoining Barbers Point Naval Air Station. Ford Island in the middle of Pearl Harbor, where I served my first years as a newly commissioned navy ensign is now almost devoid of navy life. And I'll never forget the U.S.S. *Arizona,* which I had seen in prewar days tied up at Ford Island. Now it lies a sunken hulk under a concrete memorial to a war which brought the world closer together and forever changed the life of all Pacific peoples.

Although I found the urban areas changing for the worse, I also found the rural areas changed but still retaining a tropical charm. There may be few bargains left in Hawaii for yachties to take advantage of, but a fifty-cent bus ride around Oahu is certainly one of them. Betty and I took off one day on a bus to see windward Oahu. Across Nuuanu Pali to beautiful coral fringed Kaneohe Bay, then north along the shoreline where tradewinds provide a naturally air-conditioned climate. This is also the wet side of Oahu, and greenery thrives in gardens, fields and on the slopes of the Koolau mountain range. The bus continues its winding starting-and-stopping route around Kahuku point the north-ernmost corner of Hawaii and then follows the southwest trending coastline to Haleiwa, which was our destination.

The North Shore of Oahu has been a surfer's paradise even before fiberglass boards, and it has attracted people who, to a large extent, try to live off the land while they surf off the sea. In short, the communities have become communally-oriented much to the dismay of some of the local citizens. Beer and "grass" are much in abundance in this far-out community, supported in part by macrame and handicraft stores. While it provides its own unique atmosphere, it is hardly what one would call either a good residential or tourist scene.

Haleiwa does have a small boat harbor cut into the head of Waialua Bay with slips for small boats but larger craft moor to pilings. Visiting boats must anchor out in the bay. Waialua Bay is more of an open bight at the outlet of Anahulu Stream, and during the winter months high waves and surge become a menace to the harbor. It will take a few million years of patience for the coral reef to develop and offer some protection to this pleasant little harbor.

Following a late lunch at Haleiwa we boarded another bus for the last half of our trip. The route took us down the center of the island through the rich sugar and pineapple fields, which are still Hawaii's principal source of income. Late afternoon found us back on city streets in time to catch the evening rush traffic. The bus wound its way through the suburbs of Honolulu, finally reaching Ala Moana Center where our bargain tour of Oahu started and ended. We were pleased to have seen some of rural Oahu and its less hectic pace of life.

The summer months were wearing on and changes were taking place at Ala Wai harbor. No longer were there new arrivals from the mainland, instead, departures were the common events. Some lucky boats were heading south and west to see the great South Pacific which we had just left. Others were departing for the mainland including friends like *Troubador, Amazing Grace,* and *Lauree Sue,* which had shared the same Pacific waters with us all the way to New Zealand. Now it was our turn to think about the long passage to California.

All this while Roger had enjoyed associating with other crews around the harbor and we weren't surprised when one day, coming back from Waikiki Beach, we found him in the process of moving out. We were in a sense relieved, for out relations had become strained and, although we had agreed to take him all the way to California, it would have been less than a happy boat.

The evening's happy hour was more relaxed than usual for we had had a good day at the beach and had solved a problem. The question of crew was left in limbo, for we knew Honolulu had a big crew pool from which to choose. For the moment though we relaxed and let the events of the day lead us into a bit of reminiscing of our Hawaiian visit. We recalled in particular:

—sitting in quarantine on our country's 200th birthday
—the luxuriant growth of plant life on the windward slopes
—The desolation of the recent lava flows on the young island of Hawaii

—the early way of Hawaiian life so well displayed at the City of Refuge National Park

—orchids of many varieties growing wild in the forests

—Banyan trees with their immense spread of branches and multiple trunks

—sharp differences in climate such as between Hulopoe and Manele Bays at Lanai

—tantalizing aromas pervading the air from Kona coffee, macadamia nuts, pikake, pineapples, and plumeria

—living at the bottom of a fishbowl while docked at Ala Wai in the shadows of the high rise hotels

—Bishop Museum and its wealth of knowledge on the islands and peoples of the Pacific

—the contrast between artificial tourist Hawaii and peaceful natural Hawaii

—Oahu's only free visitors' attraction—the U.S.S. *Arizona* Memorial

—Polynesian friendliness such as we found the Pacific over

14

The Eventful Passage Home

August was wearing on rapidly and it was time for us to plan our passage to the mainland. We had earlier set September 1 as the latest departure date, giving us one month in which to make the passage before the October build-up of gales along the route. I also recalled that our now-defunct insurance policy had contained a few lines of small print which excluded coverage of yachts traveling from Hawaii to the mainland after October 15. While my negative attitude toward the insurance industry had not improved since Samoa, I was willing to use their self-protective clauses to our advantage. We had experienced only one gale in our Pacific travels so far and didn't want to stretch our luck on the last leg, so we set about in earnest to get *Horizon* ready and maybe even leave a few days before September 1.

Now we really appreciated the use of Carol and David's car, affectionately called by them "Gopher," since it was used to "go-fer this and go-fer that." We had learned of a wholesale grocery business near Honolulu Harbor and a produce dealer near Kewalo Boat Harbor where we could get substantial discounts on quantity purchases. It took two trips to each place to satisfy our needs. One, to place the order from the catalog and the other to pick up the groceries. Poor "Gopher"—she was loaded so heavily that, like her namesake, she appeared to sink right into the ground. But she bravely struggled back to Ala Wai, where Betty and I made many long treks from parking lot to boat carrying the groceries. Once again we vowed to have a durable shopping cart aboard *Horizon* on our next cruise. It certainly would have proven more useful than the two folding bicycles we had carried as far as New Zealand. But we managed to get the cases of canned food, bags of flour and boxes of apples safely aboard. In the process we felt, once again, the stirrings of new adventures.

Our crew position still remained unfilled in spite of numerous crew-wanted cards I had posted about the marina and in local marine stores. Not that we didn't have a lot of applicants, but having had two crewmen previously, we were now more cagey in our selection. In fact, our experience led to writing the following set of guidelines for boats seeking a crew:

Check the applicant out as thoroughly as possible beforehand, since it is better to delay departure or to do without than have a stranger spoil your fun.

Be frank with the applicant at the interview and demand that he or she be the same, because you will both pay for deception in the end.

If you are confident of your own abilities, don't demand experience—go for personality and a willingness to learn.

Take only one unknown person at a time: don't load up on potential trouble.

Agree only to take the crewman to the next port and be sure he or she has a valid passport and sufficient finances (airline ticket at least) to travel on from there.

Don't let a crewman's seasickness get your passage off to a bad start, insist that he or she take a motion-sickness remedy for a few days ahead and a few days after departure. This will be a good test of cooperativeness.

If he or she is on a medication be certain you know what it is, the reason for it, and that an ample supply is available for the intended period.

Try to determine if there are any hangups which may make your crew a liability at sea. Can he or she go aloft to help replace a broken halyard? Is he or she at home in the water? Is diet a problem? Above all, is your intended crew clean in both a hygienic sense and in habit?

Crew people wandering the Pacific are not the most stable individuals we have met. Many are wanderers who want a life without responsibility, and others are escapists who can't adjust to the realities of life. We wanted neither, so our search continued.

One day a young man showed up who simply wanted the experience of sailing to California. He was working at Waikiki pedaling a "pedicab." This told us that he was not a free-loader but had some initiative. As we talked we also sensed a compatible personality and, when he volunteered that he had no boating experience whatsoever, we concluded he was honest also. This applicant was promising, so we continued to probe his background.

Chris was a recent graduate of the University of California at Santa Barbara who had arrived here via Japan where he had flown for a vacation. Now, on his way back to California to seek work, he had stopped over in Honolulu for more vacation and to earn money to pay his air fare to the mainland. Chris looked good to us even without any experience, since he seemed willing and able to learn. I checked him out by telephone with the head of the Santa Barbara Parks and Recreation Department, where he had worked supporting himself while in school. The reference was favorable so we signed him up without further ado. He was to become our favorite crewman.

Between periods of getting provisions aboard and talking with crew applicants, we charted our homeward course. Landfall was set for San Francisco so that we could see the Bay Area once again and renew acquaintances with some of our friends who live there. Our sailing strategy would be simple—steer north hard on a starboard tack and turn east at the top of the Pacific high pressure cell. The strategy also included filling our diesel fuel tank since winds through the Pacific High at this season range from light to none at all. This passage would take us out of the tradewind belt and into the region of variable winds, which we had last experienced in the New Zealand–Austral Islands passage. It would also take us out of the balmy tropics with its comfortable way of life.

Many of our cruising friends had already departed and we were psyched up for sailing, so, we arbitrarily set Monday, August 23, as our departure date.

Sunday we made a trip to the NOAA Weather Center at Honolulu Airport to get the latest weather prognostications. The Pacific high pressure area was sitting NNW of Hawaii, which was abnormally far west and meant we probably would not round it in textbook fashion. This was not expected to change in the next 72 hours, which was as far out on the weather limb as the meteorologists would venture. We once again came to the conclusion that sail boats travel so slowly that once your passage is started, most weather forecasts have little relevance and you are concerned principally with the weather you see and feel. We did establish that weather for a Monday departure looked fair, there was no likelihood of hurricane activity from the Eastern Pacific, and gales were at a minimum. So, let's go!

We departed Ala Wai at 1125 Monday, casting into the waters our going-away leis. As we watched them leisurely drift toward shore we took encouragement from this omen that we, too, would again return. Our course took us west around Barbers Point and then north along the leeward side of the island. We departed Kaena Point at 2100 and Betty took up her first regular 2100–midnight watch. Winds were light at force 2 from the ENE.

Horizon's log records five days of pleasant sailing before we hit our first windless period. That occurred on the 28th and we motored for 15 hours in glassy seas deviating occasionally from course to pick up Japanese glass fishing floats. Our course, with intermittent motoring, continued NNE until September 4 when the winds shifted to the SE and we were able to sail due east at last. Days were warm but nights were cool enough for long trousers. On our fourteenth day out, 1351 miles from Honolulu with 1190 miles to Point Reyes above San Francisco, the speedometer quit working. Chris volunteered to clear it, so, with bathing suit and safety harness, he clambered over the side into the blue Pacific. It didn't take him long to see the trouble—plastic twine had wrapped itself around the small propeller and stopped it. Chris came up for a knife and he soon had it cleared and working. We raised sails and continued on our way.

The barometer had climbed from 1018 millibars to a maximum of 1028 on our sixteenth day out and we were obviously crossing the Pacific High, but winds were erratic. Occasionally they reached force 5 but mostly about force 2 and as often from the southeast as from the northwest. It kept us busy changing sails to keep *Horizon* moving toward California.

It wasn't until the twenty-second day out of Honolulu (September 14) that the vaunted northwest wind positively set in and then with a vengeance to make up for its lateness. By nightfall we were broad reaching to the east at 6 knots under working jib and mizzen only. The barometer continued to drop and the size of the waves became noticeably larger. By midnight we were down to storm job and reefed mizzen, still doing 4 knots and headed east. *Horizon* rode comfortably over these large quartering waves under the positive control of the Polaris self-steering rudder. The skies remained clear, but blowing spray and an occasional slapping wave prompted us to close all hatches and ports, leaving only the main companionway hatch open, since it was protected by the windscreen and dodger.

At daybreak I shot Saturn and Rigel from the safety of the cockpit since the seas were too rough to stand higher. Betty prepared breakfast, after which we all went about our morning duties—Betty putting the galley in order and preparing to bake bread, Chris minding the cockpit, and I in the aft cabin computing the morning sights. I was eager to get a position since dead reckoning put us only 100 miles away from land, which we could make in 24 hours with reasonable wind.

At approximately 0830 *Horizon* rose to the top of still another large wave, rolling moderately to starboard. As the wave passed under us in a fury of foam we rolled back to port, sliding smoothly down the back side of the wave. Chris, who had been fascinated with waves since our departure and marveled at their "awesome power," next recalled looking to weather and seeing an immense wave tailgating the first. Before he could close the remaining open hatch, we had rolled up the face of that wave onto our starboard side and fallen with a resounding thud onto our beam end into the trough. The crest broke over us. The wave passed and *Horizon* quickly rolled upright to resume her earlier easy rolling motion.

First to recover from this rolldown was Betty, who called aft from the galley, "Earl, are you all right?" With some uncertainty I answered in the affirmative. She then called to the cockpit: "Chris, are you all right?" Chris, calm but wet, replied, "All okay in the cockpit." Her next words told me the state of things up forward—"Man the bilge pumps!" Chris jumped to the cockpit pump while I unlimbered the big Edson emergency pump in the aft cabin. In doing so, I noted very little water in the bilge sump and no apparent flow into the bilge, so I took the opportunity for a quick look topside. There was Chris completely enveloped in yards of Acrilan fabric. Nothing less than the entire windscreen, dodger and awning—all completely shredded. Little else remained in the cockpit. Everything loose—brushes, fish cleaning board, cushions, and even a heavy winch handle from its own holder had managed to find a way overboard. But Chris was unhurt and, like us, thankful that he had followed the boat's rule to attach your personal safety harness whenever alone in the cockpit or in heavy weather.

A quick survey of the boat showed no obvious structural damage, no broken ports, and no apparent leaking. But there was Betty in the salon standing ankle deep in water and waist high in assorted furnishings and food. Everything from the port side of the cabin which had not been securely anchored down had found its way to the starboard side. Even double-latched drawers managed to find a way out of their restraints to join the cushions, canned goods, apples and oranges, silverware, and other gear making up a three-foot-deep pile of assorted stuff.

Finding that the hull and sailing rig were still sound and the crew unhurt, I asked Chris to turn downwind and lower the reefed mizzen sail. Betty and I then turned to the task of cleaning up the main cabin. Books and cushions were thrown into the dry forecastle. Canned goods were randomly placed in lockers and storage bins. Broken glass from kerosene lamps and other broken articles were thrown overboard. Eventually we got to the bottom of the pile and found the sponge rubber-backed shag rug thoroughly soaked, so we jettisoned it in order to continue with our cleanup of the cabin. Drawers were replaced and locked again. Paper goods, paper boxes, and dried foods had fared badly, and much went over the side.

After clearing the cabin sole of debris we bailed with buckets to empty the water out of the main cabin which for some strange design reason had no drainage into the bilge. Later and with some hesitation, Betty suggested that we check the refrigerated ice chest. Opening the lid, we found that it was completely filled with sea water and its contents were afloat. The starboard side rolldown had opened the ice chest lid just as the breaking wave came through the main companionway hatch. Besides drenching the cabin, the wave had filled the 17-cubic-foot chest whose lid closed neatly again as we rolled upright. I uncorked the drain but by then a large amount of paper had come loose and immediately plugged it, so we started bailing again to salvage our beer, butter, and cheese.

The morning wore on and we started to breathe a little easier as we made headway. Betty continued to clean the main cabin while I went aft to see what had happened in the aft cabin. It was evident that the absence of built-ins had allowed boxes, duffle bags, navigation books, papers, and island souvenirs to hurl themselves across the cabin. But it was the unrestrained skipper who had done the most damage. I had been catapulted across the cabin colliding with the open head door, breaking panels and frame. There was little water in the aft cabin as it had been buttoned up tightly. Cleanup was limited to restowing duffle bags, locating and putting back the navigation equipment, and filing books and charts back in their proper places.

With the boat sailing comfortably downwind, Chris reasonably happy in the sunshine, and both cabins fairly well straightened up, I started a thorough inspection of the boat from stem-head to transom. I could find absolutely no hull damage or signs of leaks in hull or ports. Chris and I took a careful look at the rigging and there was no damage to any of it. Exterior damage was limited to the awning, dodger, windscreen and four weather cloths which were all in shreds. Three of the starboard lifeline stanchions were bent 20 to 30 degrees and the starboard life ring holder looked like a pretzel.

It was mid-afternoon before wind and wave abated so that we could have a three-way conversation in the cockpit about the morning's excitement. While the early morning Coast Guard weather report from San Francisco reported 15 to 25 knot winds in our area, we had logged them at Beaufort force 7—28 to 33 knots—a moderate gale. The waves were impressively high and it appeared to Chris, who had been observing them, that a double-crested wave with a very short distance between crests had done us in. Certainly, even a full gale couldn't have knocked us down with the small sail area we were carrying. After the first crest passed under us we had simply rolled up the face of the immediate following wave with no apparent resistance from hull stability. Now in a trough, the sails were also blanketed. When the boat reached 90 degrees, having no more support from the water, it simply fell down the face of the wave onto the starboard beam end. To add insult to injury, the crest of the wave then broke on top of us.

After arriving in San Francisco two days later, I visited the NOAA Forecast Center at Redwood City and reviewed with the marine forecaster the synoptic charts for September 15. They showed a high of 1028 mbs located 600 miles WNW of our position and a low of 1008 mbs located 250 miles east of us. Our barometer had read 1013 mbs and we were located in the midst of a steep pressure gradient towards the low with locally higher winds than reported. The synoptic data showed waves to be 5 to 6 feet high and a swell to 13 feet. But of greater interest was the fact that both swell and wave were shown as having natural periods of less than 5 seconds. (Swells normally run 12 to 16 seconds.) At dockside I made a simple determination of the rolling period of *Horizon* as well as several other sailboats finding it approximately 4 seconds. It was now possible to reason that with the wave motion period and the boat's natural period in roll about equal, that no natural restoring moment would come into play and we simply rolled 90 degrees in phase with the wave. We have since pondered the question—would a deep keel instead of our shoal draft keel have tripped us in the fall and triggered a 360 degree roll? It's happened before.

In retrospect we were probably negligent in not closing all hatches when force 7 winds were reached. This would have minimized water damage below. But the rolldown remained a freak coincidence of wave action. However, I think I will consider more running than reaching under similar conditions in the future. We were thankful afterwards for a staunch boat that could right itself quickly. We also looked back four years to our original procurement criteria calling for a low profile and small ports. The one-in-a-million occurred but *Horizon* brought us through.

The following day, wind and seas abated and we opened the boat fully and put everything out to dry. The sun shone and we all felt better in the moderate seas. We cheerfully accepted the one extra day of passage time caused by the gale which forced us to run south while we recovered from the damage. At nightfall we sighted the light on Farallon Island guarding the outer entrance to San Francisco.

Light winds continued through the night and progress was slow. At daybreak the breeze quit entirely and we ignominiously motored through the Golden Gate. Our Pacific cruise was over. We had only to traverse the 400 miles from San Francisco to Los Angeles to end our odyssey.

At the Alameda Marina we were visited by many San Francisco friends of long standing with whom we shared our latest adventure. But evenings by ourselves, for Chris had now left us, we relived our most exciting passage recalling:

—quietly watching our leis drift shoreward as we left Ala Wai harbor

—a growing nostalgia feeling sailing out of Polynesian waters, which had been our homeland for 16 months

—windless days in the Pacific High

—watching the barometer climb to new heights and descend slowly as we traversed the high pressure region

—the pleasing company of our new crewman

—the instant of terror felt when we were rolled down by the big wave

—followed by a great sense of relief to find no personal injuries or significant boat damage

—wondering if maybe the wave was telling us not to go home

—the welcome sight of the Golden Gate after a 25 day, 2555-mile passage

Epilogue

Even though land-bound and a hundred miles from *Horizon*, our 17,000-mile odyssey remains a living part of us. In retrospect it all seems so simple. The routine of long passages makes one delightful day at sea like the next but always leading to that smudge on the horizon that says you have navigated to a new land. Anticipation of new scenery, interesting people, and days swinging lazily at anchor in sparkling waters makes you quickly forget the 24-hour schedule that you lived with enroute. You are pleased with yourself, your crew, and your boat, and your confidence is subtly bolstered by yet another passage to still another island paradise. It can become an endless way of life and the Pacific Ocean could occupy your days to eternity.

We are satisfied with our accomplishment. We took a stock boat like so many gracing the waters of our crowded marinas, and with our own resources converted it to a first-rate cruising boat. Much weekend sailing experience plus some rational planning enabled us to properly equip and provision it for a 17,000-mile adventure. Nothing professional to start with—we learned by doing in our shakedown cruise.

Most of the boats cruising the waters of the world are manned by amateurs like ourselves. They come from all walks of life and a multitude of countries. At your first island anchorage you will become a bona fide member of the world cruising fraternity. We were pleased with our acceptance by veteran cruising people who have been at sea longer than we had been thinking about our trip. And we were doubly pleased with our acceptance by the youthful crews who took all this adventure stuff less seriously than we did. They just had fun.

Our timing was not perfect. We should have done it earlier in life so that we could repeat it many times. But our timing wasn't wrong either, for we were able to enjoy the vigorous sailing life and convert our previous sedentary selves into trim sailors.

We had no problems that couldn't be satisfactorily solved along the way. Health posed no concern and we observed that the common yachtie was, without doubt, more healthy than the landlubber. Besides living 24 hours a day in an outdoor environment, the yachtie combines a simple diet with plenty of exercise to maintain his well-being as our Creator had intended.

And there were other benefits to this simple way of life. Our records show an approximate monthly expenditure enroute of about $450.00 for all purposes, including food and drink for a crew of three, personal and goodwill expenses for Betty and myself, plus all maintenance costs on *Horizon*. Spartan you say? Not on your life! We lived in the grandeur of the sun and the sea surrounded by nature's finest flora and fauna to say nothing of the true kinship of the other yachties.

But occasionally a pall would be cast over our fun, for mail-call would bring word of the death of a work associate, a friend, or relative. Many, like us, in their prime, but who never stepped back to take a broader look at life. Others, our seniors, who just let time slip by and never sought the big adventure while they could. We take some consolation knowing that they at least shared in our travels through the newsletters which we mailed from ports of call.

Only when the yachtie makes his arrival at a new port do the fetters of civilization challenge his well-being. For most, if not all, require that yachts properly check in (and out) at predesignated ports in order that their countries may control immigration as well as prevent illicit trade. (Some yachties are not above earning a dishonest buck.) While it often proved a challenge, it was also an interesting experience, for these were our first contacts with the peoples of a new island or port. Our problems with officialdom were few. We learned that it was an advantage to be prompt, neat, and well prepared in our meetings with immigration, customs, port captains, and agriculture. I say "we," because Betty's presence always added amiability to the discussion, suppressing any signs of undesirable antagonism. One should not underestimate the influence of the female in official negotiations. It often took patience beyond belief to contain our enthusiasm to see the wonders of a new port while the officials methodically pursued paperwork. But it is their country and you are well advised to be courteous to your hosts.

World cruising is a return to a primordial society wherein the individual is free to choose both his friends and his environment. The sailboat, however slow, gives mobility to seek ports and anchorage, which accord the most satisfaction to yachtsmen. The yachtsman lives the simple life wherein the world of nature is his playground and his daily life is unfettered by over concern with goal and ambitions. One can say that cruising is one of the last refuges for the individual to exercise independence in his own way.

But as we found out there is an ever-present spectre hovering over this idyllic life. Some day that cruise will come to an end and the realities of civilization will have to be faced. On our return we sensed a trauma in urban living that we had not noticed before, probably because we had grown up with it. Now we had developed an exterior point of view which told us that it is not good. The noise of the urban world literally leaves one's ears ringing and the soft speech with which we conversed at sea could not be heard on land. The automobile traffic had certainly gotten worse as people apparently forgot the threat of a gasoline shortage—or were they simply using up their share before it disappeared? Air pollution, the by-product of a seemingly aimless hustling about by motorcar was still there and, in fact, was spreading over formerly untainted areas of the coastline. Open spaces were surrendering to land developers as once proud city centers deteriorated through neglect. Land, like products of the factory, had become enmeshed in an appalling throwaway economy. While we Americans had never been faced with a lack of raw materials from which to fashion things to make life more pleasant, the future may be different. Little New Zealand, with few natural resources, showed us that the maintenance of hard goods and the recycling of materials can meet the needs of the consumer as well as provide jobs to the wage earner. To them conservation has already become a way of life.

More apparent to us now is the artificial way of life in the cities. On our return we were awed by the range of products for sale in the modern shopping centers of Hawaii and California, which I am certain is nothing more than typical of the entire United States. Gee-gaws of endless and indescribable variety fill the market shelves, and you are led to believe that life cannot exist without them. And maybe the big city can't, for we also observed more artificial entertainment than we had ever remembered. Pioneered by Disneyland (known the Pacific over!) there now seems no end to small worlds of adventure to amuse one for a few hours with little expenditure of personal energy. Except for the hippie minority, a natural way of life no longer appears to be an objective of society.

Cautious individuals that Betty and I have always been, our concerns about the security of *Horizon* in new ports turned out to be largely needless. Aside from some unique island social customs concerning communal property, the islanders are respectful of visitors and certainly posed no threat to our bodily security. I wish I could say that for my own America. For again, the exterior viewpoint tells me that people in the U.S. are fearful—probably more so of lawsuits than of crime in the streets, which is seemingly now an accepted risk of urban life. Insurance, once considered a hedge against physical loss of car, house or life, now emphasizes protection against lawsuits for misdeeds,

What do we do for an encore? (PHOTO: AEROSPACE CORPORATION)

neglect, spontaneous action and even inaction in emergencies. The level of such fear certainly increased during our absence, as evidenced by the numerous private police forces, security fences, and burglar alarms being sold the public. The right to live a private and safe life on land appears seriously imperiled at this point.

But here we are back in the big city and what do we do for an encore? Our attachment to the world of cruising is obvious and one which we will continue to nurture. Land bound for a while, we can live with our reminiscences of the pleasures of sailing to new ports of call, meeting new peoples, and encountering cruising friends from earlier ports. We cannot predict the future, but it would be nice to have one more opportunity to sail before sunset. And we still advise others: Go now! Sail soon! Go before it's too late.

APPENDIX A

The Anatomy of Horizon

One has only to look at the variety of cruising boats at anchor in overseas harbors to realize that there is little commonality to world cruising boat design or construction. While ketch rigs, diesel engines, and long keels seem to show up most often, one is hard pressed to further define the nature of the ideal world cruising boat. All across the Pacific we sought a common design denominator and found none of general acceptance. One yachtsman claimed that the typical cruising boat was built by the owner. Another said that it was what you had when the urge struck, a third observed that the only thing in common was that the boats were paid for. To these we add our own observation that the boats with which we have shared many beautiful Pacific anchorages have all been fitted out for efficient handling by small crews (1, 2, or 3 persons) and were equipped for self-sufficiency over long periods of time. Sailboats they are, for only the wind can give you the range to cover the vast ocean distances reaching to the exotic and fabled islands of adventure. To this almost indescribable confusion of design and construction we have added another choice and that is the stock production boat modified for long range cruising.

Stock production boats are somewhat of a novelty on the world cruising scene; most cruising boats are, in fact, custom built variations of traditional Atkins, Hanna, Archer, Herreshoff, Garden, or similar designs. Papeete, the crossroads of the Pacific, brought many questions from other yachts on the suitability of *Horizon*. In particular, those yachtsmen from the Caribbean who had seen many Out Island 41s in charter service were interested in our opinion. Now, with over 17,000 miles of water under the keel, we can answer their questions with confidence.

Our reasons for seeking a stock boat were threefold: (1) to take advantage of cost savings which accrue from production; (2) to benefit from design improvements found necessary on earlier models; and (3) to be able to obtain a boat on short notice to meet our personal schedule. But the real question was, could we find a suitable stock boat for this purpose?

To guide our search we created a list of criteria to sort out possibilities on paper and thin down to a manageable size the ranks of those worth seeing. These criteria were:

—30-foot waterline (minimum), but not longer than 40 feet overall
—long keel, inside ballast, and attached rudder capable of safe grounding
—low profile with a moderate freeboard and small ports
—fiberglass hull and decks with moderate use of wood trim
—separable living quarters with internal passages
—6'6" headroom and bunk length
—cool interior with good ventilation
—large stowage volume
—ketch rig with aluminum spars and stainless steel rigging
—diesel engine in worldwide service
—good engine accessibility but protected from the weather
—500 mile (minimum) powered cruising range
—120 gals (minimum) fresh water tankage

Since no one boat could possibly meet all these criteria, we made a graded evaluation of the design features of each candidate boat asking ourselves (a) can we comfortably live and sail with this feature as is? or (b) can it be modified to meet our criteria? or (c) if missing, can it be reasonably added? Three consecutive negative answers eliminated that boat from further consideration. In fact, it took only a casual assessment of the modern racing designs to determine that fin keels, spade rudders, and lightweight construction were incompatible with coral heads, small crews, and long passages.

This still left us with many design possibilities in the racing/cruising and charter cruising classes, so we applied a few other discriminants to further narrow the field. One was, it had to be a U.S. built hull to enable carrying passengers for hire if later opportunity arose. Another was that the boat had to be a recent design to benefit from the performance and technology advances made by the boating industry. Lastly, it had to be in large scale production so that we could order one off the line already embodying production improvements found necessary by actual use.

The search for our future home took one year of correspondence, boat shows, factory visits, and talks with owners and brokers. As that year progressed, our search gravitated to the new center cockpit designs being introduced then for charter cruising in the Caribbean. Finally one rose to the top of the list and that was the Morgan Out Island 41. It met most of our criteria and we were able to visualize the modifications we would have to make to meet the others—assuming that the builder would cooperate.

Customizing on a production line tends to be counterproductive and this was to be no exception. But after some give and take discussions through the broker, Morgan Yachts agreed not to install anything that would later interfere with our modification plan. An outstanding example of this cooperation followed our insistence on having an inside passage between saloon and aft cabin. Morgan designers carefully left a clearway on the starboard side of the engine room, which allowed us to later construct a 42-inch-high crawl through between galley and aft head. Our unwavering insistence on this passageway probably added further impetus to his developing a walk-through optional cabin arrangement for the production boat.

The builder offered a long list of equipment options which we carefully considered, as these would not only save us time but they were quite economical if factory installed. Of the 124 options which were then available (excluding sails) we selected 30 but ordered only 20, since the other ten, such as extra handrails, bilge pump, and three-bladed prop had all become standard in the meantime and we were seeing our first benefits from production experience. Most of the remaining options were intended for dockside living or weekend sailing and not of interest to us. One option that we have dearly regretted not taking was their "genoa package." Our broker had assured us (and we could not deal with Morgan direct) that the genoa package could be installed at commissioning and the remaining deck fittings could then be purchased individually to our own liking. This was not to be the case since the interior headliner prevented access to through-bolt the track, and we had to settle for fixed position lead blocks.

Our major equipment option was the ketch rig. Probably no other part of the boat has received as much admiration as this strong sailing rig and it certainly has given us a sense of well-being. With the exception of a shorter mainsail boom, the ketch mainmast rig is identical to that of the well-developed sloop. The mizzen rigging, however, was not well developed and the stock running backstays equipped with pelican hooks proved totally impractical to use. They were soon replaced with adjustable block and tackle stays, which, while not sophisticated, can be set from the cockpit and ably carry the forward load of the mizzen genoa luff. Likewise, the archaic midships sheeting of the mizzen boom was replaced in New Zealand with separate port and starboard sheets permitting precise sail shaping from the cockpit as well as holding the mizzen boom steady in sloppy seas. (Since we didn't use the mainsail as much, we didn't bother to change its sheeting.)

A second major option selected was the 175-gallon fuel tank in place of the standard 60-gallon tank. (The two 60-gallon tank option was not feasible in view of our insistence on an internal passageway.) While we certainly were pleased to have the resulting 1000-mile-plus cruising range under power, the larger tank, located on the port side of the engine room seriously impaired access to the fuel injection pump, lube oil filter, the port auxiliary water tank and part of the steering cable run.

Paradoxically, sales appeal worked both for and against the adaptation of this stock boat to world cruising. There is great aesthetic appeal from the beautiful sweeping curves of the cockpit coaming and the nicely rounded cabin corners of shining gel coat. But on a wet sloppy night at sea when you have to go forward alone to change a headsail you would rather have traction than aesthetics. The selective use of pressure-sensitive nonskid tape alleviated this problem to some extent. We also gave the cockpit area additional safety features of a mid-ships pulpit and windscreen spanning the forward cockpit coaming, a gallows to support the main boom when the sail is furled, and an awning to give relief from the hot tropic sun.

Internally, the floating fiberglass headliner provided a clean, light appearance, but it also made equipment attachment difficult without creating unsightly cutouts. However, the thermal insulating qualities of the floating headliner far outweighed any of its shortcomings as we found out in the hot and humid climates of the Samoan and Tongan Islands.

Making reasonable modifications and additions to this stock boat were relatively easy because production design yielded an uncomplicated construction. In making modifications it also became clear to us that the key similarity between this popular charter boat and our concept of a world cruising design was volume. The standard accommodations for nine persons became readily convertible to stowage space for a long-range cruising complement of three persons. First to be converted was the starboard pilot berth, which became a three-unit cabinet providing 21 cubic feet of volume with additional tray space on top. Next, the two cavernous forward hanging lockers were equipped with shelves outboard and below, while still retaining the clothes hanging capability. The forward locker was also fitted with a bonded stores compartment. The space under the aft companionway ladder became an oilskin locker, and, since it is located directly over the bilge sump, it was also an ideal place to locate the big Edson emergency bilge pump.

Part of this large internal volume had to be made into a navigation station, which was lacking in the stock design and woefully inadequate in all competing designs that we evaluated. We wanted a 32 x 42 inch chart table with 4 inches of chart stowage. Space was found in the aft cabin by locating the table amidships in place of the standard cushion used for 'thwartship sleeping. It was built to standing height giving the needed surface area and chart stowage space plus a bonus of two more drawers and a linen locker underneath. Emergency steering, not present in the stock boat, now became more complicated, since the head end of the rudder post was now under the navigation table. This conflict was resolved with a dogleg-shaped emergency tiller handle (removeable) extending through the side of the navigation table and operated by the helmsman at the aft cabin hatch opening. Even though his outside visibility is restricted, he can steer by an auxiliary compass until repairs can be made. While this table has all the features of a good navigator's station, we really believe it should be located in the main cabin alongside the companionway ladder—right where our 17-cubic-foot refrigerated ice chest is.

The stock boat while having a great volume had a serious lack of built-in cabinets and drawers. For charter work, casually piled duffle and loose boxes may be acceptable, but not for the long-range cruise. Take that 14-foot beam at the galley, it yields 2-foot-deep stowage spaces outboard of ice chest and stove but they are not reachable with a normal human arm. We made six slideout trays 2 feet long to take advantage of that space. And that large top opening ice chest was only half useable because of man's limited arm length. We stored cases of beer, butter, and cheese in the hard-to-get-at aft end and bottom so as not to waste the space.

While volume was generally convertible for cruising modifications, weight was not. With three month's provisions on board, 170 gallons of water and 175 gallons of fuel, *Horizon* sat 4 to 6 inches lower in the water than in casual weekend sailing, with the result that the deep galley sinks would no longer drain by gravity. We found this after departing Los Angeles, so in San Diego we installed a Whale sink drain pump that solved the unexpected plumbing problem.

Ventilation was a neglected item on all boat designs that we had evaluated, probably because it is so hard to implement. Nevertheless, it was essential to comfortable living below, so we attacked the problem in several ways. First, the small, plastic water-trap cowl vents installed for the heads were replaced by our own design high-volume, closeable cowl vents. The builder agreed to omit installation of the standard fixed ports in the aft cabin trunk so that we could install Vetus opening ports. For these and all other openings and hatchways we provided Velcro-attached fiberglass screens, which proved to be a wise move. Internally, we ventilated locker and head doors with either large holes cut in the top and bottom frames or with inset louvered panels. We had no mildew problems, but we don't know whether it was due to our additional ventilation schemes or the fact that with the engineroom doors open, the internal cabin air circulation is good regardless of outside wind direction.

A last major modification was the installation of dependable ground tackle to handle a variety of anchoring situations. For this we selected a 60-pound CQR plow anchor on 240 feet of ⅜-inch chain as our working anchor, keeping the standard 35-pound CQR with nylon rode as a spare. The 60-pound CQR worked nicely off the standard stemhead roller chock even though it was made for the 35-pound plow. The windlass is a manual Simpson-Lawrence 555, capable of handling both the working anchor chain and the spare anchor rope rode. The voluminous forepeak of the boat was easily divided into separate lockers for chain and rope, but the deck above had to be heavily reinforced internally with aluminum angles to carry the load from the windlass. The ground tackle arrangements have been very satisfactory, and the stemhead roller chock was an invaluable part of our successful anchoring in Pacific harbors.

Structural integrity is one of the expected benefits of production design and testing, and our hull, number 95 in the series, embodied several improvements found necessary by earlier experience. But, alas, even 94 trial horses were insufficient to eliminate all problems. Early in our 28-day passage from Mazatlan to the Marquesas Islands, a water leak developed, which we were unable to stop from the interior. In fact, we could not even find it because the suspect hull-deck mating joint was neatly hidden behind the interior head-liner and hull-liner. Underway, the bow wave would force water behind the hollow rub-rail covering the hull-deck joint, where it would flow aft until it found a gap in the epoxied joint to flow inside the boat. Leakage was about one quart per hour and, once inside, it flowed through lockers, into storage bins, and finally across the full length of the main cabin sole where it was sponged up by the person on watch. Temporary sealing with duct tape was done at Nuku Hiva, and at Papeete we acquired a nonhardening butyl mastic that we liberally squeezed through the external gaps to help fill the interior voids from stem to stern. This apparently overcame the production fault because we no longer found wet carpets, rusty canned goods, and sodden books.

On the plus side of the ledger we can point to an auxiliary power plant installation made for cruising. This should come as no surprise since auxiliary power plant demands for tightly scheduled charter and weekend cruising are probably much more severe than in long distance cruising. In 17,000 miles of sailing plus earlier local sailing we only reached our 800th engine hour—a goodly share of this time had been used in battery charging and refrigeration. The Westerbeke 4-107 diesel, Paragon transmission, and 3-bladed propeller are well matched to the hull. Our average fuel consumption has been ⅔ gallon per hour, burning whatever was available in Mexico, Samoa, and New Zealand. The automobile-type voltage regulator supplied with the engine was inadequate for daily battery charging on a one-hour-or-less running time, so a manual charge control was added. This permitted continuous charge of up to 40 amps to match electrical needs. Unfortunately, we have found the maintenance and spare part manuals furnished with the engine woefully inadequate to solve problems.

Custom-designed long-range cruising boats have for many years incorporated separate engine rooms, and they make a lot of sense in a boat of this size. Corrosion of mechanical and electrical equipment from salt or fresh water is virtually eliminated in this layout. Further, maintenance work can be performed underway in most weather without interfering with sailing or galley operation. As an example, I replaced an ailing fuel lift pump sailing between Tonga and New Zealand as easily as if we were dockside. The engine room environment is, in fact, the most benign of the entire boat and a good place to dry wet shoes after a rainy watch.

One of the unusual design features of the Out Island 41 is its shallow 4′ 2″ draft and no centerboard. We were not particularly enamored of this feature, but we were willing to face the prospect of more difficult upwind sailing in return for the other design advantages of the boat. We have since come to enjoy this shallow draft with excursions into waters that have raised the eyebrows of many onlookers. And the sailing performance upwind? We beat that problem, too. After a series of sail configuration tests, we proved to our satisfaction that the mainsail was the major cause of leeway in upwind sailing and should be left furled. We further found that a genoa sail specifically fitted to the mizzen mast would give us an increment of speed over the mainsail without any leeway penalty. As a result of those tests we have subsequently done all of our upwind sailing using a 130 percent genoa, a 110 percent mizzen genoa, and the mizzen. Off the wind the mizzen genoa is tacked to weather and used as a staysail. This bald-headed ketch configuration has conclusively proven its improved sailing ability, and we no longer use the mainsail—which also greatly simplifies sail handling. Self steering with the James Ogg designed Polaris wind vane has worked most satisfactorily with this sail rig.

APPENDIX B

Our Maintenance Plan

The ingenuity of a sailor probably shows to no better advantage than in keeping his boat going on an extended cruise. There must be some pioneering spirit left in all of us, for the cruising sailors we know seem to enjoy doing maintenance themselves. Away from chandleries, repair shops, and technicians, they are truly on their own. But as boats get more complex in design and equipment, it is no longer sufficient to have oakum, nails, and rope for repairs. Now you need epoxy, wire cable, and a multitude of factory-made spare parts.

Modern boat technology and design have given us an advantage in that failures are fewer, but at the same time it has made failures more difficult to repair. *Horizon,* for instance, had a spares inventory of nearly $2,000. Fortunately, most of it returned home with us. There were, however, unforeseen side benefits in economy to carrying this large inventory, for parts and supplies are far cheaper in the United States than in Pacific ports, and certainly, if you add inflationary price increases, they are a good investment.

The well-stocked parts inventory was not, by itself, the complete answer. Shop manuals for all complex equipment such as engine, transmission, winches and windlass, refrigeration, toilets, pumps, stoves, etc. were included with the spares. In fact, training manuals prepared for the technician's education were ideal adjuncts to shop manuals. Few of us are experts in all fields and knowledge of the fundamentals can improve the quality of maintenance. I have also found it convenient to know the address of the manufacturer's plant for each of the principal mechanical and electrical units aboard *Horizon*. On a few occasions I have sought their advice or needed special parts which they handled by mail in a timely fashion.

Finally, in precruise preparations, it is important to keep in mind that the United States is one of the last countries using the foot-pound-gallon (English) measuring system. Overseas you are confronted with metric-designed parts, tools, and standards. Bolts are not only of different diameters, but they have different threads. In fact, bolt and screw selections are much narrowed, because few countries can afford the multiplicity of fastenings in common use in the United States. Some recent converts to the metric system, like New Zealand, are still able to satisfy many needs, but others like French Polynesia are already 100 percent metric.

One good way we found to minimize your maintenance and repair work was through regular mechanical and electrical inspections. We are accustomed to this in automobiles and airplanes but hardly think of it in casual weekend sailing. On an extended cruise, however, the service hours on the boat and its equipment accumulate very rapidly. *Horizon* accrued 4,000 hours of actual sailing time in less than two years of cruising, while the rigging probably experienced several times that amount, since in many anchorages the boat was never still and the rigging was continually working.

A routine electro-mechanical inspection was evolved, which was both simple and fast and took the following form:

Daily (usually before battery and refrigerator charge)

   a. inspect engine visually
   b. check oil level (engine and transmission)
   c. check drip pan for foreign matter
   d. inspect bilge
   e. inspect rigging (use binoculars for aloft)

Weekly

   a. check battery water level and specific gravity
   b. check engine cooling fresh water
   c. check engine propeller shaft

  d. close and open all seacocks
  e. tighten hose clamps if loose
  f. test emergency warning circuits
  g. inspect steering system

Enroute or at anchor, the same inspection routine was followed to catch small problems before they became big ones.

Did it pay off? All of our inspection efforts were amply rewarded on the one day in which our routine binocular inspection of things aloft showed the forestay parting at the masthead. We not only were able to save the mast, but we saved ourselves the needless problem of having to sail with a jerry-rigged mast.

We had given serious thought to tools and spare parts for, in order of importance, hull, rigging, steering, propulsion, and lastly accessories. Our philosophy was to be able to repair or replace any item aboard short of catastrophic damage to hull, mast or engine. While we carried the best in emergency life raft, provisions, and equipment, we had no desire to use them short of total loss. We felt it better to keep 40 feet going than to sit idle in 8 feet.

Cruising safety took a big step forward with the advent of the fiberglass hull. It is virtually indestructable in the open water and, kept sealed, can survive practically any weather. Other than smashing the hull on a reef, we were prepared to reseal, patch or plug any hole in the hull above or below the waterline.

Before our cruise was over we had practically every leak stopped except—you guessed it—the hatches. Designed for looks rather than function, most acrylic, metal alloy, and molded fiberglass hatches depend on sponge rubber for sealing. With no interlocking design features to form flow barriers, water soon finds its way inside. We were never able to seal our $275 deluxe metal and smoked acrylic dinette hatch in spite of a new rubber seal sent to us in New Zealand by the manufacturer.

Routine maintenance above the waterline mostly involves stopping those irritating water leaks, while below the waterline the ancient problem of marine growth is dominant. But in tropical waters what can be more refreshing and fun than a plunge into a sparkling lagoon and a few minutes spent in brushing away the new growth? It worked for a while, but eventually the bottom needed new antifouling paint. We had taken along a couple gallons of bottom paint that we eventually applied.

Rigging spares were a close second priority to the hull because the oceans are vast and movement by the wind is the only dependable power source. All the rigging—standing and running—as well as the sails, are subject to continuous dynamic loads, so that wear and fatigue rather than stress are the causes of failure. We experienced two rigging failures—a backstay and the forestay. Both were caused by fatigue and both were repairable at sea due to our complete rigging spares complement.

Attaching a shroud or stay to the masthead 55 feet above a turbulent sea is a real challenge at best, but ours was made considerably easier through a series of photographs of the masthead assembly that I had taken before leaving San Pedro. By studying the photographs from all angles, we were able to collect on deck the proper tools and parts for the needed fix. Later in Honolulu, when I installed the missing toggle along with a new forestay, I rephotographed the masthead assembly with a Polaroid camera to keep the album up to date.

Our standing rigging spares inventory, which worked so well, was developed with the aid of a rigging shop specializing in ship, dock, and mobile crane equipment. They fabricated three 7 x 19 galvanized wire rope cables (¼, ⁵⁄₁₆, ⅜ inches in diameter) with thimbles at one end only. Each was long enough to replace its longest in-use counterparts. To install these, a variety of high-quality wire thimbles, cable clamps, and shackles were provided to create any possible end configuration that we needed. We also had aboard a handy billy block and tackle with which we could tighten and hold a cable in position while making up the lower end attachment. Mainly, the handy billy served as our mizzen genoa sheet winch, but we found it to be a most valuable rigging tool.

Besides cable, *Horizon* carried an assortment of "original equipment" forged bronze turnbuckles and toggles plus stainless steel shackles, none of which were ever needed. All the turnbuckles in use had been lubricated before departure with a molybdenum grease, Never-Seez, and we never had a turnbuckle resist hand adjustment. Conversely, we kept them securely cotter-pinned so that they wouldn't unscrew themselves. For catastrophic failures we also carried a heavy-duty cable cutter and a banding tool.

Running rigging spares consisted of bulk lengths of dacron rope for halyards and sheets, spare blocks (we did experience two breakages) and a winch repair kit, which, except for lubrication, went unused. The spare blocks and rope, however, found occasional uses as we experimented with alternate ways to rig sheets, running backstays, whisker pole, etc.

Mechanical spares for the engine, refrigerator, and steering system were stocked in abundance to permit at least a one-time replacement of most critical items. The engine and refrigeration builders' recommendations for spares kits were followed, but I also consulted with local servicemen to find out their commonly experienced problems with these systems. The combined spares inventory assembled by this approach worked out well, and I would change but one aspect of it. Where a particular unit was judged vulnerable to failure, for instance a salt water pump or fuel lift pump, I would have not only the repair kit (with instructions!) but one completely assembled unit on hand. At sea it is not too difficult to replace an ailing part, but it may be hard to rebuild that part. It is really much better to rebuild it when at a quiet anchorage with plenty of time to do a proper job.

As for getting major mechanical work done in foreign ports, you can't depend on it. In very few places will you find competent mechanics and in even fewer places will there be parts available. While we experienced none of the major mechanical problems like total engine or transmission failure, we learned from other's sad experiences the absolute need for carrying comprehensive shop manuals as well as complete parts lists. With these and a reasonably competent local mechanic, you can identify the parts needing replacement and order them from the nearest supply point if you don't have them aboard. Throughout the Pacific it appeared more expeditious and dependable to order any needed parts by radio telephone from the United States and have them air shipped to your port. Unless local dealers have them on hand, your chances of expedited delivery from the United States are much better than the local mechanic's.

Of all the diesel engine failures we heard about, the majority were due to corrosion of the oil heat exchangers, allowing water to enter the oil system. In every one of these cases, the owner was unaware of the need for a zinc rod in the salt water cooling circuit. In fact, some of the Perkins engines had no provisions for installing such a rod. On our Westerbeke we need to replace the heat exchanger zinc rod about every six months, which is a whole lot easier than the alternative. While you're at it, give some thought to your hull and propeller zincs even though you are far away from marinas with their stray electrical currents.

Keeping the engine going also means keeping the electrical system in good order. Its importance depends on the number of uses that you put it to. Besides engine starting, your navigation and cabin lights depend on it as do the speedometers and emergency warning systems and a whole host of electronic gear that can't function without electric power. Certainly primitive cruising without electricity can be fun and safe but it can be considerably more fun and much safer with electric power.

Horizon's electrical system was simple—a 12-volt dual bank of automobile batteries charged by a common automobile alternator on the engine. One thing that is standard throughout the world is the 12-volt automobile electric system, and, if you stick to that, you can always get parts or repairs made in a foreign port. You can still have 110-volt AC electricity for small power tools, sewing machines, vacuum cleaners, and the like through use of a solid state inverter.

Moisture and the resulting corrosion has to be the number-one enemy of the electrical system, so keep it dry to keep it going. To prevent electrical resistance build-up at wire connectors, soldered joints are preferred to crimped connectors. So, also carry a 12-volt soldering iron with an extension cord to reach any part of the boat and a 12-volt work light. These and many other good pieces of equipment can be obtained at a recreational vehicle supply house. For trouble-shooting the electrical system, a volt-ohmmeter is an essential item in your electrical kit. Cynically, we can always quote Murphy's law in defense of failure: "If anything can go wrong, it will." But isn't it more practical to catch failures before they happen through inspection and maintenance? A well-maintained boat is no guarantee that you won't have trouble, but your chances are much improved, and when you are caught in a gale you can devote your thoughts to surviving through good seamanship rather than worrying whether your boat will hold together.

Horizon's inventory of cruising spares in approximate order of importance was as follows:

Hull and cabin

fiberglass cloth, four- and six-inch fiberglass tapes, polyester resin with catalyst, solvent, epoxy filler, polyester gel coat repair, underwater epoxy, silicone sealant, caulking rubber, bedding compound, duct tape, sponge rubber gasket strips, bottom paint, teak oil, paint thinner, ½ inch exterior plywood, one-inch teak board, softwood bungs, assorted bronze wood screws, stainless steel sheet metal screws, machine screws with washers and nuts, bronze nails, epoxy cement, wood glue, hull zincs

Standing rigging

rigging plan, 7 x 19 galvanized wire ropes with swaged eye on one end (30' x ⅜", 55' x ⅜", 55' x ⁵⁄₁₆"), wire rope clips (³⁄₁₆, ¼, ⁵⁄₁₆, ⅜" diameter), galvanized shackles (¼, ⁵⁄₁₆, ⅜, ⁷⁄₁₆" diameter), "original equipment" turnbuckles, toggles and clevis pins, cotter pins, safety wire, molybdenum grease, assorted stainless bolts, washers, and nuts (¼ to ½" in diameter and 2 to 4 inches long)

Running rigging

Dacron rope for mainsheet, jib sheets and halyard tails, spare all-rope halyards and blocks permanently installed on both masts, stainless steel wire rope and Nicropress fittings for halyards, ³⁄₁₆-inch nylon braid (500 feet), whipping line, light marline, heavy marline, utility blocks, stainless steel shackles, winch repair kit

Sail repair

Sail plan, ditty bag with track slides, bronze thimbles, brass rings, jib snaps, sail bag with Dacron cloth, self-adhesive nylon cloth and tape, Dacron hand-stitching and sewing machine threads, beeswax, ¹⁄₁₆-inch-thick soft leather, batten material

Steering system

replacement cable and clamps, chain links (standard and cable end), spare tiller, wind-vane paddle and shear pins

Ground tackle

Spare anchor with length of chain, chain repair links, chain shackles (⁵⁄₁₆, ³⁄₈, ⁷⁄₁₆-inch), rope thimbles (closed, round), galvanized safety wire, heavy leather and canvas chafing pieces, 600 feet of ¾-inch nylon warp

Propulsion (diesel)

manuals and parts lists, fuel lift pump assembly and parts kit, injector assemblies, injector piping set, fuel line tubing and end fittings, fuel filter elements and gaskets, anti-bacterial fuel additive, salt water pump assembly and parts kit, heat exchanger zinc anodes, drive belt, cooling system preservative, thermostat, hoses and clamps, water resistant grease, oil filter elements, engine oil, transmission oil, starter motor and solenoid, alternator and voltage regulator, distilled water, propeller shaft bearing grease, log packing, zinc anodes, engine gasket set, sheet gasket material, (fiber and asbestos), gasket compound, miscellaneous steel bolts, nuts, plain and lock washers, exhaust hose and clamps

Stove and lamps

stove parts list, burner assembly and parts kit, stove fuel filter element, lamp wicks, pressurized lamp-repair kit, mantles

General plumbing

parts list and repair kits for fresh and salt water hand pumps, toilets, bilge pumps, sink drain pumps, hoses and clamps for fresh and salt water lines, Teflon tape and pipe joint compound, neoprene sheet gasket, assorted O-rings

Electrical

bulbs and fuses (indexed), dry cells for flashlights and transistor devices, electric wire (50 feet each No. $\frac{16}{2}$, No. $\frac{12}{2}$, No. 18 single), assorted terminal lugs, rosin core solder, vinyl tape, diodes for inverter, heat conducting gasket paste, Sumlog cable, wind direction vane

Refrigeration

service manual and parts list, refrigerant, dryer, leak detector fluid, compressor oil, drive belt, compressor shaft seal

APPENDIX C

Horizon *in Retrospect*

Looking back, we see that many improvements could be made to the boat, its equipment, and our method of operating it. We also see where modern day cruising has made some significant breaks with traditional sailing ideas and how it differs drastically from weekend and coastal cruising.

One's earliest dreams of cruising envision a boat of character design, possibly even a picturesque schooner, speeding across the sparkling blue waters with a bone in her teeth and the wind abaft the beam. Without such dreams, few of us would ever entertain the idea of long-range cruising. But the unfortunate fact of the matter is, more often than not, the wind is forward of the beam!

On the one hand, the prevailing global winds circulating in their immense pattern over the open ocean tell you to go west in the tropics and return east above 40° latitude; go poleward at the western ocean boundaries and head for the equator at the eastern ocean boundaries. So, unless you are entertaining thoughts of a westward circumnavigation in the tropics or an eastward one in the Roaring Forties, you will find yourself, sooner or later, beating against the prevailing winds or working your way though the belt of variable winds that separate them.

Add to this, then, the cruising sailor's increasing interest in visiting islands off the beaten path of the tradewinds and you can see a real need for the cruising boat to have a reasonable windward sailing ability. Many skippers also have economic, educational, or professional needs to return to their starting points in a couple of years, and this may require additional windward sailing to make the most of the available time.

Horizon is not a traditional design in any sense of the word. With its shoal draft it had a poor windward performance until we developed the mizzen genoa to replace the mainsail for sailing to weather. Without it, our Pacific adventure would have been confined to the more common ports of call along the path to leeward.

As one example, we were one of the few boats in 1976 able to visit the Austral Islands on the passage east from New Zealand because of the unusually persistent easterly winds that kept us on a beat for most of the 2200 miles. Many boats with a poor windward ability could only reach north to the Cook Islands or, at best, lay Tahiti direct. Unusually common among these boats were the traditional cruising designs with salty good looks and sea-kindly hulls, but without the ability to go well to weather.

Although cruising should not be a matter of speed or schedule, one always looks forward to shortening the long passages and enjoying more time on the beaches or gunkholing inside the reefs. Should you be out looking for your ideal cruising boat, keep in mind that there are modern boat designs with both seakindly hulls and good windward performance, which will make your cruise itinerary much more flexible and less wearing on the crew.

A word of caution, though, lest the pendulum of cruising boat design swing too far to weather. Centerboards, fin keels, and spade rudders may be great for high performance racing boats with gung ho crews, but they are not compatible with shoal waters, coral heads, and small, relaxed cruising crews. The designer, indeed, is called upon to tread a narrow line between performance and simplicity of design in order to come up with the ideal cruising boat.

Next to a suitable hull design, the sails are probably the most important. We were quite satisfied with our inventory consisting of a 130-percent genoa, working jib, and storm jib as headsails plus mainsail, mizzensail, and that uncanny mizzen genoa. In many of our hours of drifting on windless waters we thought how nice it would be to have a nylon drifter just to keep steerageway. But our sail inventory already took up half of the forecastle and we couldn't see adding another sail unless we could also subtract one. So our desire remained unfulfilled.

All of our downwind sailing (which wasn't really much) was done with the genoa clewed to the single whisker pole, and we found little reason for a more sophisticated downwind rig. Sometime in the future, though, we will permanently mount the pole on a forward facing track on the mast to ease its handling in lumpy seas.

But more important than any new sail was the frequent need we found to shorten sail quickly and by one person in the face of a rising wind. Here the ketch rig certainly helped but we still had a large single headsail to contend with, and it had to be removed from the headstay before we could hank on a smaller jib. This proved both time consuming and difficult for one person. Since most of the headsail shortening takes place between the genoa and working jib, this is the combination to be improved.

A thought that comes immediately to mind is the use of reef points in the genoa. This may not only be the solution to the sail shortening problem, but it may also help to restrain the sail inventory relieving the budget as well as saving valuable stowage space below decks.

Another alternative is the use of double headsails as in the cutter rig in which the large (outer) jib can be quickly dropped and secured on deck leaving the inner staysail drawing by itself in the heavier wind. In this manner one is never without a functioning headsail for good control.

Roller furling jibs are a possible third alternative, but I doubt that the roller furling gear would stand up to gales or that the sail could be kept furled, much less reefed, in a gale. In Hawaii we saw several roller furling rigs that had not survived the single passage from California, so they don't appear to be adequately developed yet for extended cruising.

Both our mainsail and mizzen were fitted with jiffy reefing to shorten sail. We found this simple and effective once we had developed our technique and all of the reefing lines were cut to proper length and marked.

We were well satisfied with the modern sailmaking techniques using dacron materials and triple stitching. Sail wear in more than 4000 hours of sailing was minimal. This probably represents at least 10 years of sailing for the average boatowner. Some sail design features did not work out well in practice. Go-fast leach and foot adjustment cords were neither durable nor easy to use, and I can really see no need for them on well-cut cruising sails. There is little incentive to fool around with them on passages of long duration.

Mainsail and mizzen battens tended to foul topping lifts, so in the future they will be sewn into close-fitting pockets instead of being tied in place. We had two jib tack pendants made of ³⁄₁₆-inch 7x19 stainless steel cable break from fatigue, and they were replaced with rope pendants which are still with us. Jib hanks wore badly on the dacron cloth wrapping the luff wire, and all of them eventually had leather chafing inserts sewn in. The leather we used, incidentally, was a jacket grade material purchased in La Paz, Mexico, at $10 for a full hide, and this turned out to be a very useful addition to our canvas and sail repair kits. Early in the cruise we had attached baggy-wrinkle to shrouds and back stays to reduce wear but ended up removing it in favor of snap-on plastic tubing which was neater and provided adequate protection.

Radio communications for long-range cruising seem to have little in common with current marine radiotelephone developments. We, in fact, carried no radiotelephone and felt not in the least disadvantaged. The usual arguments of weather information, boat-to-boat communications, and safety all take on a different perspective when you are a thousand or more miles from anywhere. Boats travel so slowly that once your passage is started, most weather forecasts have little impact on you and you are concerned principally with the weather you see and feel. The one-minute time slot weather reports of WWV covering gales and more severe storms are valuable and a good all-band radio receiver will suffice for this need as well as giving you time ticks for navigation and, occasionally, a little entertainment.

Communications with other boats or shore stations usually take place over great distances which are beyond reliable capabilities of conventional marine band radiotelephones. We observed that only those boats equipped with mobile ham rigs were able to have satisfactory boat-to-boat and boat-to-shore communications. (You need an amateur radio license to use these sets.) So many boats are now equipped with ham rigs that a ham net has been established in the South Pacific which ties together the boats with interested shore stations in New Zealand, Fiji, Samoa, and other island groups of this area. The shore-based operators provide weather reports from their areas (good for the local boats) as well as boat and personal news of interest.

From a safety standpoint, I feel that a call on a ham frequency would be the only chance one would have of obtaining emergency help on the high seas or at an isolated atoll. Aside from a mobile ham rig, a VHF set might occasionally be useful to announce your arrival to English-speaking harbormasters or to talk to a passing freighter.

Obviously the radio, as well as lights and some modern day luxuries you may want on board, will depend on the reliability of the boat's electric power source. Our experience and that of many others is that it can fail for a variety of reasons. Most boats charge batteries with their engine and when it or the generator fails, they are without electric power. From New Guinea to the Galapagos we knew of seven boats (including *Horizon*) whose engines were out of order at one time or another. Troubles were basically cooling oriented. All were fresh water cooled diesel engines which, in itself, was not the problem. It was always the salt water cooling circuit that was at fault. That old devil corrosion attacked the transmission and lubricating oil heat exchangers until leakage developed and water got into the gearbox or crankcase, resulting in the highly loaded bearings freezing up.

Horizon's problem was slightly different in that the exhaust cooling standpipe had corroded through, allowing water to seep into the exhaust manifold when the engine was shut down. The effects were all the same—no battery recharge capability.

Our backup for this situation was to use kerosene lamps (both cabin and running) which, when we were faced with the problem, turned out not to be a good solution. Not only were they too inconvenient and messy, but the lights are a logistic, mounting and storage problem. Those boats with radiotelephones (several were mobile ham rigs) also lost communication in addition to the lights as soon as their stored energy was used up. On the plus side, however, all of us learned to be better sailors without reliance on the iron jib.

While there is little remedy at sea for a frozen engine, I now believe that the properly equipped cruising boat should have a backup electrical generator rather than backup kerosene lamps. My current thoughts turn to a small hand-started, air-cooled, four-cycle diesel engine driving the spare 12-volt alternator carried for the primary engine. Permanently installed and drawing its fuel from the boat's tank, it would be an unsophisticated source of emergency electric power to keep the sophisticated electric systems going to the next port.

Primary engine failure can also result in the loss of refrigeration. The auxiliary generator would be of no help in the case of a mechanical compressor and probably would be too small to drive most electrically-powered refrigerators unless their duty cycles were cut down. We learned to live without refrigeration during the passage between the Austral Islands and Tahiti when our engine was inoperative and we now question whether refrigeration was even a wise investment. Most cruising boats do not have refrigeration and thereby avoid significant initial costs and maintenance problems. In retrospect, I think we could have spent the $1300 more wisely.

I can't help but think of the famous phrase which makes the rounds in cruising circles: All the big boats have the maintenance problems while all the small boats have the fun.

One problem which we had not anticipated was with our "shoreboat." Ours was a popular model inflatable dinghy, which we felt would keep the deck clear for sunning and sailing but we soon learned that it took up too much space below decks and was not easily inflated or repacked. While we got used to less room in the forecastle and allowed ourselves extra time to get the dinghy ready for use, we were never happy trying to row it against the wind and wave or for long distances to explore an interesting tropical shoreline. An outboard motor would solve the rowing problem, but it would only compound the stowage or readiness problem.

We are now looking for a hard-bottom fiberglass dinghy with two rowing stations (forward and middle thwart), full bilges for stability, and a modest keel for good tracking. We would carry it inverted in fitted chocks over the forward cabin and offload it with the spare jib halyard. It would not be davit mounted. The need for an outboard motor becomes less with a handier hard-bottom dinghy. We saw such a dinghy in New Zealand, but because fiberglass products there are so expensive, we decided to wait and investigate the U.S. market.

A more subtle part of the shoreboat system which needs improvement for cruising is the boarding (swimming) ladder. We had the common type of plastic and aluminum ladder, which did not engender a feeling of security when you climbed on it. We eventually quit using it in favor of scrambling up the shrouds, but this was not particularly attractive to guests nor is it easy even for the experienced when carrying precious supplies. Safety, besides ease of climbing, dictates a better ladder, probably of stainless steel tubing and possibly even permanently mounted on the transom to solve its stowage and availability problems.

Looking back, we note that most of our hardware decisions gone wrong involved complication rather than simplicity. While it is getting more and more difficult to get rugged marine hardware, it may be wiser to do without than expose yourself to potential fun-killing problems on your cruise. We had our share of problems, but we also had more than our share of fun on our 17,000 mile shakedown cruise.

APPENDIX D

Navigation

Navigation on *Horizon* was more formal than it is on most cruising boats because it had always been my hobby and I am a professional engineer, which leads to disciplined practices. We probably had an easier time at navigation and fewer worries because we stuck to a very thorough approach. Learning to navigate the right way from the beginning made our 165 days of navigating a pleasure, and our landfalls were precise and safe.

Celestial Navigation

In the early 1970s, the HO 229 method of sight reduction came into being and I immediately learned the process. It differed very little from the older HO 214. Either method gives a navigator complete flexibility to choose celestial bodies for sights with virtually no restrictions. The sight reduction process is always the same and your thinking process is indelibly set, so there is less chance of mistakes.

Our daily procedure called for taking planet or star sights in the morning, reserving the sun or moon for back up in case of morning clouds. On the outbound voyage celestial position-fixing was shared by the crewman and myself. Whoever had the 0300 to 0600 watch took the sights and reduced them. These were compared with an 0600 DR position to give us a measure of the current each day and to update our DR plot for that day.

A continuous DR plot was maintained. The DR plot was based on log entries that were made every hour by the person on watch. New DR positions were plotted four times a day, interrupted only by celestial updates. DR positions were plotted at 0600, 1200, 1800, and 2400. If we were near land, an Estimated Position, based on the last current data, was also plotted. Noon positions were transcribed to small-scale ocean charts, and the whole crew followed those daily positions across the Pacific. On a trackless ocean, the noon chart positions are all you have to show progress.

We did not neglect the use of the sun. On cloudy mornings it became our next choice, and even a single line of position from one sun sight was welcome. Because of the ease with which the noon sun sight can be made, we often took it to verify our latitude and to keep our sextant technique sharp.

If we missed both morning sights and sun sights, we would try for evening planets or stars. These were never really enjoyed, because they had to be calculated by artificial light and they cut into valuable sleeping time. If we were approaching a landfall, there was no question that we would take evening star sights, even if we already had a full round of morning stars and daytime sun. In this manner we were able to track the currents with reasonable confidence and to know we would not be getting into trouble during the night.

As the days went by, celestial navigation became easier, and we felt it was also more precise. Eventually we stopped taking sights on more than two bodies. Instead, we used the available twilight to get precise sextant readings on just two bodies. I continued this practice through the rest of the cruise.

Sight timing was done mostly with the aid of a stop watch and a quartz chronometer. Occasionally we would use the time signals of WWVH directly. The chronometer was calibrated daily against WWVH when we checked the Pacific weather picture.

Chart Procurement

Before starting the cruise we obtained charts for the ocean areas and archipelagoes we thought we would visit, hoping to supplement them as we went along and as our itinerary changed. It worked, and it didn't work. What did work was great. We got the best charts of French Polynesia in Papeete. They were French charts and far better than the available U.S. charts. In New Zealand we bought New Zealand charts, and they were excellent. Their cartographic techniques were more imaginative than those found on U.S. charts.

What *didn't* work about getting charts en route was the few places one could buy them. Papeete and New Zealand were the only places we found along our route. We traded some charts with other boats, but that isn't a good practice, for you may trade a chart you will need later.

I formed a philosophy about charts and navigation books for specific geographic areas, and that is buy them from the government that has surveyed the area and is currently responsible for it—French charts of French possessions, or New Zealand charts of their areas. This also includes Sailing Directions for their waters. At any rate, *don't skimp:* the safety of your boat and crew depends on accurate and complete knowledge of the local area, especially when making landfalls.

Landfalls at Night

This brings us to the subject of making landfalls at night. *Don't!* Time is not so precious that you should jeopardize your boat and its crew to save a few hours. We had to stand off Nuku Hiva, Pago Pago, and Rangiroa until daylight hours to make safe entries, but we entered Papeete, with its reefs, at night because we had been there before. We knew the harbor well, and it was a clear night with soft tropical breezes. Both Hana Menu and the Bay of Islands were entered at dusk, which is as marginal as I want to get. We clearly saw their entrances from seaward in daylight and there were no reef problems for either; it was a clear run in. But that was the limit of our night entrances.

What do you do for ten hours while you're in the shadow of your destination? One way is to drop your sails and sit. We did that at Nuku Hiva and Pago Pago, where we could clearly see the island and observe our position. Approaching Rangiroa there was no way to see the atoll at night until you are on top of it, and that is much too close. In that instance, we sailed as close to it as our EP plot would allow, then we turned 180 degrees and sailed away for several hours, back into waters we knew were clear of hazards. Judging our speed carefully, we returned to our original course (corrected by current estimates) during the night and sailed directly toward the atoll, timing our arrival for just after daybreak. It worked, and I felt better through the night, for I was controlling the destiny of the boat rather than just drifting along with the current.

Atoll Navigation

Approaching an atoll requires extreme care, day or night. The land is not distinguishable until you are almost up to it and by then you have probably encountered the reef. A depth finder is of little value in finding a coral reef, because they rise almost perpendicularly from the depths. Visually, your only key to the nearness of an atoll is the tops of the palm trees. If there are no trees, there *may* be clouds above the atoll—but I wouldn't depend on it.

Passes to atolls are generally located on their leeward sides, sheltered from the prevailing winds and swells. Because the prevailing winds are from the east, flow through the passes is usually deflected to the westerly side, which suggests that making an east-of-center approach will generally be the safest. Whether the current is flooding (which is rare) or ebbing (which is common), there will be a vigorous race where the flow exits into smoother water. The race can be rough, but if you can stay out of it by hugging the eastern shore, you may have an easier ride.

It is advisable to transit an atoll pass at a fairly good speed, especially if there is an outflowing stream. Whirlpools and eddies from the irregular sides and bottom of the pass demand good steering control, which only adequate speed can give. There are usually no coral heads rising to the surface in a pass, but they may be found at the inner approaches, so it is advisable to post a lookout in the rigging.

During prevailing trade wind periods, the outgoing stream from a lagoon is noticeably stronger than the incoming stream. The swells on the windward side of the atoll break over the reef and flood the lagoon, and the high water inside is seeking a way out through the pass. After a lengthy period of strong prevailing winds and heavy swells, the outflowing stream may overwhelm the lunar tides for several days, eliminating slack water or flood currents.

Observations of currents in the passes have produced a generalized guide that may be helpful if you are entering a pass during normal prevailing wind conditions. The rules of thumb given in the British *Pacific Islands Pilot* read:

Time	*Current in pass*
Moonrise minus one hour	Slack water of short duration with beginning of outflowing stream
Moonrise plus three or four hours	Slack water again
Moonrise plus four hours	Inflowing stream begins

Moonset minus one hour	Outflowing stream begins
Moonset plus three or four hours	Slack water again
Moon's lower meridian passage minus one hour	Inflowing stream begins

Horizon entered and departed both Rangiroa and Ahe atolls using these rules of thumb as a timing guide, and the flows were in the directions we had anticipated. Because of a strong inflowing stream in Rangiroa's Avatoru Pass, the race at the inside was well developed and the motion at the spreaders caused the lookout to hold on with both hands.

Once inside a lagoon is the most peaceful of worlds, and the only hazards are coral reefs and coral heads in many of the lagoons. Those that were used during World War II for ship anchorages or seaplane landing areas were dragged or blasted clean of coral heads. Bora Bora lagoon is one of these. Nothing has prevented a slow regrowth, and some coral heads may be approaching keel depth in the shallows.

Eyeball navigation from the spreaders is the only safe way to transit a lagoon. It is preferable, almost mandatory, to have the sun at your back to do a good job. As an assist, Polaroid glasses seem to penetrate the surface reflection and give better depth perspective.

Atolls are the most fascinating land masses of the Pacific, but they claim more than their share of yachts. Care in approaching, entering, and crossing the lagoon is essential if you hope to enjoy their peace and beauty.

APPENDIX E

Navigation Supplies and Equipment

The Offshore Log (copyright by author), a working logbook.
Navigation workbook—a student's notebook.
Sight log and reduction book—a stenographer's notebook.
Sight Solver (copyright by author), which eliminates the need for paper
    forms.
Universal plotting sheets.
One-degree celestial position plotting sheets.
Mk II Navy surplus sextant with 4-power scope.
Davis plastic sextant as a back up.
HO 2102 Star Finder
Hand-bearing compass.
Ritchie 5-inch binnacle compass.
VDO Sumlog.
Stop-watch.
Quartz chronometer.
HO 229—Volumes I, II, and III (0° to 45° latitude).
HO 211 (easiest for determining great circle distances).
Sailing Directions.
Harbor, coastal, and ocean charts.
Miscellaneous plotting tools.

APPENDIX F

Route Planning

Probably the most important aspect of planning a cruise is the weather. We go to the tropics because it is warm. The trade winds are followed because they make the easiest work of sailing. And we try to avoid storms. Unfortunately, within the tropics and the trade wind belts are also found those violent storms known as tropical cyclones. They are generated over the warm waters of the tropics and, generally, they spend their short lives there. Occasionally they pass from the tropics into the temperate zone, where they are known as extra-tropical cyclones.

A cyclone is a "closed circulation" with respect to the weather system (isobars). Winds cross the isobars and spiral in toward the center (eye). The clouds also show this spiraling effect, but on such a grand scale that it is only visible in satellite pictures. The tropical cyclone is of tropical oceanic origin. It has no weather fronts per se and derives its energy from the ocean waters with temperatures in excess of 80°F. Hence, they rarely generate outside of the tropics, although they are known to travel poleward outside of the tropics.

Tropical Storms

A cyclone starts as a tropical depression with winds of less than 34 knots. At sea you might think it is only a small gale, but if you have been listening to WWVH, you will have been alerted to the fact that there was a tropical depression in your vicinity and the winds would have verified it.

As the winds increase from 34 to 63 knots, the depression is reclassified as a tropical storm, and the waves, clouds, and winds will become threatening. By that time the barometer will have dropped to 1000 mbs. If the barometer continues to drop, you are in for a fully developed hurricane, with winds going from 64 knots to 100 knots or higher. In the immature stage hurricane-force winds will exist within a circle of 50 miles or so. At full force, winds of a mature hurricane may reach out to a radius of 400 miles.

Tropical cyclones at any stage are not a yachtsman's friend, so care should be taken to avoid them. Regions experiencing cyclones are well defined and the chart, Tropical Cyclones of the Pacific Ocean from Navy's *"Climatic* Atlas of Tropical Storms," shows the principal regions and periods of tropical cyclones. This publication is based on historical data and covers up to one hundred years of record keeping in some areas.

Horizon's trip from California to New Zealand involved cruising through two cyclonic regions—the Eastern North Pacific and the Southwest Pacific. We departed the Mexican coast in mid-May to safely cross the Eastern North Pacific hurricane region, which begins in earnest in June. Our next schedule for staying out of trouble involved the South Pacific hurricane season of November to March. Note that this is one month earlier than those shown on the chart. The best information from other yachties is that, north of New Zealand, the season starts about a month earlier than it does closer to Australia, and it lets up one month earlier to the east of New Zealand. We elected to be off the ocean by the first of November and to spend the Southern Hemisphere summer in New Zealand.

Along the popular South Pacific cruising route there are few real hurricane holes. Pago Pago is probably the best, but you will still need excellent ground tackle to ride out a real blow, in the harbor. Vava'u is probably next best, with a somewhat better holding bottom. A number of boats stay at Suva's Bay of Islands, where they go up a river in case of a severe blow.

Departing New Zealand we felt safe in heading east in March, since the dominant hurricane activity is west of New Zealand. Boats that were planning northerly or westerly courses from New Zealand stayed put until April. Even then the storms were not completely over and in 1976 several boats were severely damaged by the tag ends of unpredictable extra-tropical cyclones.

Doldrums

A second global weather feature of interest to cruising yachtsmen is the area known as the Inter-tropical Convergence Zone—the doldrums. This is an area of low atmospheric pressure, where the northeast and southeast trade winds meet. Unlike tropical cyclones, they are not to be feared, only endured and understood.

The doldrums are a region of light airs and periodic squalls. They are at their widest (north-south) in the Eastern Pacific and they may narrow to nothing in the Western Pacific. They generally follow the sun, being in the Northern Hemisphere in its summer and in the Southern Hemisphere in its summer. *Horizon* experienced little trouble in getting through the doldrums on its passages, but some yachts have been becalmed for days. Some have resorted to motoring to work their way out. Plenty of water and a good sunshade are essential to doldrum passages.

Using the Tradewinds

The popular cruising routes still follow the trade winds and the Pilot Charts are still your best guide. You will find that the average wind patterns described by the Pilot Charts may be disturbed locally by fronts or nearby storms, but don't give up on Matthew Fontaine Maury, who founded the Pilot Chart; it happens to everyone. A boat that goes well to weather will not be restricted to the down wind cruising routes that have made the Marquesas and Tahiti so crowded. If you can go to weather, you are free to choose a new destination and experience contacts with peoples who are not blasé about cruising yachts. There are more than 10,000 islands in the Pacific, so if your boat can go to weather, you will have many more options to stray from the beaten path.

Unless you are on a circumnavigation, you should also plan the best way to get back to your home port. From the Southwest Pacific to the United States is almost all uphill sailing, which can be dispiriting after months of lazy downhill sailing. The notable on-the-wind passages are from New Zealand to Tahiti, Tahiti to Hawaii, or direct to the United States if you favor a single long passage home. There is one outbound passage that is also all windward work, and that is Hawaii to French Polynesia.

The secret to windward passages is to forget the great circle route and study those Pilot Charts carefully. Your wind-directed courses will take you far from either the great circle or rhumb line, so they may take 25 to 30 per cent longer, but there is no alternative except shipping your boat home. No self-respecting cruising sailor would do that, would they?

Horizon's first long on-the-wind passage was New Zealand to the Austral Islands—21 days on the wind. Except for a constant heel, it wasn't all that difficult. Perseverance was the byword, and we did see Raivavae, which few boats ever visit. Most boats end up in the Cook Islands, Samoa, or Tahiti, which they had visited on the downhill run.

Our next uphill run was Ahe to Hawaii, and for that we stood well east of the rhumb-line to use the Southeast trades as long as possible and then pick up the Northeast trades for the run to Hilo. It worked fine and was only 10 percent longer than the great-circle route.

Our last uphill run was the Honolulu-to-San Francisco passage, which swings north of the Pacific high pressure area between Hawaii and the Pacific Coast. Depending on how well your boat goes to weather, you can short-cut the northerly swing somewhat. *Horizon*'s route was 22 per cent longer than the great-circle distance, and it took us to 40°N latitude. This was reasonable, though we motored on some really flat days.

Route Statistics

There can be no single set of statistics for cruising, because of the differences between boats and crews and the variability of winds. The following table of statistics from *Horizon*'s cruise tells you how one boat did it:

Statistics on **Horizon's Cruise**

Overall cruise data:

Distance traveled	16,946 nm
Time at sea	165 days
Average speed	103 mpd
Time in port	468 days
(Approximately three days in port for every day at sea)	
Longest stay in port (New Zealand)	5 months, 10 days

Outbound summary:

Distance traveled	8,161 miles
Time en route	84 days
Average speed	97 nm
Best day	175 nm

Return summary:

Distance traveled	8,785 nm
Time en route	81 days
Average speed	108 mpd
Best day	160 nm

Most motoring (Honolulu to San Francisco)　　　85 hours (total)

Long Passage Data

	Mazatlan/Nuku Hiva	New Zealand/Raivavae	Ahe/Hilo	Honolulu/San Francisco
Passage length	2,845 nm	2,200 nm	2,375 nm	2,555 nm
Great circle distance	2,700 nm	2,100 nm	2,150 nm	2,091 nm
Time en route	27 days	21¼ days	18½ days	25 days
Average speed	105 mpd	104 mpd	129 mpd	102 mpd
Best day's run	175 nm	147 nm	160 nm	150 nm
Slowest day	41 nm	55 nm	75 nm	60 nm
Maximum current encountered	2.4 knots	1.4 knots	1.3 knots	1 knot
Average current	1.3 knots	1 knot	.7 knots	.5 knots
Doldrums width	10°50'N - 6°45'N	—	2°08'N - 5°03'N	—
Boat speed in doldrums	68 mpd	—	92 mpd	—

APPENDIX G

Provisioning

by
Betty Hinz

The following list of provisions represents the basic foods *Horizon* had aboard to give three people three meals a day for ninety days. The numbers on the left of the column represent the actual amount we carried. The numbers in parentheses after the item represent the amount we will take on our next long cruise. There are great differences in some of the items—especially the canned meats. You cannot get quality fresh meat for canning except in New Zealand—and perhaps in Australia.

Food is also a good investment. The prices are high, but they'll never get lower. Therefore, the numbers on the right would be sufficient for three people for six to ten months. The cans will stay in good condition if you wipe each with WD-40 as you stow it. Then check each can every week. Needless to say, this quantity of food can only be carried on larger boats.

Provisions

Canned Fruit

12 fruit cocktail (25) 20 oz.
22 pineapple (15) 20 oz.
22 peaches (25) 20 oz.
22 pears (15) 20 oz.
12 apricots (10) 20 oz.

Canned Vegetables

15 potatoes (20) 20 oz.
20 peas (30) 20 oz.
12 carrots (20) 20 oz.
4 corn (20) 20 oz.
12 beans (30)—green, waxed, kidney, etc. 20 oz.
14 assorted (25)—beets, spinach, okra, sauerkraut, etc. 20 oz.

Starch Foods

12 large boxes dehydrated potatoes
20 large boxes rice
18 large boxes noodles (18 small)
20 large boxes spaghetti
20 large boxes macaroni (10 large and 10 small)
10 large boxes navy beans

Heavy Weather Meals—heat & serve

12 large size beef stew (24)
6 large size chili (6 large & 12 small)
6 large size chow mein (10)
6 large size spaghetti & meatballs (10)

Canned Soups

15 large-size hearty soups with lots of meat, chicken, vegetables, etc.
    (30)
20 regular-size cooking soups—Cream of Mushroom, etc. (50)

Canned Meats

25 cans 1 lb. bacon (50)

20 cans tuna (2 cases 6½ oz. and 20 cans 12½ oz.)
10 cans Spam (20)
10 2-lb. cans Wilson's beef (20)
10 2-lb. cans Wilson's ham (20)
10 2-lb. cans Wilson's pork (20)
10 2-lb. cans Wilson's turkey (20)
5 2-lb. cans Wilson's miniribs (10)
5 2-lb. cans Wilson's beef brisket (15)
5 cans Vienna sausages (25)
5 large cans corn beef hash (10 cans plus 10 cans beef hash)

Cereal, Flours, etc.

2 2-lb. boxes quick-cooking oatmeal (5)
2 1-lb. boxes quick-cooking Cream of Wheat (5)
2 large boxes of granola cold cereal (10)
1 large box Grapenuts (3)
1 large box Wheat Chex (2)
1 large box Shredded Wheat (2)
2 medium-size boxes pancake mix
1 large box Bisquick (10)
10 lb. white flour (30)
10 lb. cornmeal (10)
5 boxes roll mix
10 boxes cake mix (30 of the 1-layer size. Chocolate, white, yellow, &
    Stir & Bake)
10 pkg. cookie mix (30)
5 lbs. sugar (30)
1 lb. brown sugar (10)

General canned and bottled foods

20 cans evaporated milk (10)
23 46-oz. cans fruit juice (40)
10 29-oz. tomato sauce (15 plus 30 small cans of seasoned sauce)
10 12-oz. cans tomato paste (15)
10 29-oz. cans stewed tomatoes (20)
4 large plastic bottles pancake syrup (10)
3 3-lb. cans honey
5 jars jelly (5 3-lb. cans)
90 pkg. dried milk - each pkg. makes 1 qt. (Just enough to get to the
    South Pacific. New Zealand powdered milk is far superior.)
3 large jars of Tang (5)
5 cans chicken spread (10)

5 cans deviled ham spread (10)
5 cans Braunschweiger spread (10)
20 cans pudding (For heavy-weather treats.)
7 large cans drink mixes (7 lemonade and 3 cherry)
20 pkg. each beef, pork, turkey, and chicken gravy mix
20 pkg. each spaghetti, tuna, stew seasoning mix
20 pkg. each misc. hot dish mixes (Spanish rice, etc.)

Miscellaneous

Mincemeat (5 pkg.) (Remember, you'll be away on Thanksgiving)
Pumpkin pie (5 cans)
3 cans mushrooms (25)
2 cans Garbanzo beans (15 small cans)
Brown bread (5 cans)
5 cans cranberry sauce (10)
hard sauce (3 cans) (You'll be gone Christmas too!)
20 3-oz. pkg. Jell-O (50 6-oz.)
20 3-oz. pkg. pudding (25 6-oz. plus 25 6 oz. *instant)*
2 1-lb. boxes raisins (3 1-lb. plus 90 tiny boxes for night watch)
2 1-lb. boxes pitted dates (4 1-lb. boxes plus 4 boxes of date pieces)
2 cans vacuum-packed prunes (4 cans)
6 1-qt. jars of pickles (20)
3 large jars stuffed olives (10 medium)
5 small cans ripe olives (5 large cans whole plus 10 small cans sliced)
barbeque sauce (2 bottles)
5 large ketsup (10)
1 bottle horseradish (10)
2 bottles chili sauce
3 large bottles Worcestershire sauce (5)
cheese sauce (10 cans)
white sauce (10 cans)
5 jars mustard (10 plastic bottles)
2 48-oz. jars Miracle Whip (5)
2 48-oz. jars sandwich spread with pickles (5)
3 1-lb. cans instant cocoa (5)
5 bottles soy sauce (2)
5 7-oz. cans green chili salsa (15)
1 large bottle Tabasco sauce
taco sauce (3 bottles)
2 16-oz. bottle white vinegar (1 16-oz. bottle plus 1 gallon)
2 16-oz. bottle brown vinegar (1 16-oz. bottle plus 1 gallon)
2 5-oz. bottles olive oil (4 16-oz. bottles)

2 16-oz. bottles Wesson oil (1 16-oz. plus 1 gallon)
1 16-oz. dark molasses (3)
1 bottle liquid smoke (2)
10 cans Bordens sweetened condensed milk (25)
36 3-lb. cans regular ground coffee (24 large jars Sanka, 24 large jars regular instant plus 10 1-lb. cans). Fine gifts for island chefs.
5 boxes tea bags (0)
1 8-oz. bottle vanilla (4 16-oz. bottles—plastic)
4 boxes salt
20 pkg. dry yeast (100) (You'll find you bake a lot!)
1 lg. can baking powder (4)
3 lg. cans popcorn (10)
1 pkg. small marshmallows (5)
1 16-oz. pkg. shelled walnuts (4 plus 10 cans walnuts)
liquid brown sugar (2)
5 cans cake frosting (10 chocolate plus 10 white)
20 pkg. gum (360 sticks plus a few pkg. to hide for use during heavy weather when your throat gets dry)
30 candy bars (360 small ones—like you give on Halloween for night watches.)
5 jars peanuts (360 small pkg. and 5 cans salted mixed nuts for night watches.)
1 lb. individually wrapped fruit candy (5 lb. plus 5 cans hard candy for night watches.)
Herbs & spices (Double what you think you will need.)
2 boxes baking soda (10 large)
2 boxes graham crackers (5)
2 boxes soda crackers
2 cans Parmesan cheese (3)
3 1-lb. jars peanut butter (5 2-lb. jars)
2 boxes Reddi Whip (5 boxes)
24 plastic bottles lime juice
24 plastic bottles lemon juice
1 large can pepper (4)
2 cans BacO Bits (4 plus PepO Bits)
1 lg. jar dried onions (4)
1 jar garlic bits (4)

Partial list of Household and Personal Items

15 bars Vel Soap (25) (great for salt water baths)
1 can Borax hand-cleaning powder (3 cans plus 1 can Borax paste)

2 gal. Chlorox (4 gallons) (To purify water.)
6 large tubes toothpaste (10) (A nice change from salt and soda.)
30 toothbrushes (Visitors and crew always forget them.)
1 box 3-M plastic pan scrapers (4 boxes or 48 pads)
10 brushes of various sizes (20)
2 boxes lg. Zip Lok bags (5)
1 lg. bottle Lysol (3 lg. Lysol plus 1 lg. Hexol)
2 lg. bottles Mr. Kleen (2 gal. Fantastic), and 1 small one with the
     spray attachment.
copper-pan cleaners (2 boxes)
10 sponges of various sizes (20)
2 boxes sandwich-size Zip Lok bags (4)
5 boxes strong-plastic food-storage bags (10)
2 boxes regular sandwich bags (5)
All the large-size paper grocery bags you can collect.
5 various size & shape plastic funnels (20)
50 rolls toilet paper (75)
12 rolls paper towels (24) (One roll lasts 1 week.) Cost twice as much
     elsewhere.
4 pkg. disposable dish cloths (10)
1 gallon mouth wash
2 gallons liquid shampoo (Cheapest suds best in sea water.)
6 dozen sturdy clothes pins (12 dozen)
1 kitchen shears (2) one for galley use only
1 dozen cotton diapers for dish towels (4 doz.)
1 laundry bag full of rags (take 4 bags) (The engine room uses a lot.)
2 sturdy plastic buckets (4)
2 plastic dish pans (4)
1 6-qt. pressure cooker (1 6-qt. and 1 12-qt.) (Be sure it is a safe
     one.)
1 box heavy trash-can bags (5)
2 small mesh bags with plastic zipper (take 4) (Put Vel soap in and
     use as wash cloth during fantail shower)
1 scrub board with glass scrub area
Folding grocery cart (Be sure to take one. Before you get back home
     you will carry tons of papaya, pineapple, bananas, and other
     goodies for miles and miles.)
1 gal. good liquid laundry soap (2 gal.—more if you have room)
3 rolls aluminum foil (10 rolls)

Fresh

Only you can decide what you need. Below is a list of just a few.

We took 12 dozen eggs (take 24 dozen.) Get them strictly fresh and unrefrigerated. Coat with Vaseline, return to cartons, stack in plastic ventilated crate, turn upside down once a week, and they will last 6 months.

10 lbs. oleo (take just enough to get you to French Polynesia. New Zealand canned butter is excellent and as inexpensive as Oleo.)

1 head lettuce (3) (Does not keep well. Eat a lot the first few days and then forget about it.)

2 pkg. carrots (10) (Keep very well and give you the crunchy chewing you begin to miss.)

1 head of cabbage (take 3 or more) (Keeps well.)

2 cucumbers (take a dozen) (Keep well and smell fresh.)

2 stalks celery (Doesn't keep well.)

2 lbs. bacon (5)

10 lbs. potatoes (If you have room, take 20 lbs.)

10 lbs. brown onions (20 lbs.)

2 doz. oranges (Take a case.)

2 doz. apples (Take a case.)

10 lbs. cheese with wax covering (20 lbs. at least)

3 whole Hickory Farms beef sticks (12 sticks)

3 loaves white bread (5)

3 loaves wheat bread (5)

1 can cookies (5)

5 boxes or large pkg. of cookies (at least 10)

If you can get a metal 20-lb. can of New Zealand Cabin bread, do so. (The above breads were taken only to give me time to get a routine going in the galley before I started baking from scratch.)

Did You Know?

One roll of paper towels will last at least a week, but you have to lay down the law.

Have a good big breakfast, and have the main big meal at noon. A light soup and sandwich-type meal is best at night. You will sleep much better and you won't fall asleep on watch.

Before you leave the galley after the evening meal, make a goodie bag for each person. One small candy bar, a few cookies, a stick of gum, a bag of peanuts—whatever. At least four or five items and always a piece of fruit. Apples are best. However, *that is all.* They must keep their fingers out of your supplies—or you will all be without in no time.

Take plenty of flour. Remember, after about a week you don't go to the store to restock. You bake from scratch! It is really fun, and it smells so good.

If you catch a fish, cook what you want at the moment and then put a large piece in the large pressure cooker and cook per instructions. Do not open the cooker when it is done. Let it stand in the cooker unopened until you are ready for more fish. It will last for days unrefrigerated.

Take plenty of baking soda. You use ½C in each 50-gallon water tank to keep the water fresh. Or you can use 1-pt. red wine to each 50 gallons of water to keep it fresh. Use baking soda for stings, bites, burns and rashes. A combination of ½C soda and ½C salt, followed by boiling water, cleans galley or head plumbing beautifully.

When you think you will be attacked by mosquitoes, chiggers, sand fleas, or the infamous nau-nau Flies, mix 1 part Hexol with 2 parts of baby oil and spread it on all exposed parts. You will smell like a public washroom, but you won't get the bites and infection that follows.

Regarding the packages of mixes mentioned, your family probably would not touch them at home; but they would at sea. Besides, you also have to get on watch on time.

Use seawater for cooking potatoes and other vegetables. Never use seawater for cooking pasta. Much too salty.

Rather than making a thermos of coffee for night watches, make it full of hot water only. That way the crew can choose between coffee, soup, cocoa, or whatever instant drink is available.

Take two different size cans of fruits and vegetables. The regular 20-oz.

size for the meat and potato meals. The fruit is for desserts. The 6- or 8-oz. size vegetables are for hot dishes, and the smaller cans of fruit are to add to Jell-O and cake mixes for special desserts.

Have one large pressure cooker to can meat, fruits, and vegetables along the way.

Collect plastic containers of all sizes and shapes. They can be used for anything, from quieting a noisy block to protecting an infected wound.

Take a few special civilized foods along for birthdays and national holidays. It is wonderful to celebrate Thanksgiving or the Fourth of July in a foreign country.

Bake your bread in the pressure cooker on top of the stove. Use an asbestos pad between the flame and the pan. Sprinkle the greased pan with corn meal and cover it tightly with aluminum foil.

You can expect to run out of some items, and some are difficult to carry aboard and keep fresh. The following are a few substitutions I found useful.

2⅔ tbsp cocoa + ½ tbsp shortening − 1 square chocolate
1 C bread flour − 2 tbsp = 1 C pastry flour
2 tbsp flour = 1 tbsp corn starch—for thickening puddings
¼ tsp soda + ½ tsp cream tartar = 1 tsp baking powder
1 C sugar = ¾ C molasses + ½ tsp soda
or
1 C honey + ¼ tsp soda
or
1 C pancake syrup + ¼ C corn syrup

With any of the above substitutes for sugar, reduce the liquid in the recipe by ¼ C.

(You will add to this list as you improvise while you are under way.)

Learn the metric system! Most foreign countries are way ahead of the U.S. on that score.

Have you ever wondered what to give as a gift to someone going on a long voyage?

CONSIDER:

An 18″ piece of 2x4 wood. We got one as a joke—to kill the nau-flies. It works as a small work bench, to kill a fish, or to ward off uninvited boarders. It is one of our most treasured gifts.

Paperback books. Good, bad, clean, dirty, classic, modern. ANY-THING.

1 very small jar of black caviar. Wonderful on hard-boiled eggs for the first happy hour after a storm.

A new magazine that has just come out in the past few days. Remember, the crew is busy, there is still lots of work, and there is no time for them to get to a magazine stand.